The loneliness room

Manchester University Press

Anthropology, Creative Practice and Ethnography (ACE)

Series editors: Faye Ginsburg, Paul Henley, Andrew Irving and Sarah Pink

Anthropology, Creative Practice and Ethnography provides a forum for authors and practitioners from across the digital humanities and social sciences to explore the rapidly developing opportunities offered by visual, acoustic and textual media for generating ethnographic understandings of social, cultural and political life.
It addresses both established and experimental fields of visual anthropology, including film, photography, sensory and acoustic ethnography, ethnomusicology, graphic anthropology, digital media and other creative modes of representation. The series features works that engage in the theoretical and practical interrogation of the possibilities and constraints of audiovisual media in ethnographic research, while simultaneously offering a critical analysis of the cultural, political and historical contexts.

Previously published

Paul Carter, *Translations, an autoethnography: Migration, colonial Australia and the creative encounter*

Olivia Casagrande, Claudio Alvarado Lincopi and Roberto Cayuqueo Martínez (eds), *Performing the jumbled city: Subversive aesthetics, anticolonial indigeneity and collaborative ethnography in Santiago de Chile*

Lorenzo Ferrarini and Nicola Scaldaferri, *Sonic ethnography: Identity, heritage and creative research practice in Basilicata, southern Italy*

Paul Henley, *Beyond observation: A history of authorship in ethnographic film*

David MacDougall, *The looking machine: Essays on cinema, anthropology and documentary filmmaking*

Christian Suhr, *Descending with angels: Islamic exorcism and psychiatry – A film monograph*

In association with the Granada Centre for Visual Anthropology

The loneliness room

A creative ethnography of loneliness

Sean Redmond

MANCHESTER UNIVERSITY PRESS

Copyright © Sean Redmond 2024

The right of Sean Redmond to be identified as the author of this work has been asserted in accordance with the Copyright, Designs and Patents Act 1988.

Published by Manchester University Press
Oxford Road, Manchester M13 9PL

www.manchesteruniversitypress.co.uk

British Library Cataloguing-in-Publication Data
A catalogue record for this book is available from the British Library

ISBN 978 1 5261 6144 4 hardback
ISBN 978 1 5261 9576 0 paperback

First published 2024
Paperback published 2026

The publisher has no responsibility for the persistence or accuracy of URLs for any external or third-party internet websites referred to in this book, and does not guarantee that any content on such websites is, or will remain, accurate or appropriate.

EU authorised representative for GPSR:
Easy Access System Europe – Mustamäe tee 50,
10621 Tallinn, Estonia
gpsr.requests@easproject.com

Typeset by Newgen Publishing UK

For all the lonely people

Contents

List of figures	*page* viii
Acknowledgements	ix
1 The loneliness room: a creative ethnography of loneliness	1
2 Lonely emulsion: the loneliness in photography	35
3 Dim the lights: loneliness in cinema	69
4 Lonely realities: documenting loneliness	97
5 None but the lonely heart: the sounds of loneliness	123
6 Lonely words: writing loneliness in the post-digital age	155
7 A pandemic of creative loneliness	187
Conclusion: if nobody speaks of loneliness rooms	205
Appendices	213
References	219
Index	233

Figures

1.1	The candle	*page* 6
1.2	The desk of destiny	6
1.3	Within me	7
1.4	Lonely space	22
2.1	Quiet loneliness	39
2.2	Inside my head	40
2.3	Dawn calls	41
2.4	The gloaming	42
2.5	Pulse	47
2.6	Laneway	52
2.7	Lonely in the crowd	52
2.8	Your silent face	59
2.9	It feeds my soul	64
2.10	Tranquillity	65
4.1	The tree	101
4.2	Stay positive	103
4.3	Balancing act	104
4.4	Dancing loneliness	108
4.5	Dancing loneliness	108
5.1	Sound shapes	130
8.1	Figure and window	206
8.2	Spirit garden	207
8.3	The loneliness room	210
8.4	Around-and-around	211
8.5	Bedroom blues	211

All photographs and artworks © the author and participants in the loneliness room project

Acknowledgements

To John Downie, who first mooted the idea of the loneliness room as we drove the coastal road from Kapiti to Wellington. As we talked, the swell of the ocean lapped over our lonely imaginations.

Warmly, to Andrew Irving and Sarah Pink, for recognising and supporting the design of the lonely rooms that this book dwells in. To Tom Dark and Shannon Kneis, for their excellent stewardship of the development of this monograph, from review to publication.

To Lee, for being there and for journeying with me into those rooms where the lonely imagination touched us deeply.

To my children, Joshua, Caitlin, Erin, Dylan, and Cael, for all that you gift me, for now and always.

To the participants whose artwork and stories fill the pages of this book: thank you for sharing your loneliness rooms with me.

A version of 'A Pandemic of Creative Loneliness' was published in *Continuum Journal of Media & Cultural Studies*, 36:2 (2022), 184–198.

1

The loneliness room: a creative ethnography of loneliness

Prelude: sea salt on tongue

When I am asked to define what loneliness is, a set of complex impressions and expressions are elicited. Pausing, I might respond that loneliness is an overwhelming sensation that is barely able to be expressed in words, or that it is a set of disorientating if fleeting circumstances that leaves one socially, emotionally marooned or uprooted. I may reason that loneliness is context specific, related to personal loss, or that it is caused by an unexpected catastrophic life event. I may then say that loneliness is genetic, baked into the building blocks of DNA and therefore as *essentially* 'my fault'. Darkly, I might describe loneliness as an ailing contagion that lingers like a virus on skin and bone infecting everyone else's mood.

And then, thinking more deeply, I may seek to explain loneliness in terms of exploitative economic systems and the blip-speed of contemporary existence that renders humankind as anchorless agents in an uncaring world. Here, I may identify liquid capitalism and the relentless engines of neoliberalism as the forces that produce or manufacture loneliness, since loneliness may also be seen as an industry that profits from the discourses of the alienated self. Loneliness, I would wager, is bought and sold in the health marketplaces that simultaneously audit sadness, surveil despair, and promote therapeutic solutions. I might conclude by arguing that there is profit to be had in the skin and bone of being lonely.

These binary oppositions structure most of the thinking and feeling on loneliness: it is either the fault of the individual or of the economic and social systems that leave some people behind or positioned at the margins of culture. Loneliness, however, has a longer history than the short arc of modern systems of governance and control, and a more complex set of relations than the deficit modelling used so often to define and describe it. To be lonely can be argued to be a *natural* and *essential* part of the human condition: an emotional, affective state that is home and homely within each of us. When loneliness is understood in this way, its shackles and chains fall away into rivers and seas swimming with the nutrients of complex human life.

When I imagine what loneliness means to me, I taste sea salt on my tongue. I conjure up a driftwood beach emptied of people. I feel my feet walking softly on the sand and the heat of the falling sun on my exposed neck. I sense solitude and an emptiness rising out of and over me. Salty on my skin. A weakening and a sharpening of my senses, all at the same time. And as loneliness grips me, threatens to overwhelm me, I move further towards the wetted horizon and feel miraculously replenished.

When taken together, the beach and the sea is my *loneliness room*: the experiential, creative metaphor that holds this book together.

The loneliness room is a real or imagined space where people experience loneliness as a site or location of aching despair or, conversely, as a source of regeneration or existential reincarnation. *The Loneliness Room* explores not simply the devastating isolation of chronic loneliness, but the social, creative, and experiential possibilities of the lonely imagination – which this book suggests sits comfortably within all of us. This is one of the main interventions and revelations of this work: it shows us the replenishing values of creative practice for understanding the complex contexts of what it means to be lonely in the world today.

The term 'the lonely imagination' is one that is 'reversible' and at its core, dynamic. It refers to ordinary people who draw upon creative means to express how they experience loneliness. The lonely imagination is not a term that is meant to be quantified or datafied. Rather, like the chapters found in this book, it is expressive and poetic – a term chosen to meet and match the artworks it attempts to analyse. *The Loneliness Room* is in part written creatively: its analysis is shaped and versed in the art forms that it addresses; and its 'verses' are in dialogue with the artistic work supplied by its participants, by its lonely room storytellers.

To get inside or to better understand what these lonely rooms are, the book draws upon creative participatory ethnography. Its pages are culled and curated from the creative stories of ordinary people who were asked to use the idea of the loneliness room to submit sound and music pieces, video and essay films, photography, poetry, paintings, and drawings, alongside questionnaire responses that sought to draw on their lonely imaginations. These submissions captured the participants' personal interpretation of what they *felt* were the threads and fibres of loneliness. In so doing, *The Loneliness Room* eschews the forensic voice of the 'expert', replacing it with the autonomous art forms of the ordinary lonely.

As these creative stories emerge in this book, lonely rooms appear in the most surprising of places and spaces: at the car wash on a sodden day; 'being late' on the school run; standing on a balcony at midnight under the spell of a full moon; snuggled under the comforting bed sheets as a lover leaves for their day-shift; sitting in the garden shed and drinking English tea on a warm afternoon; out at night, quickly, or slowly, walking alone, or away, from someone or something; bike riding in the evergreen lush hills; alone, hanging a colourful painting on a white wall after a relationship has ended; and curled up on a velveteen sofa as music seeps into the stillness of the stale air.

In this book, loneliness becomes a set of connecting rooms, each leading to the discovery of how personally isolating and yet also homely and communal it can be to feel lonely. As both a realistic description and a malleable metaphor for being lonely, *The Loneliness Room* enables the book's storytellers to explore their isolation in richly imaginative ways. *The Loneliness Room* shatters the limited prescriptions usually applied to loneliness, enabling us to see its manifestations newly and uniquely. The book's storytellers set loneliness free.

The Loneliness Room also works on the premise that people get their shared understanding of loneliness through cultural and artistic forms, particularly audiovisual media, and that they often express what their understanding of loneliness is through the telling of stories and embodied descriptions that are in lockstep with these creative mediums. When seeking to express how they feel about loneliness, ordinary people often refer to artists and art forms whose work swims in lonely exchanges. The artists and art chosen by the book's storytellers often overlap, so that shared themes emerge, demonstrating the ways that loneliness has collective characteristics. The artistic sounds and images of loneliness become constitutive of, and foundational to, the embodied experience of being lonely. The creative representations of loneliness, then, and one's understanding and experience of it, are essentially entangled, as *The Loneliness Room* will powerfully go on to explore and evidence.

and I taste sea salt on my tongue.

What is loneliness and why does it matter?

Loneliness everywhere

There is much evidence to suggest that across early and late capitalist societies, new and extensive forms of loneliness have emerged. Statistically speaking, in countries such as the UK, Australia, Japan, and India, people are known to have fewer companions and that community networks have broken down, or have been rendered virtual and ephemeral, signalling a retreat into the home, or to the lonely rooms found online. In this contextual triad, loneliness emerges through three supposedly 'catastrophic' intersections. First, people are increasingly seen to have limited and inconsistent friendship networks that fail to provide the succour and counselling functions that they traditionally did (Mousavi and Dehshiri, 2021). Second, this interpersonal 'fracture' is accompanied by a corresponding collapse in the public sites, spaces, and places where shared social life historically materialised (Bergefurt et al., 2019). Finally, the simultaneous rise in online connectivity has pulled the individual into the privatised home and into social media encounters and engagements that are shown to be less rewarding and, in fact, more socially isolating and alienating (Smith et al., 2021; Turkle, 2011). Together, these intersections are said to create the conditions for an epidemic in loneliness to emerge.

The evidence for this rise in loneliness seems to be everywhere. For example, in a recent report, published with Age UK, feeling lonely is linked to risk of an earlier death, depression, dementia, and poor self-rated health (Davidson and Rossall, 2015). The BBC and The University of Manchester's national survey, *The Loneliness Experiment*, revealed that levels of loneliness were highest in younger respondents, with 40% feeling lonely compared with only 27% of older respondents who completed the study (Qualter, 2018). Similarly, the *Australian Loneliness Report* (Lim, 2018) found that

> 50.5% of Australians reported they felt lonely for at least a day in the previous week; 27.6% felt lonely for three or more days. Nearly 30% rarely or never felt they were part of a group of friends. One in four (25.5%) do not feel they have a lot in common with the people around them. One in five (21.4%) rarely or never feel close to people, rarely or never feel they have someone to talk to (22.1%) and don't feel they have people they can turn to (21.4%). Nearly a quarter (24.5%) say they can't find companionship when they want it.

In contemporary Japan, the increase in loneliness is partly tied to traditional family structures falling apart, resulting in the phenomenon of kodokushi or 'lonely death', where people die alone in their homes, remaining undiscovered for an extended period of time. The expression 'muen shakai' or 'no-relationship society' has begun to be used as an umbrella term for these new and emerging forms of social isolation (Taylor, 2012), as if all of society has become one all-encompassing loneliness room.

In this age of loneliness people are increasingly seen to be self-driven isolates, caught in a perpetual state of brute individualism which denies and even prohibits meaningful connections with the social world. As George Monbiot suggests,

> A study by Independent Age shows that severe loneliness in England blights the lives of 700,000 men and 1.1m women over 50, and is rising with astonishing speed … Social isolation is as potent a cause of early death as smoking 15 cigarettes a day; loneliness, research suggests, is twice as deadly

as obesity. Dementia, high blood pressure, alcoholism and accidents – all these, like depression, paranoia, anxiety and suicide, become more prevalent when connections are cut. We cannot cope alone. Yes, factories have closed, people travel by car instead of buses, use YouTube rather than the cinema. But these shifts alone fail to explain the speed of our social collapse. These structural changes have been accompanied by a life-denying ideology, which enforces and celebrates our social isolation. The war of every man against every man – competition and individualism, in other words – is the religion of our time, justified by a mythology of lone rangers, sole traders, self-starters, self-made men and women, going it alone. For the most social of creatures, who cannot prosper without love, there is no such thing as society, only heroic individualism. What counts is to win. The rest is collateral damage.

(Monbiot, 2014)

Zygmunt Bauman takes up a similar position where he outlines how liquid modernity has stripped away a range of solid connections to be replaced with floating virtual networks, loosely formed 'neo-tribes', and just-in-time-consumption demands that seem to govern all aspects of people's lives, including love and intimacy (2000). Bauman describes this state of existence as liquefied, since individuals seem to be constantly swimming against a rising tide of systems and practices that prohibits them from mooring or anchoring.

The precarious workplace and the rise of zero-hours contracts are one such perilous sea, not only rendering workers economically unstable but socially so, since their employment ties are ever so tenuous, and their productive work is only a shallow means to a lonely consumption end. Nonetheless, the forms and formations of loneliness are complexly layered and textured, opening the concept to more hopeful, nourishing lines of insight and enquiry, as this chapter will now go on to explore.

Chronically or existentially lonely?

In his landmark account of loneliness, Robert Weiss suggests that there are two main forms: social loneliness and emotional loneliness (1974). The former is linked to an individual having a lack of access to social networks, while the latter is connected to an individual not having any deep or meaningful emotional attachments. Of course, one can have social connections but still feel emotionally lonely, like when one is standing, chatting, in a noisy room while experiencing the conversations from a position of empty disconnect.

For loneliness room participant Craig D, emotional and social loneliness are brought together and likened to a candle's flame whose shadows replace the warmth of the sun, expressed as just beyond their reach (Figures 1.1 and 1.2):

> My loneliness room exists in my head ... A darkened corner, shadows cast by a single solitary candle. Look how one single flame can both defy and define the darkness ... It is the feeling of isolation and detachment I feel from the world ... I wish I could leave and embrace the sun and learn to believe that my life is worthwhile.

Craig D's description of loneliness is 'chronic' because it is experienced as a permanent state of being, excessive and aggressive in the way it seems to perpetually drown him in feelings of alienation and isolation (de Jong-Gierveld, 1998).

In his foundational study of loneliness, Clark Moustakas argues that chronic loneliness anxiety involves rejecting or detaching from everyday life's rituals and events (1961). One retreats into rooms of the alienated self where doors are closed and locked. Loneliness anxiety is an emotional state where one is unable to relate to dominant norms around shared taste and

Figure 1.1 The candle

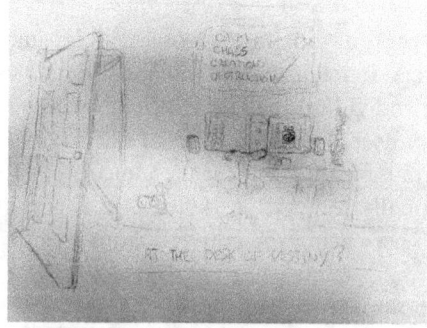

Figure 1.2 The desk of destiny

communal food; to everyday routines; to the confines of social regulation; and to abstract concepts such as home and belonging and 'with fitting in'.

When anxiously lonely, one withdraws from creative and social participation, finding such interactions anxiety inducing since there is no space for 'true identity' to emerge, or because in taking part in 'life' one is essentially abandoning 'real desires and interests' in favour 'of social, economic, and vocational rewards' (Moustakas, 1961: 32). The rooms of the anxiously lonely are felt to be more 'real' or authentic than the phoney social rooms of the constructed world. These rooms can be experienced as incredibly dark spaces, as a participant in this study responds:

> My loneliness room is a living hell. It springs to life when a person or person's, dark side appears. I may misinterpret what I read, on their face or in their words, or feel from their energy, but I don't believe so. Each time I flee to my loneliness room, another demon appears there ... No matter how hard I try to befriend these creatures, they will not respond, and remain, cold, and lifeless. The only way I know that they are alive, is by the vibration of my nervous system. When I flee to the loneliness room, my body is numb, but as soon as I enter, the room, my body becomes as if on fire. Here is a painting of that room [Figure 1.3].

Figure 1.3 Within me

This somatic, embodied response demonstrates the terrifying pull of the loneliness room, rendering the participant a material part of its horrifying environment. This is again a response that points to the chronic nature of loneliness and to the way it is felt *in the body*. Its visual and poetic representation is one that draws on expressionistic and horror conventions and awards us a powerful understanding of how loneliness grips and assaults the flesh. The book's lonely room metaphor here acts as an enabling conduit for the participant to both describe and paint it, revealing how space and body are unified in their depression.

Loneliness can also be by degree and measured by temporality. A traumatic event can bring on a sense of loneliness, such as the loss of a lifetime partner, although it may rise up momentarily, unexpectedly, to then dissipate as quickly as it was felt. This is loneliness that occurs in the moment, seemingly without root or stimulus. Moustakas terms this 'existential loneliness', a sublime state which involves a 'conscious' experience of awe and potentiality as one contemplates deeply on what 'life' and 'living' truly constitute (1961: 33).

Moustakas suggests that when one enters a state of existential loneliness a level of unprecedented self-awareness emerges: all the doubts of one's meaningless existence rear into view, at the same time as one sees an 'authentic self' emerge that is full of possibility and potential. Existential loneliness puts one in touch with both the inner self *and* the universe, 'opening a new awareness of value and relatedness to both nature and life' (Moustakas, 1961: 33).

For this participant, Lee, it is when visiting their sister's farm, in the historic gold-mining region of northern Victoria, Australia, that they experience the giddy freedom that comes from directly experiencing existential loneliness:

> The land is covered in ancient gums, beneath them, lies dried skins of old and fragile limbs, the hills sparkle as the golden light finds the quartz unearthed, I stick to the narrow sheep trails, a balancing act for an audience of bemused kookaburras. Springtime winds blow and I dance in the moment.

Existential loneliness, then, is understood to be a natural or essential part of being human and, further, that those rooms that people go to experience it may be recuperative and regenerative. Lee's description of loneliness draws on the beauty of the outdoors, and the way light, colour, and natural sounds amplify their sense of aloneness and the richness it brings them. They dance in what is, in effect, the lonely sublime.

For Lee, the loneliness room has acted as an enabling metaphor since it has allowed them to render it inside-out, and to employ it as mobile and fertile ground for their lonely imagination. Lee's response also draws attention to a distinction that some scholars want to make between loneliness and being alone. This is something that Eric Klinenberg addresses in relation to the rising phenomenon of living alone:

> Living alone helps us pursue sacred modern values – individual freedom, personal control, and self-realization – whose significance endures from adolescence to our final days. It allows us to do what we want, when we want, on our own terms. It liberates us from the constraints of a domestic partner's needs and demands, and permits us to focus on ourselves. Today, in our age of digital media and ever-expanding social networks, living alone can offer even greater benefits: the time and space for restorative solitude. This means that living alone helps us discover who we are, as well as what gives us meaning and purpose.
>
> (Klinenberg, 2013: 33)

Once we begin to unravel and reassemble the coordinates of loneliness, new understandings of it productively emerge. As Klinenberg touches upon in the above quote, one related concept is that of solitude which affords one the 'opportunity for personal reflection and growth' (Smith et al., 2022). Solitude is a form of aloneness where one does not feel anxiously lonely or isolated, but contented and calmly reflective (Gotesky, 1965).

Solitude, aloneness, and escapism

According to David A. Diekema, solitude is a 'symmetrical, wilful, cooperative social form' chosen by the individual and supported or countenanced by their community (1992: 489). At solitude's core 'is an ongoing intimacy between the individual and community, the self and the other, as while the aloneness is mutually generated, it is also acknowledged that the relationship is still existent throughout and after the solitude's duration' (Diekema, 1992: 489). Solitude provides people with the time and space to experience a productive and necessary aloneness, away from the social while still being connected to it. Solitary walking in the wilderness provides such a room, for example, while certain religious ritualistic practices, including meditation, attempt to 'cleanse' the worshipper of the atheistic toxic chatter of everyday life.

In the rooms of solitude, it is the contemplative comfort of aloneness that supposedly differentiates it from the alienating sensations of chronic loneliness. And yet, nonetheless, aloneness may itself be a form of existential loneliness, bound to the sublime and to the desire or need to leave behind the noise and regulations of the social world. As Ben Lazare Mijuskovic suggests, one may seek isolation as a 'defensive device to thwart the threat of diffusion, of the self's evaporation before the overwhelming presence of the "others" as it is assaulted by an impersonal, bureaucratic, industrialised, mechanised society or by violent and traumatic interpersonal relations' (2012: 61).

This is the position that *The Loneliness Room* adopts, led there by what it sees as the atomised tyranny of neoliberal capitalism, and by the stories and artistic creations of its participants. The book creatively evidences that aloneness and solitude exist *within* the framework of a beneficial loneliness that resists and rejects the relentless commodification and conformity of capitalised existence.

These are the anti-conformist reasons that this participant gives for walking and wandering: they seek to remove themselves from the routinised monotony of the social world:

> I find that commuting is a point in time akin to grieving, where you are both lonely and surrounded by people. It's a moving funeral without a wake. There are too many people around, too many words already to parse, too many people on download or transmit. I don't have the bandwidth for that. I would rather be alone and not listen to the incessant narcissism of others, as I already have too much information in my mind to cope with on a minute-by-minute basis. Walking helps to filter some of this ... Often walking alone is like waking up. Behind the noise of the traffic the birds sing and they get louder when the airliners, once quietened birds themselves in the pandemic, take to the skies once again as man craves command and control over his environment. We are a species of walkers, perhaps not nomadic, but need that immediate connection to the world around us. Why do we insist on machines to do the most elemental thing in the world? The more I walk, the less sense it makes.

The notion of self-defence against an uncaring corporatised world can be extended to understanding loneliness as a type of 'escapism' in which the individual rejects or denies 'the relevance of community', opting to create fantasy and fantastic rooms to live in (Diekema, 1992). Addiction and alcoholism are two escapist 'flights' from community, but so are instances of parasocial relationships with celebrities, for example, where, in the realm of fantasy, the lonely individual imagines a deep connection with their starry 'love interest' (Stever, 2009).

These fantasy rooms are not, however, necessarily shielded from chronic loneliness, but are rather built out of its qualities. The condition of anomic loneliness fosters a need to be connected to people who seem to be their antithesis: the famous occupy rooms that appear to be inherently social and spectacular. Of course, stars and celebrities can also be lonely people, fame becoming a form of relentless visibility that leaves them no room to be alone (Hoffner and Cohen, 2018). What emerges here is a tension between invisibility and detachment, and the visuality of the social. This is a theme that *The Loneliness Room* will take up across its case studies.

More broadly and as significantly, lonely escapism is deeply connected to the consumption of art forms that not only represent loneliness but provide a creative means with which to understand it. Art provides the means of expression, the representations and discourses, through which loneliness is given its cultural meaning. There is an art to being lonely, something widely ignored in the literature on loneliness but which *The Loneliness Room* goes on to advance and celebrate.

What now follows is an exploration of the central creative art forms that take loneliness as their subject matter, art forms that then become the structuring substance of the chapters that occupy the rest of the book.

The art of loneliness

Loneliness is like a tapestry that is woven through visual art and media and popular culture, texturing its pronouncements, productions, and performances with its chronic, anxious, and existential qualities and intensities. Through popular and artistic representations, people are repeatedly told and shown that they live chronically lonely lives, or, contrarily, that loneliness frees the soul from the tyranny of a banal existence. Films, songs, novels, poems, podcasts, television dramas, news reports, realist and expressionistic photography, and screen documentaries provide people with an inter-textual and extra-textual narrative about isolation and anomie. The art of loneliness depicts a world that is wetted and matted by innumerable loneliness rooms.

Neon

Neon art has been central to the representations of melancholy, loss, and loneliness, particularly in terms of capturing the anomie of urban living. Installations have been placed in city spaces that are felt to be transitory and impersonal in nature, and where the possibility of love and human connection has been seemingly muted. In Robert Montgomery's *Light Poem* series, for example, neon poems are placed in public settings that capture the sadness and liminality of social life and the dreams one might have there: 'the people you love become ghosts inside of you and like this you keep them alive' (2013). In Tracey Emin's neon artwork, we see self-disclosure, relationship breakdowns, and the past scars of her various encounters, represented in humorous, tragic, and explicit terms: 'her soft lips touched mine and every thing became hard' (2008). One is alone and lonely in viewing these light pieces since they are placed in spaces of concrete or vertical emptiness and register as carriers of the trauma of lost human connections.

The loneliness room of neon art is the modern city, cavernous in its size, seemingly empty on its insides, with city dwellers moving across its terrain like spectres.

The relationship between neon art and the modern city is connected to their shared history. The city was/is illuminated by neon, which provided advertising agencies with commercial signs that invited the urbanist to consume, consume, consume as they moved across its transactional spaces. Neon commodified the spaces of the city so that they were experienced as bought, as product, and as signifiers of the elusive American dream (Ribbat, 2013).

Nonetheless, there is beauty in neon, and neon art invites the city dweller to stand and ponder, to dwell, in effect creating a space of connection that the work suggests no longer exists. The reflective nature of neon may create the conditions for existential loneliness to emerge, its colours washing the spaces where it is found with potentiality and possibility. These are themes that are similarly taken up in paintings that explore the cross-current rivulets of loneliness.

Painting

Olivia Laing has traced art and the artist's relationship to loneliness, examining the way the city – captured in painting, photography, and sculpture – represents and embodies aloneness (2016). For example, in exploring and explaining the loneliness in Edward Hopper's paintings, Laing writes:

> The obvious answer is that his paintings tend to be populated by people alone, or in uneasy, uncommunicative groupings of twos and threes, fastened into poses that seem indicative of distress. But there's something else too; something about the way he contrives his city streets. What Hopper's urban scenes replicate is one of the central experiences of being lonely: the way a feeling of separation, of being walled off or penned in, combines with a sense of near unbearable exposure.
>
> (Laing, 2016: 11)

Laing's idea of exposure – of having one's loneliness put cruelly out in the open – is here considered to be a destructive force in Hopper's paintings. However, those isolated or contemplative individuals found in his work may also be read as engaged in escapist flights of fancy, or as being existentially uncoupled from the world, and, consequently, as being more free, more deeply human in the lonely light of their exposure. That is to say, the figures in Hopper's paintings may in fact be *comfortable* in their loneliness. Here again we can see how light and exposure is central to representations of loneliness. Hopper's anonymous subjects are both afraid of being seen, of being out in the open, and yet also hungry for self-illumination and social visibility.

This notion of exposure is taken up by this participant through the idea of embodied density where, at a certain thickness or weight, one can dissolve into or *through* loneliness:

> It would be an invisible room adjoined to [our] large vibrant bustling home. The people in the lonely room have bodies that fluctuate in density. They would only be able to enter the bustling home when their bodies were at a specific density and would disappear into loneliness when their density changed.

The idea of exposure, of visibility and invisibility, haunts a great many paintings through the way they either draw upon mirrors and reflections, or sketch their subjects without corporeal borders, as if their faces, bodies, skin are dissolving or melting into the spaces they are placed in. This is the type of representation found in the participant's 'within me' painting explored above (see Figure 1.3), and one which directly echoes Francis Bacon's horror paintings of bodily disintegration, such as *Head VI* (1949). This painting captures the lonely, tortured figure of Pope Innocent X, screaming into the void that surrounds him. Of course, it is also the texture of the paint that gives creative anguish to the participant's art and to Bacon's character studies, as if the oils they use are materially wetted with loneliness. This atomic essentialism can be applied to the inherent loneliness of the art of photography.

Photography

The art form of photography is often baked in the essential chemicals of loneliness. The photograph is always its own haunting, an absent/present medium, capturing ephemeral moments as it witnesses 'the disappearance of the present and the possibility of representing that "present" as a form of "mourning"' (Fisher, 2012: 22). The photograph memorialises the past, and yet rears memory into the present, taking the viewer back to lost moments while keeping them stuck in the reality of the here and now. By its very nature, photography is a loneliness room: a captured space, fixed in time, reminding the viewer of what once was.

Artists draw upon the melancholy of photography's form to capture and record loneliness wherever it may be found. This includes the settings and interactions found in isolated, rural communities, and the impersonal environs of sanitised and surveyed totalising institutions, such as hospitals, banks, and supermarkets. Photographers capture the beads of loneliness in the ordinary lives of those who are felt to be trapped in either catastrophic despair or existential reverie – their daily routines becoming the material for monochrome emulsification. For example, Katy Grannan's 99 series of street photographs, 'set in the parched landscape and forgotten towns along Highway 99', captures the isolated and socially fragmented lives of the marginalised, allowing the viewer to witness them 'unfold as an enormous procession of humanity – a dance macabre of marginalized and powerless members of society' (Grannan, 2014).

Conversely, photographers also find an essential beauty in loneliness, allowing them to reproduce its contemplative textures in their emulsions. For example, Nico Goodden's photographs attempt to capture the empty city at night, 'absolutely free from people and passers-by' and that 'felt abandoned'. Goodden notes, 'our society often associates solitude with sadness but for me it's quite the contrary. It brings me joy, freedom and independence but more importantly it restores my privacy' (2020).

The Loneliness Room explores this lonely dialectic, this set of oppositions and collisions, both through the photographs supplied by its participants and the work of artists who have focused their lens on the lonely. Thematically and artistically, the book reveals how amateur and professional photography draws out loneliness in similarly creative ways. This is a dialectic of loneliness that is also found in the art of cinema.

Cinema

Cinema is a venue and an art form that provides the physical and imaginative space for lonely rooms to appear. Its architectural and dramatic features combine to create a theatre for the various qualities of loneliness to be felt and performed. The drama of the movie theatre sets the scene for it to become a loneliness room: one sits among a crowd but views the film in isolation. As the lights slowly fade, and as the curtains are slowly drawn open, one faces an enormous moving screen that is more dark than light, more sound than image. Cinema is magically or cosmically of a higher order: it offers one a direct escape from the world and all its troubles.

The lone patron who visits the cinema on a Tuesday afternoon speaks to the different conditions of loneliness. Either out of work, or with acres of leisure time available to them; either looking for the company of cinema, or secure and happy in their self-chosen moment of aloneness, they sit unfulfilled but with their heart ready to be filled with the transformatory power of the moving image.

Of course, when the film begins, loneliness can emerge through its subject matter: across its forms and genres, stories of the lonely populate its fictions. Melancholy, introspection, meditation, detachment, isolation, and atomisation are found across film's global production axes, staining its transnational spotlights with the hues and cries of those who anxiously, chronically, or existentially find themselves adrift.

In *City Lights* (Chaplin, 1931), Charlie Chaplin is but a lonely "tramp" who finds his lonely flower girl: together their love extinguishes their isolated despair. Jean Renoir's *A Day in the Country* (Renoir, 1946) is a reverie on romantic companionship that is marked by deep pockets of loneliness: we witness the lovers first kiss taste like it is their last. In the film noir *Gilda* (Vidor, 1946), Gilda (Rita Hayworth) desires Johnny (Glenn Ford), but Johnny may only be interested in the homoerotically charged Balam (George Macready). At the end of the film, when Gilda and Johnny walk off together, the impression lingers that it is to a lonely, incompatible future. In *Late Spring* (Ozu, 1949), single parent Shukichi (Chishu Ryu) arranges for his 27-year-old daughter, Noriko (Setsuko Hara), to get married. He is worried that she will be alone and lonely when he eventually dies. Shukichi and Noriko have spent their entire lives together: the film captures them sharing memories in shared spaces, always framed in familial intimate proximity. After the wedding, Shukichi is shot peeling an apple while sitting alone on Noriko's bentwood chair – his loneliness cutting into the apple and into the empty space where she would normally be.

When asked to choose a film that for them expressed what it felt like to be lonely, this participant chose *Brokeback Mountain* (Lee, 2005) since it is about

> a man trapped in time, waiting for nothing, when it is too late to acknowledge his dead lover. More than any other film I can think of, *Brokeback Mountain* captured that hopeless, lonely feeling for me. I think it is significant that a film about a gay couple has defined this for my straight self ... At the end of the film, when Ennis, alone in his trailer, says 'Jack, I swear', looks at the photo of the mountain, and carefully buttons Jack's old shirt: it's loneliness and regret captured in images and words ... gut wrenching (particularly with music by Gustavo Santaolalla).

Robert Kolker has more broadly defined a 'cinema of loneliness' in terms of American auteurs such as Arthur Penn, Oliver Stone, Stanley Kubrick, Martin Scorsese, Stephen Spielberg, and Robert Altman (2011). In their films, often realistically imagined, lonely male protagonists struggle to connect or maturate in a world which renders them mute or powerless. As we will go on to explore in this book, gender will prove to be crucial to the critical and creative findings of *The Loneliness Room*. We will see its female participants exploring their isolation through the strictures of patriarchy, and its male participants describing themselves as like 'waste' and 'refuse'.

We constantly see, visit, and dwell in lonely spaces in film, where female and male protagonists are set against alienating, disconnecting environments, or else 'find themselves' in these existential sites of recovery. American film noir of the 1940s very often used the city as a mausoleum for those alienated from the world, while the 1980s British heritage film employed the grandeur and yet tight constraints of the mansion house to show how suffocated progressive female characters were because of their societal obligations. In science fiction, loneliness enters the fictional world through end-of-time scenarios in which there may only be one 'man' left alive, and yet the genre's expansiveness connects it to the cosmos, suturing its melancholy to existential openness. In science fiction, loneliness becomes the starry cloth of the universe.

In *The Loneliness Room*, we find that film expresses the different ways that loneliness manifests in people. However, its fictions do not simply reflect the loneliness of the participants but provide them with the creative canvas with which to express and understand their lonely feelings. Film genre is shown to operate as a means to dialogue with the participants' loneliness, affording them the opportunity to use story, script, and scene to dramatise the coordinates of their lonely imagination. While fiction is essential to the loneliness rooms found in this book, so too are the optics of the real.

The documentary

The documentary film regularly takes loneliness as its object of study. Its realism and investigative and exploratory nature are seen as a natural and non-hierarchical way for the stories, causes, and consequences of loneliness to be outlined, shared, and negotiated. Irrespective of the documentary mode, filmmakers readily take their cameras into environments where loneliness is powerfully situated and encountered. They do this as a form of activism, to mobilise political responses to the scourge of chronic loneliness, and to capture the affective intimacy of the ordinary, of the banal, of the 'truly lived'. The documentary film supposedly gives an authentic voice to lonely people that is very often taken from them by health science professionals whose reports and investigations often leave their words behind. The documentary film is also able to shine a light on the way realism and creativity have a role to play in understanding loneliness.

For example, in *Breaking Loneliness*, filmmaker Brandy Yanchyk follows four people: 'Indigenous Peer Support Worker John Chief Moon, 2SLGBTQ+ Liaison and Peer Support Worker Jace Laing-Schroeder, volunteer Tom Greyson and ESL teacher Julie Kraychy – who have worked to overcome their own loneliness and social isolation and are now helping others to battle theirs' (Yanchyk, 2019). Filmed in Edmonton, Calgary, and on the Blood Reserve in Southern Alberta, Canada, the documentary details both the causes of chronic loneliness and the creative and communal ways that ordinary people have overcome it.

These lonely room documentaries, however, can also pathologise loneliness as singularly chronic and destructive – their focus squarely set on the 'damaged' individual. When this is the case, they fail to explore the causes of extreme loneliness as stemming from the systemic failures found in neoliberal capitalism's political and economic systems. *The Loneliness Room* documents this 'gap' and provides a new critical and creative lens with which to view loneliness: one where capitalism creates the conditions for the chronically lonely to emerge, and yet where the participants' creative artworks become forms of protest and resistance against this oppressive machine.

Sound and song

It is also the sound worlds of screen media that capture the qualities and intensities of loneliness. These melodies and symphonies of loneliness can be heard and felt diegetically, their lonely notes emanating from the screen world's drama; and they can be carried through the score and soundtrack that anchors the lonely images that they play over. For example, in the science fiction film *Under the Skin* (Glazer, 2013), a particular microtonal music structure is employed to capture the urban decay of Glasgow and the existential void of the lonely men found there. The soundtrack's fragmented 'scrape of the strings' melody cuts through the alienating gloom of its city streets so that, at times, it is as if the film is itself expressing its own alienation and loss through its weeping musical chords. In this example, we can see how space and place – a decaying, lonesome Glasgow – is given its representational power through the way its soundscape expresses what is being physically and emotionally encountered on screen.

The sounds of loneliness can, of course, be silent, where nothing is heard or spoken. A dramatic scene can be emptied of sound to capture the isolation that is being characterised or dramatised. This silencing of screen space is meant to echo the way lonely people either crave human sound, chatter, so isolated have they become, or else it represents the type of silence that emerges in the existential moment where one encounters the universe as truly awesome.

Nonetheless, sound and song can also be used to undermine a filmic representation. For example, at the end of *Happy Together* (Kar-Wai, 1997), the Turtle's song 'Happy Together' is used over shots of Lai Yiu-Fai (Tony Leung Chiu-Wai) as he returns to Hong Kong alone, without his love interest, Ho Po-Wing (Leslie Cheung). As the song plays over the scene, Lai Yiu-Fai is filmed sitting on an empty bus as flashes of the city fuse with his fragmented memories of Wing. The song's lyrics,

> Imagine me and you, I do
> I think about you day and night, it's only right
> To think about the girl you love and hold her tight
> So happy together

> If I should call you up, invest a dime
> And you say you belong to me and ease my mind
> Imagine how the world could be, so very fine
> So happy together

reveal that the love expressed by the song's narrator – here transposed onto Lai Yiu-Fai – is not reciprocated by the other person, and that the happiness being narrated is from a base of lonely longing.

This discontinuity between sound and image, song and mood, is something that can shape the imagination of the lonely who are looking for love or who have lost a romantic connection. Music does this more generally: it provides people with stories and memories that are about loneliness, or which allow us to feel lonely. For this participant, unrequited love is their song of loneliness, choosing The Cure's 'Pictures of You' as their lonely room track: 'The song is about someone missing someone else. It has these really heartfelt lyrics. I picture someone in a lonely place just wishing someone else was there'.

In all its artistic and generic forms, music charts lonely relationships or encounters, or becomes a memorial membrane in which hearing a song brings one back to a time when loneliness wrapped itself around the core self. There are songs and overtures that are either about loneliness or, in their composition, melodies, and harmonies, 'sound out' chronic or existential loneliness. And yet, conversely, music does not have to sound lonely or be about loneliness to have lonesome effects/affects. In fact, a song that might be associated with a happy memory can elicit loneliness since in hearing it one is reminded of what once was, or of what has been lost, even as its oration and instrumentation acts as a conduit of self-regeneration.

Of course, performing music, or taking active part in song and dance, connects the body to the social, and lifts one's emotional state. Even if one is separated by distance and decree, active and collective music-making quietens the melodies of loneliness (Schäfer et al., 2020). Music is often used for 'relationship building' and 'immersing in emotions', fostering a sense of positive well-being in the world (Papinczak et al., 2015). Music can provide a soundscape for loneliness that is enabling, freeing, as *The Loneliness Room* will go on to explore in its chapters. We can see how the written word also embodies the contrasting nature of how people experience loneliness.

Words

The novel, the play, the diary, the memoir, and the poem are conduits for the lonely imagination, employing the poetics and politics of language to furnish their own versions of the loneliness room. They express, nonetheless, in similar ways to the art forms already mentioned above, the differing conditions of loneliness and the contradictory qualities it possesses.

Sometimes fictional characters are so inflicted by the state of loneliness that they wish to die, such as is the case with Holden Caulfield in *The Catcher in the Rye* (Salinger, 1951/1969), who says, 'I felt so lonesome, all of a sudden, I almost wished I was dead'.

In Sylvia Plath's *The Bell Jar*, the book's narrator, Esther Greenwood, struggles with loneliness and mental illness while they are trying to write a novel (1972). They attempt suicide but recover, seemingly coming to terms with their lonely state. Plath, of course, directly writes about loneliness in her poetry. For example, in 'Tulips' (1965), composed after a stay in hospital while recovering from an appendectomy, Plath is found lying in a blindingly white, sterile room, as she draws on the colour and textures of 'red' to describe the bouquet of tulips next to her:

> The tulips are too red in the first place, they hurt me.
> Even through the gift paper I could hear them breathe
> Lightly, through their white swaddlings, like an awful baby.
> Their redness talks to my wound, it corresponds.
> They are subtle: they seem to float, though they weigh me down,
> Upsetting me with their sudden tongues and their color,
> A dozen red lead sinkers round my neck.
>
> Nobody watched me before, now I am watched.
> The tulips turn to me, and the window behind me
> Where once a day the light slowly widens and slowly thins,
> And I see myself, flat, ridiculous, a cut-paper shadow
> Between the eye of the sun and the eyes of the tulips,
> And I have no face, I have wanted to efface myself.
> The vivid tulips eat my oxygen.

Here the tulips are both life and death, a part of Plath and yet distinct and separate from her. They are impressionably surveyor and surveyed, and they capture the violence she feels exists not only in the world around her – that is smothering her – but in her lonely, isolated being. Plath's body becomes the tulip, the tulip becomes the loneliness room, sandwiched between birth and death, light and shadow, suffocation and oxygen.

The poem that this participant submitted sees loneliness as also constituting a state where the other half of a natural pair or binary is missing:

> *Everyday Loneliness*
> On Sunday, loneliness is a prayer room, in need of hope.
> On Monday, loneliness is a hallway, in need of light.
> On Tuesday, loneliness is a morning room, in need of conversation.
> On Wednesday, loneliness is a post room, in need of a message.
> On Thursday, loneliness is a vault, in need of treasure.
> On Friday, loneliness is a bedroom, in need of caressing.
> On Saturday, loneliness is an old barn, in need of support.

In this poem, loneliness travels across and into various public and private settings, with each day of the week being given a particular room for its lonesome expression. The poem repeats the refrain that each of its spaces is 'in need' of that which is missing, so that its perceived sociality is muted, darkened, isolated. Space is personified in the poem so that the relationship between environment and loneliness is humanised while being at the same time defined as bleak. This personification of the loneliness room, of its imaginative mobility, is something carried across the pages of this book.

The very process or act of reading can be lonely. The 'alone' reader escapes their loneliness through the written word, or they use it to explore how it manifests fictionally, if only to better experience and understand it personally. The rituals and practices of reading take one outside the social into a cocoon or hermit-like space that is homely to the reader. Lights are dimmed. Curtains are drawn. Cushions are positioned or replaced. The room folds in on itself, like a cloak warming the entire space. The temperature of the air changes. Sounds are softened. *Hush*. Reading lonely begins.

And when people write about their own loneliness, the process is both confessional and therapeutic – it is a way for them to define the type of loneliness that they are experiencing and a means to creatively explore their own feelings and senses. The lonely letters, diary entries, or social media posts that people often write can either be decidedly private or public, intended to be confidential or shared. However, the 'incitement to discourse' (Foucault, 1990), to confess one's lonely state, begins to return us to the question that heads this entire section, namely: what is loneliness, and why does it matter?

One of the answers to the second part of this question is tautological: it is because we are told and counselled that it matters. The confessional, therapeutic, and self-healing discourses that run rampant across modern society ask or compel us to reveal our inner thoughts and to let out our lonely feelings. It will help we are told. We will feel much better, we are countenanced. In this context, the lonely confessional can be understood as a strategy of centring dissatisfaction on the individual body rather than as a consequence of the dislocating forces of neoliberal capitalism, or as the responsibility of the state. The lonely confession is here understood as a negative example of biopower or one of the 'numerous and diverse techniques for achieving the subjugations of bodies and the control of populations' (Foucault, 1990: 140). As Furedi suggests:

> In a larger context, disclosure represents the point of departure in the act of seeking help – an act of virtue in therapeutic culture. Help-seeking also constitutes the precondition for the management of people's emotions. That is

why there are such strong cultural pressures on the individual to 'acknowledge pain' and 'share'. Confession, preferably through therapy, relieves the burden of responsibility and offers a route to public acceptance – even acclaim.

(Furedi, 2003)

This approach, nonetheless, is not the complete answer to the 'why and what of loneliness'? As so far discussed, loneliness is not simply or singularly a deficit value and neither does it necessarily serve the therapeutic industries or the governance regimes just outlined. Rather, the creativity involved in writing, filming, sounding, painting, or photographing one's loneliness enables it to 'escape' its limitations, allowing each of us to ponder deeply on its existential axes and to question those very discourses that attempt to 'discipline' it. These are the creative qualities of the lonely imagination – something that the design and method for this book intends to innovatively establish.

Methods and design

What is a (lonely) room?

A room can be a physical space, one that has an entrance or a doorway, with walls or boundary markers. A room can be closed or open plan and can be furnished to be homely, or uninviting and threatening, as is the case with prison cells. Its light source, natural or artificial, colours the way the room is felt or inhabited. A room becomes lived in when it is filled with furniture, design choices, mementoes, keepsakes, and memory objects. A room comes-into-being through the way people use it, fall into it, make it their own.

Culturally, rooms are often designated as high or low, their spatial positioning lofty or claustrophobic. The attic and the basement are two types of room which, representationally speaking, are involved in violent excesses of power – horror is often found brooding in both. A room can call attention to its use or function and to the discourses that shape its design. The international airport, an atrium of consumption, an any-space-whatever, encourages one to eat, drink, and shop, and to put on a tourist's gaze before one has even boarded the plane. The airport often refuses connections even as it pretends to be a space to allow people to reconnect.

Institutionalised rooms such as the courtroom, the prison cell, or the classroom are designed to demarcate power relations and to allow the rituals of its governing body to take control. These operations can be resisted of course, with ownership or stewardship of the room making it a contested space. Children very often refuse to conform to the totalising 'bricks' found in their school environments.

A room doesn't need to have a ceiling. The garden is a room: its picket fence, brick wall, or grass edge separating it from the next-door neighbours, or the urban fringe it buttresses against. The garden is often an 'Eden' set next to the 'wilderness': a safe heaven, a place to grow things, or a nurturing space of play.

The beach is a room, natural and sometimes wild, its terrain marked by the lips of the ocean and blankets of sand, as one walks over its granulated floors. The tent and caravan are also rooms, as is the car, the train, and bus. These mobile rooms, these transient spaces, allow one to settle even as one is on the move. We take our rooms with us and make spaces into rooms wherever we roam. As this participant demonstrates, the university bus can become a vehicle of loneliness:

> This is a university bus (only runs on campus to transport students and staff from one building to another). Many Chinese universities have very huge campuses and have on-campus buses. The photo was shot before the driver boarded. Someone sitting in the co-driver seat (a student or a staff) was listening to music to enjoy the temporary loneliness.

They title their photograph, 'Lonely space' (Figure 1.4).

A room doesn't need to be a physical location, however: they exist in our imaginations, daydreams, and nightmares, and their elasticity or plasticity enables them to be shaped through both utopian and dystopian sentiments.

Figure 1.4 Lonely space

We create rooms to house our thoughts, to engage with possibility, to change our present course. We imaginatively enter rooms we know, have recently been in, to do something different, to feel its homely nature or to reject its oppressive or lonesome structures. Rooms, then, can be terribly and existentially lonely. Rooms demonstrate a powerful hold on the way we inhabit the world and can be used as a creative means with which to think and feel our lives differently.

Lonely methods

The loneliness room has all the traces, imprints, limitations, and possibilities of the rooms just described. Loneliness is associated with certain places and spaces; is found housed in the rooms of the real and in the imaginary; and one can consciously take one's loneliness to interior and exterior environments in order to dwell and reflect on its intensities. The loneliness room is not a fixed or singular physical space: it is also mental, associative, and transitory. A space can be lonely, felt as lonely for one, but not another. A space or place that was once happy may become a loneliness room, as one presently re-remembers it, and of what has since been lost or left behind. The loneliness room is both 'out there' in the social world and within one, drawn upon in the psychological realm to make sense of life and of living. All these spatial, temporal, and affective qualities were taken into the book's interventionist approach to fieldwork.

Interventions into fieldwork

As the structuring device of this book, the loneliness room is employed to shine a critical and creative light on where, when, how, and why loneliness is encountered. It intends to provide a new creative canvas with which to better understand how people live, providing them with the artistic space to represent their loneliness. *The Loneliness Room* is an example of participatory culture, of co-creation, since it is the lonely artwork of ordinary people which in part fills the 'lungs' of its pages. In so doing, the book extends and enriches the boundaries of creative ethnography since these lifeworld practices newly re-imagine what it means to be lonely.

The book's fieldwork involved five methods or approaches.

First, it asked participants to respond to the idea of the loneliness room through either sharing their creative responses, and/or completing a short questionnaire. Participants were not required to do both, however: they could respond creatively, or by filling out the questionnaire. The requested creative responses took in various forms: photographs (with or without captions); short videos; drawings; paintings; diary entries; social media posts;

hand-written letters/notes (which could have been posted to me); music or sound compositions; and audio recordings or recorded performances. As noted above, these creative submissions were supported by responses to four separate questionnaires: the first asked participants to outline what their loneliness room is, the context for their choice, and to name an artist or art piece that for them best captured their sense of loneliness (see Appendix 1). The second questionnaire asked participants to choose one film and a key scene or sequence that for them best captured loneliness (see Appendix 2). The third questionnaire asked participants to choose one photographer and/or photograph that secured the qualities of loneliness in its subject matter (see Appendix 3). The final questionnaire asked participants to name one song that made them feel lonely, or which for them contextually was connected to a time when they felt a deep well of aloneness consume or overcome them (see Appendix 4). Over 100 creative submissions were received, and over 350 questionnaires were completed during the life of the project, which ran between 2019 and 2022.

Second, it held an interactive workshop with a group of men who attended Coventry Men's Shed in England. The workshop lasted two hours and involved the men creating paintings that represented their loneliness room. The men also talked through what their loneliness room felt like, and these responses were transcribed.

Third, a Reddit sub-community, r/lonely, was followed and interacted with over a three-month timespan, and intensively over a 24-hour period on 2 May 2021. The r/lonely community users were asked to describe their loneliness room; devise haiku poems that captured their loneliness room, and to choose a film or song that best expressed loneliness for them. During 2 May, I followed the posts that were 'upvoted' on my feed.

Fourth, it draws upon creative autoethnography. The stories, memories, and creative impressions of the author are threaded throughout the book to both deepen its co-creative sentiments and to enable the researcher's own lonely imagination to underpin the writing.

Finally, it explores the creative art forms that the participants have either commented upon in their questionnaire responses, or which were utilised in their creative submissions. Photography and painting; film and cinema; the documentary and documentation; sound and music; and writing and posting are the art forms that the book's loneliness rooms are built upon.

The twin drivers of *The Loneliness Room* are the submitted creative work and questionnaire responses, and the published art it refers or alludes to. This duality enables the book to explore how creative practices – professional and commercial, home-made and personal – relate to one another, and are intimately connected in chains of lonely repetition.

The entangled research questions that energise *The Loneliness Room* are

1. What types of loneliness are imagined in and through the work of its participants?
2. How has/does art represent loneliness?
3. What thematic relationships and differences emerge between published or professional art and the art produced for the project?
4. How does the conceit of the loneliness room operationalise our experience of the lonely imagination?

These are the contours of *The Loneliness Room*, a book that reimagines the way loneliness is understood, handing its voice, eyes, and ears – its creative memories – to the participants who embraced its conceit.

But what rooms will we enter and spend time in?

Blocking and threading: the lonely rooms of the book

Each chapter of this book can be read as a room that we enter, observing the way loneliness emerges in the creative forms it represents. These rooms are interconnected: they belong relationally, in the same home, and so the stories that emerge are heard, seen, and felt like we are walking around the same lonely house.

The lonely rooms of the book are best understood as being in a *blocking and threading* relationship. That is to say, each chapter takes a singular art form, such as photography, but weaves into its exploration both professional examples and the work of its participants. These binding 'threads' then go on to connect with the art forms of the other chapters, enabling themes to emerge, stories to grow, loneliness to be creatively penetrated.

Each chapter is divided into three main but connected parts. They begin with a creative prelude that poetically stories the lonely art form that is to be explored. The art form is then analysed in terms of its relationship to loneliness and to loneliness rooms, and is connected to, and entangled with, the creative submissions and questionnaire responses that have been submitted by its participants. Finally, each chapter explores two in-depth case studies, and these weighted illustrations are again threaded or connected as the book moves from chapter to chapter, from room to room.

Chapter 2: Lonely emulsion: the loneliness in photography

Since photography's inception, photographers and photographic movements have powerfully captured loneliness and its associated forms. Taking the still lens to the city, the suburb, the rural, and the wild, photographers have captured loneliness as both claustrophobic and expansive, and as spatialised, set within prescribed horizontal and vertical axes. These spatial locators have been connected to age, ethnicity, and social class so that loneliness is tied to identity positions, to becoming youth and to isolated aging; to diaspora alienation; and to marginalisation and separation due to the politics of gender, sexuality, and social class. Further, photographers have captured the spontaneity of loneliness: the way it can suddenly emerge out of the sunlit cracks of an unplanned encounter.

The loneliness of photography stems also from its ontological past-ness and to the way it enacts a form of emulsified reminiscentia, since memories eternally hold the photograph in a slow dance of regret and not-forgetting. The beauty of loneliness and its power to translate pain as an affective assemblage rises up in photography's spatiality and temporality, and in its haptic sense. The photograph doesn't just represent loneliness but *embodies* it. In this chapter, then, I take the reader through the different ways that photographers and the project's participants have captured loneliness, drawing attention to the shared 'rooms' that frame their melancholy. The chapter has two central case studies.

Case study 1: (Alley) Loneliness in the Street *photographs of Maika Elan*

Vietnamese photographer Maika Elan captures the isolated lives of the hikikomori, young Japanese men who haven't participated in society, or shown a desire to do so, for at least a year. They rely instead on their parents to take care of them. Shut off from the external world they exist in a series of physical and mental loneliness rooms. In *Inside Hanoi,* Elan captures the everyday life of the thousands of people who live in the small alleys: her photos 'try to describe the people, the living space, the joy and sadness at the end of the alley in the heart of Hanoi' (2015).

Case study 2: Alec Soth's loners

American photographer Alec Soth's work captures 'loners and dreamers' and the 'off-beat, hauntingly banal images of modern America'. In *Sleeping by the Mississippi* (2004), for example, Soth began to follow the Mississippi River in his car, driving from place to place, letting himself progress towards locations he had vaguely researched and 'using the river as a route to connect with strangers along the way' (O'Toole, 2019).

These two studies offer the book contrasting geographies of loneliness, from the urban to the rural, from the 'East' to the 'West'. Soth's work captures the way loneliness 'travels' across rural America, while Elan's photographs depict the claustrophobia of loneliness in the deprived parts of Chiba and Hanoi. Both artists work through cultural myths, and locate loneliness in terms of the economic conditions that prevail in the country where they are set.

The two case studies offer the chapter contrasting aesthetics, but they are connected by the role of young strangers who populate their work – people who are both inside and outside the environments they are framed in (Simmel, 1950). The theme of the lonely stranger is also central to the way loneliness is explored in cinema, providing the book with a thematic and conceptual link to Chapter 3.

Chapter 3: Dim the lights: loneliness in cinema

There is a long history of exploring loneliness in cinema: it is found in genre filmmaking such as the melodrama and science fiction, in social realism and modernism, and in the work of auteurs such as Wong Kar-wai and Lynne Ramsay. One can periodise loneliness in cinema, such as the way Kolker (2011), mentioned above, has done when looking at the failed masculinity of urban dwellers found in 1970s American cinema, and films such as *Taxi Driver* (Scorsese, 1976). Loneliness is also aesthetic, crafted into the high and low, inner and outer spatial metaphors of city films, and is given sonic agency, since isolation can be heard as a cinematic 'silence' in the dead of the night. There are age and gender markers to the way loneliness is played out and signified, where loss is carried through aging transformations. As the book's participants observe, cinema itself is a loneliness room: people go there to experience isolation, to be alone, since the theatre of cinema calls forth the expressions of privatised experience.

In this chapter, I chart the way loneliness is fictionalised in contemporary cinema, drawing upon such films as *Under the Skin* (Glazer, 2004), *Her* (Jonze, 2013), *Red Road* (Arnold, 2006), *Ghost World* (Zwigoff, 2001), and *Lost in Translation* (Coppola, 2003). I also explore the lonely video work supplied by the participants, seeing and hearing cinematic 'sirens' between them. The chapter has two central case studies.

Case study 1: Arrested development: the lonesome films of Yorgos Lanthimos

Auteur Yorgos Lanthimos creates film worlds composed of misfits, outliers, and the socially disconnected. Moving across forms and genres, his work explores the barriers to communication, the perversion at the heart of the middle class, and the way the senses are uncoupled from the noise of modern life. Lanthimos is fascinated by the drive for mastery – in both its mundanities and extremes – and by the inscrutability of human behaviour. The director's loneliness rooms are found in abandoned hotels and apartment complexes, in everyday life rituals, in suburbia, and the regulated routines of habitual living. Films under analysis include *Dogtooth* (2009), *Alps* (2011), *The Lobster* (2015), and *The Killing of a Sacred Deer* (2017).

Case study 2: Lost in space: the loneliness of science fiction

In this case study I explore the way popular science fiction film and television create the conduits of loneliness through 'the last man on earth' motif, human apocalypse, time travel, and future-set social isolation. As a genre, through its future possibility permutations, science fiction explores the issues that most concern the present, and it is the vectors of loneliness that dominate its outpourings today. When science fiction takes us to the end of time, where loneliness blossoms, new participatory cultures soon emerge. The rooms of loneliness in science fiction are wasted fields, ruined cities, cargo vessels, deep space, black holes, surveillance cameras, and AI interfaces. Films under analysis include *Solaris* (Tarkovsky, 1972), *Gravity* (Cuarón, 2013), *Children of Men* (Cuarón, 2006), and *Blade Runner* (Scott, 1982).

These two studies allow the book to extend its analysis to illustrations that work across national cultures, as is the case with the study of science fiction, and to authors and texts which are non-realist. In both case studies, loneliness exists in an alternative or future reality, enabling the representations of loneliness to be expressed through metaphorical signifiers. Further, the spatial dynamics of the two case studies 'open out' and 'close down': the expansive geographies of science fiction take loneliness into outer space, while the confined cartographies of Lanthimos's work shuts space down. The two case studies then spatially 'echo' but extend the studies found in the preceding chapter. Finally, the two case studies move the conduits of loneliness from the lonely young strangers of Chapter 2 to considerations of gender and social class; the figure of the last man and the gendered AI in science fiction; and to the 'broken' or traumatised middle-class families found in Lanthimos's film work. The participants' work entangles with these themes, foregrounding how their own social position defines the type of loneliness they experience and how they seek to creatively express it. The themes of gender and social class are then picked up and carried forward in Chapter 4.

Chapter 4: Lonely realities: documenting loneliness

In this chapter I discuss the way the screen documentary takes the moving camera to the street, to directly engage with the social reality of loneliness to effect change. Documenting loneliness is a political weapon. The documentary is also an affective assemblage, inviting viewers to experience the everyday reality it is filming: as it moves across the lives of ordinary individuals, it *activates* the lonely senses.

British social realism, *cinéma vérité*, and direct cinema are examples of documentary forms which have captured the conditions of loneliness and isolation, whether it be slum dwellers, inmates, or youth subcultures. In contemporary terms, the digital video diary and the compressed short video documentary have enabled non-professionals to record their own stories and share and stream them. Documenting loneliness has become a form of creative self-expression: an attempt by the lonely to make connections.

These realist works are also connected to DIY celebrity culture, where the glamour and connectedness of fame not only make isolated people feel lonelier, but create the conditions for them to crave renown for themselves. Ordinary people 'document' their loneliness rooms to become visible, trapping themselves in a cycle of disappointment since being seen is not the same as achieving renown. The chapter has two central case studies.

Case study 1: Amy's loneliness room (Amy, Asif Kapadia, 2015)

Amy, Asif Kapadia's documentary on fame, loneliness, and mental illness, charts Amy Winehouse's story from her childhood in Southgate, North London, to her death from alcohol poisoning in 2011. The director avoids showing his interviewees on screen, and instead mixes archive footage with audio from new interviews with Amy's parents, childhood friends, and her ex-husband, Blake Fielder-Civil. The singer – who struggled with drug and alcohol addiction, depression, and bulimia – was plagued by the attention of the press and shocked by the attention that her bluntly honest songs and remarkable voice attracted. 'I don't think I'm going to be at all famous', says a pre-fame Winehouse. She became, of course, extraordinarily famous and this renown transformed into her loneliness room, as I will go on to argue.

Case study 2: Lonely children in The 3 Rooms of Melancholia *(Honkasalo, 2004)*

This award-winning documentary film captures how the Chechen War has psychologically affected children in Russia and in Chechnya. Divided into three episodes or 'rooms', the film is characterised by an 'elegantly paced observational style, which uses little dialog, minimal voice-over commentary and a spare but evocative musical score' (Icarus Films, nd). *The 3 Rooms of Melancholia*, which poetically blends sustained close-ups of children's faces with grey, fog-shrouded landscapes, illuminates the emotional devastation wrought on young children who have little or no understanding of the historical and political reasons for the bitter conflict.

These two studies highlight two of the conditions through which contemporary loneliness powerfully emerges: conflict and violence, and the 'frenzy of renown' of celebrity culture. *The 3 Rooms of Melancholia* explores conflict through the way it affects young children: their loneliness rooms both literalised and emotionalised in the film's title. This study also reconnects the book with the photographs of Maika Elan, analysed in Chapter 2, and the dispossessed condition that many people face today. In Elan's photographs, it is young migrant Japanese men, while here is it is the children of war. *Amy* stands in sharp contrast to *The 3 Rooms of Melancholia*, swapping bitter conflict for the tears of fame. Nonetheless, celebrity culture increasingly drives the aspirations and goals of young people, and the failure to achieve fame or notoriety has a corresponding lessening in the way the self is valued (Mendick et al., 2015). Amy Winehouse embodies this tension: she craved fame and yet it made her lonely. As a role model this loneliness connected with her fans in deeply meaningful ways. Of course, it was Amy's music, her voice, that sounded out loneliness.

Chapter 5: None but the lonely heart: the sounds of loneliness

In this chapter I explore the way sound is mobilised to capture and communicate what it feels like to be lonely. Engaging centrally with popular music, the sound design of screen media, and the conversational address of podcasts, I look at the way the auditory values of loneliness mark people's lives and powerfully shape the form and content of art forms. As our participants attest, popular songs very often carry narrative stories about loneliness, and they can be connected to rituals and events where in hearing 'that song' a lonely memory is elicited. These lonely songs are often encountered in spaces or places which come to embody and carry forth the melodies of loneliness, becoming auditory loneliness rooms. Individual biographies emerge when sounding loneliness, but this exists alongside the cultural 'chatter' that is found across aural forms, such as the radio and the podcast, in which experts and laypeople give their advice, and bare their lonely souls. The chapter has two central case studies.

Case study 1: *The sounds of loneliness:* Joker's loneliness room

Joker (Phillips, 2019) is organised and dissected by spatial collisions: it is marked by the 'non-place', 'the-any-space-whatever', and by a number of high and low spatial metaphors that stand as affective and effective registers of social alienation, communal break-down, and privatised living. These wasted spaces are full of dreadful sounds, as if the sonic spaces carry forth the film's lonely despair. Audiences get to see and hear these urban spaces through the movement of Arthur Fleck/The Joker, whose point of view moves the film forward. Movement as well as moving is important here since it is precisely because of the way that Arthur embodies space that we get to know its corrosive and then liberating possibilities. Arthur first moves like a ghost or a zombie, but as the film progresses and fantasies collide, there is a spring in his step, reverie in his gestures, an animalism in his walk – all captured through a metered sound design and a musical score that powerfully rhythms Arthur and the spaces that he encounters. When Arthur dances through space, he transforms it, showing us the possibility of affective action even as he/it becomes ever more grotesque. The film entangles melody with madness, madness with alienated space, alienated space with noise, as the lonely world goes increasingly insane.

Case study 2: Alone Together, A Curious Exploration of Loneliness

In the podcast series, *Alone Together*, host Peg Fong asks 'experts and researchers around the world' to 'share their insights about what we know about loneliness'. Running over two seasons, the series examines loneliness in various cultural and social contexts, explores its psychology and biology, and navigates its relationship to historical and contemporary habitus. In so doing, *Alone Together* not only aurally takes loneliness into various 'rooms' but operates out of its own lonely cocoon – its aesthetics and formatting create an intimate space for lonesome discourses to sound.

This chapter's two case studies establish the way music, sound design, and the talk of loneliness shape its impressions and articulations. They stand as markers for not only the way sound has become central to our understanding of loneliness, but for the tensions and ambiguities in these discourses. Both *Joker* and *Alone Together* can be 'heard' as representing loneliness as anxious, chronic, and existential, contributing to and resisting the loneliness pandemic that marks much of contemporary culture. These ideas of loneliness being everywhere are taken up in the next chapter, where the ubiquity of social media provides both the deep well for loneliness to develop, and a way to escape its confines.

Chapter 6: Lonely words: writing loneliness in the post-digital age

In one sense, we have never been more connected: numerous digital interfaces enable us to connect in real time over vast spaces (Baruah, 2012). Facebook, TikTok, Snapchat, and Instagram have become engines for connection and belonging, allowing people to share personal videos, photographs, memes, and forms of creative bricolage. Of course, as noted above, empirical research suggests that social media increases one's loneliness and feelings of anxiety and depression, particularly for young people (Woods and Scott, 2016). Bedroom Instagrammers, influencers, and Facebookers find that it often becomes their shrine to loneliness. In this chapter I explore this oxymoron – social loneliness – looking at the way these communal digital interfaces operate. The chapter will both narrate the empirical evidence on the relationship between social media and will textually analyse a range of sites where loneliness has been curated. It will draw upon the writings that participants submitted, revealing in their confessions the way loneliness gripped and released them.

Case study 1: r/lonely

On this sub-community Reddit page, people can post their messages of loneliness. The page carries the posts of the broken hearted, the socially alienated, the marginalised, and the 'damaged'. Like all Reddit communities it offers a chronology of loneliness, but when read like a newsfeed, as some users do, it becomes a storeroom of loneliness. However, the postings are often not a shout out to despair, but the very means to reconnect and to speak to and with other lonely people.

Case study 2: the lonely intimacy of The Red Hand Files

In Nick Cave's weekly email letter responses to fans' questions, he seeks to establish intimate, spiritual connections. Laid out on what resembles watermarked paper and as if they have been typed, there is a material, embodied intimacy to not only the way the letters appear, as if they are scented analogue exchanges in a dematerialised digital world, but in their imagined two-wayness, as if fan and Cave are privately conversing. Topics discussed range from religion to death, love and longing, and to the taste distinctions that one might make over art, literature, music, and poetry. It is these letters that I analyse in this chapter, finding love and loneliness across their sheets.

The Reddit r/lonely community attracts posts from young people around the world. They share their stories of loneliness, key 'lonely' events, and comment and rate each other's posts. Loneliness is both conferred but also communed. By contrast, *The Red Hand Files* is formed from questions raised by Nick Cave's wider fan-base, but whose demographic is decidedly older. The two case studies, then, show us oscillating ends of the age spectrum, but with connections to the way social media allows them to engage in communication otherwise found wanting. By focusing on Cave, we also return the book to the question of fame and belonging and the feeling that one is lonely *without* renown, and yet the sharing of loneliness on these platforms ignites it, transforms it into empowering modes of confession.

Chapter 7: A pandemic of creative loneliness

The loneliness room project was started before the COVID-19 outbreak and the subsequent closure of international borders and the numerous lockdown, isolation, and quarantine measures that kept people indoors, unable to socialise in ways that they were accustomed to. What these events afforded the research was both a canvas in which new forms of 'collective' creativity emerged and a set of contexts where people newly experienced loneliness or felt it in ways that rendered them affectively thin and fragile against the tradewinds of the pandemic. The loneliness room became a particularly apt metaphor for people to hang their lonely coats on since the idea of the room – literal, figurative, and creative – seemed to enter everyday consciousness and the four-walled coordinates of one's habitus.

In this chapter I explore the way that everyday forms of creativity responded to the first wave of the coronavirus pandemic. I argue that these creative responses did two things. First, they demonstrated the rich agency that ordinary people had in shaping and sharing their experience of lonely isolation. Second, through the creative works generated and circulated, a critical lens was placed on the way that the pandemic carried forward the inequalities inherent in modern systems of the governance of loneliness. The chapter is divided into two main sections: the first looks at a range of creative works made by ordinary people to reconnect them to the social world. The second section looks at the creative works that were explicitly politicised and activist in nature, turning loneliness into a political project.

This last chapter, then, not only draws on multiple art forms and everyday practices, bringing together into one interconnected space the creative material that has been previously analysed separately, but refocuses on the tensions between different types of loneliness and the capitalist systems that try to manufacture and control their form.

Conclusion: if nobody speaks of loneliness rooms

In the conclusion, I draw together the diverse themes and threads of the book, situating it within my own creative practice. I look to celebrate the ordinariness of loneliness while recognising the unequal forms and formations that it materialises from. I reflect on the journey of the project, on the rooms it visited, and the stories that it was gifted.

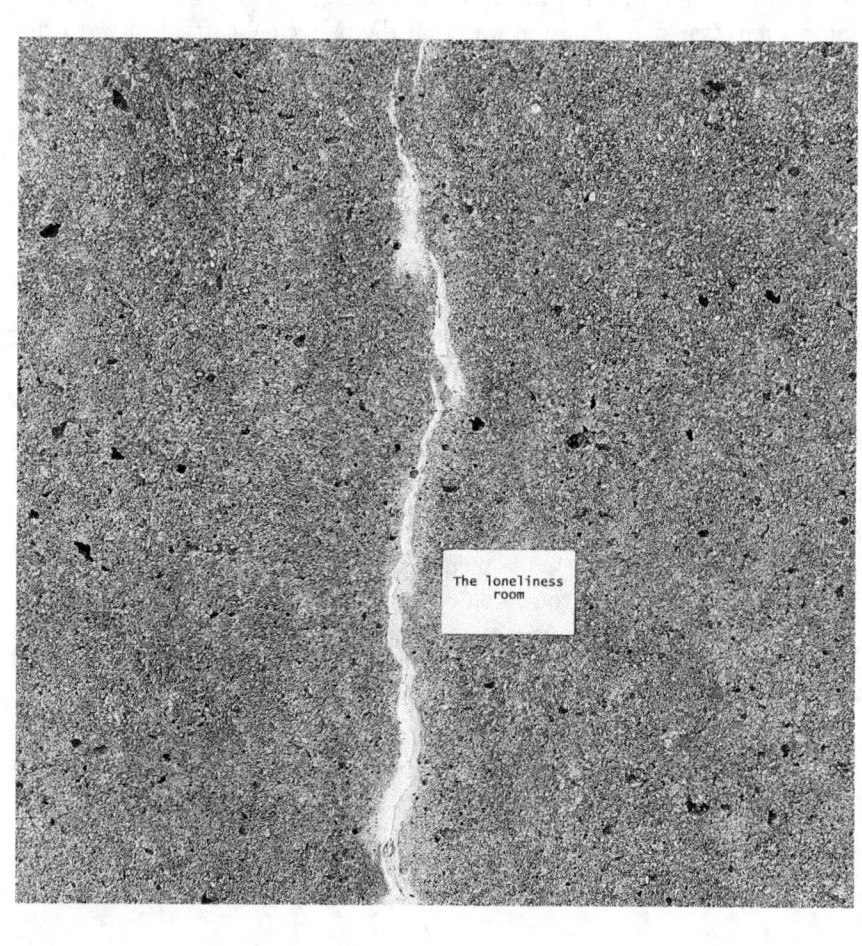

2

Lonely emulsion: the loneliness in photography

Prelude: lonely emulsion

The darkroom sits at the end of a long corridor with its neon sign, 'Darkroom in Use', illuminated. A quietness surrounds its door: one knows not to enter. Inside, in the semi-darkness, a red safelight casts crimson across the walls, ceiling, and floor. Along the back wall is a sink and a run of three trays filled with chemicals. The aroma of vinegar and metals blends, staining the air with the scents of emulsified photography. On a taut clothesline a series of photographs are pegged: their black and white shadows have been left to dry in the red dark.

In the first tray, a hand holding a tong begins to wash a sheet of orthochromatic paper. Partially blind to the red light, the paper slowly develops its invisible image, conjuring up its hidden ghosts as it does so. A clock ticks as time moves forwards and then freezes, its alarm a wake-up call to move the photograph along. Into the next tray it falls, enabling its now visible image to merge with the ripples of the fixer, finally giving away its photographic story.

The photographer examines this becoming-image, registering its exposure, light and shade. They are thrown back in time to the initial point of capture, to their point of view, and to the way their hands held the camera and curated the shot. As lines and shapes emerge, they are able to fill in the gaps before the full ontology of the photograph appears. The photographer feels both the melancholy of this loss and the joy of seeing these images newly return.

In the darkroom the photographer is by nature existentially lonely: they exist in a sublime state of becoming, seeing the world as both absence and as potential and possibility. Ghosts rise out of the acetic acid, pouring themselves onto the paper and into the hands of the photographer. These ghosts also embody the moment when they were not there: they are photographically wetted with their loneliness. The silence of the darkroom resembles the start of a wake or funeral, but life is here resurrected and the prints, holding the wet traces of past human events, are awakened.

The darkroom is a loneliness room: shut off from the outside world it is a space of introspection and revelation; it wallows in its own aloneness and isolation; and it produces photographs that are always haunted by their own lonely absences. Photographs capture the moments, environments, and the relations of loneliness, becoming an art form that represents and embodies its qualities and intensities.

The darkroom is a loneliness room because it is, mostly, no more. With the digital age, and with the ubiquity of the camera in mobile phones, photographs exist as living data: present and accessible from the moment they are taken. Photographs may well now be lonely for the slow time of the analogue age.

Today's photographers find themselves in a rush of images, which fall out of their camera into social media settings, rendering absence an ever presence, creating digital ghosts that are constantly in the light. And yet, perhaps, the photographer, like the ghosts of images, still retreats into the darkroom of their imagination, to wash their hands in lonely emulsion, to enjoy their escapist time of being alone.

The photographer washes the photograph and pegs it to the clothesline – leaving its shapes and shadows to dry in the red dark.

The loneliness in photography

Feeling and voicing photographs

By their very nature, photographs offer up a relationship to loneliness. From the moment of photographic capture to their display in private, communal, and public settings, they seem knitted to processes, impressions, and memories that dwell in the well of the lonely imagination. The commercial photographer, for example, is both removed and a part of the environment they seek to capture. They belong and they don't. They are present in the scene but very often attempt to remove themselves so that they are not noticed, are not really there. They become non-participant observers to whatever stands or moves before their camera.

For example, the wedding photographer, employed to capture the happy moments of the day, exists as an outsider to this event ritual. The manufacture of 'spectacle' moments, such as capturing the 'happy couple' in an opulent or Edenic setting, extends their embodied distance and becomes for them – because of endless repetition – inherently banal, inevitably joyless. Their photographs, and their relationship to them, exist at the level of the 'studium' or mere political or cultural convention with an 'average affect' (Barthes, 1981).

Nonetheless, when we look *into* photographs, to see beyond their surface level, we can reach for, or be sensorially assaulted by, the 'punctum'. When viewing the molecular details of certain photographs, a highly personalised response may emerge resulting in an 'accident which pricks me (but also bruises me, is poignant to me)' (Barthes, 1981: 26–27). The punctum cuts through photographic code and the cultural training that shapes reception, revealing itself to the viewer as an open wound and as a pathfinder to the memorial and the embodied. One can look upon a 'banal' or 'generic' photograph and witness it reveal something of the viewer's heart, of their longings, losses, and traumas – one can *feel* its cutting images soliciting an affective and somatic response. One can look into a photograph and see one's very own loneliness room emerge.

In this respect, the wedding photographer may only be partially caught in the closed, representational web of the studium since what always remains is the chance that they are wounded by a moment that reveals more than it captures, such as their own reflection, accidently caught in a mirror or on a surface, staring sadly back at them. This is true for all members of the wedding party. What they see in the photographs are the lived, experiential minutiae of the day as they experienced or felt it. Of course, wedding celebration photographs also reveal the nature of the lonely imagination: this day is meant to be the pinnacle of one's life journey but, as such, accidently reveals the ordinariness of everything that sits either side of it. These photographs are made of longing and of loss even as they dance in the joy of romantic love.

Family albums are full of photographs that offer wounding moments and thus also become narrated or storied loneliness rooms. Filling the album's pages are familial conflicts, lost opportunities, break-ups, themed dramas, alongside the chronology of growing up, moving on, and growing old. The family album is full of dividing rooms and connecting doorways so that as one's fingers run over familiar faces and yesterday's dramas, the 'touching' of that photograph registers deeply within, igniting a profound sense of existential loneliness. As Elizabeth Edwards contends, 'Not only are photographs touched, but they are also enmeshed in a fluid continuum of touch and gesture by means of which groups of interlocutors are made to cohere ... photographs are viewed in groups: bodies touching, proximate sense of an interpreting community' (2009: 44).

Family albums can reveal loneliness for other reasons, such as it being a document that recounts isolation, entrapment, or incarceration. For example, in Adria L. Imada's exploration of the medical incarceration of patients with leprosy, sent to a remote settlement on the island of Molokai, Hawaii, she notes how the family album became a site that revealed the shared 'kinship' that came from the loneliness they were jointly experiencing. Viewing the album created by Franklin Mark, a Chinese immigrant descendant, Imada suggests:

> Mark's visions mingled joyous occasions with mourning for relationships aborted or unfulfilled. On another album page, a group of men and women laugh on a beach in a scene bathed in light, and the overexposure of the photo also increases this effect … However, above on the same page, Mark sits next to another male friend in a far darker and moodier scene. The young men wear light-colored shirts, but the composition is dense with shadowy detail – a dark wood-panelled house and foliage frames their expressions, Mark inscribed, 'Two pals, lonely and sad.' Mark further accented this theme of darkness and light, loss and joy with a photograph of the Kalaupapa lighthouse perched above the coast. As he wrote, 'Without this guiding light, ships will be helpless during the night'.
>
> (Imada, 2018: 305)

The centrality of loss to the loneliness of photography is doubled in these subaltern family albums: there is the loss of one's freedom and of connection to wider society; and there is the loss of losing friends as they pass or are moved on. However, it is the textures and absences in these photographs which create its lonely rooms: the play with shadow; claustrophobic framing; and closed borders, set alongside the longing for open space, sea travel, and the 'lights' beyond the caged horizon. One imagines the 'interpreting community' – those fellow sufferers of leprosy – touching and being touched by these photographic 'gestures' with each shot affectively confirming their lonely state.

However, it is Imada who here provides the analysis of these photographs, so that she is in effect the interpreting community, providing the reading that undresses the photographs. It is Imada's own understanding of loneliness which caresses the images she analyses. Her voice sounds out the meaning of these lonely family album images, directly drawing in the researcher to these stories of lonely imaginings.

The research method of the photovoice takes up a different position: it invites its participants to take their own photographs and to select the ones they would like to analyse or explain. Organised around a theme, participants are asked to 'reflect upon and explore the reasons, emotions and experiences that have guided their chosen images' (Wang and Burris, 1997: 370). Such a co-creative method works well with loneliness, of course, since it enables the participant to set their own understanding of it, and to use located, personal images to represent their relationship to feeling lonely.

In Ashleigh Charles and Anne Felton's remarkable photovoice research, *Exploring Young People's Experiences and Perceptions of Mental Health and Well-being*, they show how an image of an empty fridge taken by their participant is described as 'sometimes I feel empty, this shows times when

I'm upset sometimes there's nothing there, nothingness, I try and feel something but nothing takes over'. Similarly,

> Another image displayed the benches outside their college, and the young person used this as a visual metaphor to describe their experience: 'although I've met some great people at college I do sometimes feel slightly excluded at times, I feel that the photo represents exactly how I feel when I feel like I'm on my own'.
>
> (Charles and Felton, 2020: 15)

While photovoice was not the explicit method of this book's research, the centrality of creation and critical autonomy to understanding loneliness are, as are the themes of loss, longing, and marginality found in the photographs and related questionnaire responses submitted for the project. My voice, my feelings, also find their way into the loneliness rooms revealed.

Bedrooms, cars, and moons: loss, longing, and suburbia

Ke Chen, a final-year undergraduate student at Heilongjiang University in China, submitted a photograph titled 'Quiet loneliness' (Figure 2.1). The photograph was taken on campus with his mobile phone as he went back to

Figure 2.1 Quiet loneliness

his university dorm after studying in the library for the entrance examination to the graduate school – a very competitive, nationwide exam in China. Chen 'felt very lonely during the period of exam preparation as my future was uncertain and I had a lot of pressure from parents and myself'. He thinks that the 'loneliness room' is an extension of 'loners'.

For Maryyam, it is the relative silence and solitude of their bedroom that enables it to be their loneliness room:

> My bedroom, when it's quiet and nobody else is in it except myself. Sometimes to have a moment of silence, sometimes to lay in bed and rest (without sleeping), to think about whatever is on my mind especially if I am feeling overwhelmed by several things or a problem that is weighing on me. Its gently lit with natural light, usually filtered slightly by the pulled curtains. The only sound is that of the fan running and the birds outside – maybe the odd passing car. The scuttle of the house just barely comes through from downstairs so I can easily ignore it. The sheets on the bed are cool, the pillow always feels soft somehow ... All the objects in the room are familiar to me, and if there's ever something new in my room I like to ignore it. Everything smells familiar too; like myself, so it feels like I am inside my head.

These notions of plenitude, safety, and interiority are represented in their photograph (Figure 2.2). Invisible in the shot, the point-of-view photograph captures Maryyam observing the street outside as early evening or morning arrives.

Figure 2.2 Inside my head

The loneliness in photography 41

Maryyam's description of her bedroom is sensory: light, weight, temperature, touch, and smell are employed to bring it into textual, imaginary view. We are able to see it, walk around it, feel the coolness of the bedsheets that are described. Creative method here brings the full experiential weight of the room into existence, providing us with the affective mood that is being highlighted.

In Dan's photograph (Figure 2.3), we are also presented with a twilight scene: a point-of-view shot from his perspective, looking up from his bed and towards the partially drawn curtains. A shaft of light enters the bedroom, invading the dark and calling the dawn forwards. For Dan, this moment is one he dreads, since

> my loneliness room is my bedroom during the small morning hours. That gloom period between 6 and 8am. Light sneaks through the shades and begins to softly let me know that rest and certainty are drawing to an end. Modern living requires me to break with the bonds of sleep and the beautiful form of my sleeping wife against my will. I must leave this sanctuary in order to maintain it. I caress Michele and wish her a soft good morning with the bittersweet notion that soon I will be thrust to the outside world. Things will be less certain than they are here. I yearn to be able to say no. To stay. In that moment, the feeling of isolation is never more noticeable to me.

Dan goes on to suggest, however, that his bedroom 'morphs' since 'it's my rest room, my desire room, my sick bed, my "ate too much" room, my

Figure 2.3 Dawn calls

comfort room. It is a place of darkness and of light. It envelops me and sends me to sleep. It startles me awake. A place of contradictions'. Again, we can see how the description of the bedroom demonstrates the two sides of loneliness: existential reverie and despondent gloom. Dan has these forces walking its floor, getting into bed with him, so that we see loneliness over a period of shifting contexts.

In a similar vein of contrast and tension, Rhonda submitted the following photograph (Figure 2.4) and poetic stanza:

> *The Gloaming*
> Between night and day, drive the gloaming.
> When the light beckons the ink dark – My loneliness room.

The temporal nature of Maryyam's, Dan's, and Rhonda's photographs places their loneliness in liminal time zones: between night and day, day and night. Rhonda's photograph has been worked upon: it is sepia tinted and emulsified so that it resembles an image resurrected from the analogue age. It is a photograph of time past as much as time becoming. For Rhonda,

Figure 2.4 The gloaming

loneliness emerges on the drive home as the night falls and the road narrows, and as the clouds melt into the inked sky.

The centrality of the car as a loneliness room is also a recurring space for a number of the lonely room participants. It acts as a private, mobile cocoon, where one can exit the world and leave behind the troubles and dramas that it may contain. For this participant,

> My loneliness room is a car interior, in which a double-sided cassette plays albums by The Dirty Three, over and over, ad infinitum, as the world goes by my windows ... I travel in my car interior, gliding at one speed, under glass, as I drive around, alone. I'm a lonelier version of Iggy Pop's 'The Passenger'. Outside is not a site of endless night-time possibility, but a place in which all the other people live, beyond reach. It's a horrible kind of funny that they don't know.

Again, movement and speed, interiority and exteriority shape the sentiments of this lonely room imagining. One can *hear* 'The Passenger' blasting out of the car speakers; one can *see* the neon lights of the city rushing by; one can *feel* the isolation the driver feels as the smudges of people they drive past remain out of reach.

For Sophia, the car is her loneliness room because it enables her to engage in a one-way conversation that cannot be interrupted or overheard, and which allows her to both question who she is, and to ruminate on missed opportunities, on plans gone wrong:

> When I turn the radio volume down, I'm not only on my own, but alone. And while I'm driving, and concentrating on the road, with nothing else to listen to, my mind entertains me. It shows me scenes from my life. My car is my loneliness room, cornering me like an excited new friend at a dinner party, telling me the same stories over and over while the more exciting guests meander further and further away. 'Do you remember the one where you had surgery, but nobody knew you were even sick? It's weird that you didn't tell anybody, but still felt entitled to be lonely', the car tells me. 'Maybe you secretly like it here'. Sometimes when I've had enough of talking to my car, I turn the sound up and have a big cry. The problem with therapy is that it requires more than just one person to be there. When most of your waking and dreaming life is spent in the company of others, there's rare chances to be alone with yourself. Then when those opportunities finally present themselves, you feel unprepared for the impending self-talk. 'Urgh, you again', it feels. 'Time for you to go', it says, as you slide your phone out from your pocket. The fact is, though, that idle time isn't the same as being alone, or being restful. When I'm in my loneliness room I have no choice but to confront it. 'Remember the time ... How about this one ...? Stop me if you've heard this one before ... Just kidding! I don't think you've properly dealt with this one yet' ... My car wasn't always this place for me, but now it's so a part of my routine I can't remember how

> I used to think about these things before I had one. Sometimes I feel so lonely I just go out and sit there. I might drive to the top of the hill with a cup of coffee and just ruminate, or sit in the Coles car park for way longer than I need to for a trip to get two tomatoes.

As with Dan, Sophia experiences the two sides of the loneliness room: possibility and prohibition. The car offers her a space to open up and reflect on her loneliness, but it also becomes a space that produces or solicits negative lonely feelings. Her response draws attention to the way social life leaves its imprint on the relational self and the need to debrief away from the noise of the world. This is the same for this participant, but here it is the kids' school run and an unhappy marriage which shapes their experience of the car as a loneliness room:

> I use the space to think about who I want to be. It's a recurring thought process, of admitting and denying, of understanding I married someone I didn't know properly, of seeing how brilliant a father he is, of being witness to the love he shares with our children and being unable to take part in this, of wondering if it would be better to break this or carry on and being stuck in the stasis.

The car is here situational: the loneliness being countenanced is to do with a relationship that has begun to fail. It is also gendered: the participant imagines their selfhood in relation to the confines and discourses associated with a patriarchal marriage and traditional parenting roles.

The centrality of gender to the loneliness room is something Erin picks up when responding to the question, 'what photographer best captures loneliness for you?' She responds:

> Carol Jerrems: An Australian feminist photographer, who died young and whose art practice was well-ahead of its time, the look-back of her self-portraits betray a sense of separation of her experience and life from that of her peers, and her portraits of other women in Australian suburbia in the 60s and 70s reflects a desperate limitation and yearning (the loneliness of an unfulfilling life).

Erin goes on to reference *Vale Street* (1975) as one example from Jerrem's work that 'suggests the loneliness of the photographer in the context of her peers, and how she is distanced from them. It suggests the price of being defiant, an artist, as well as a woman is loneliness (through difference and social exclusion)'. In Erin's response, it is space and time that take hold of loneliness. She sees the confines of Australian suburbia in the 1960s and 1970s as alienating (married) women – who had been forced or conditioned to live limited lives – and for creating a climate where radical women artists were socially excluded.

Jerrem's loneliness room is captured in her photographs through distance and difference techniques. In *Vale Street* she appears topless, in front of and between two bare-chested and tattooed men. All three return the gaze, staring back at the viewer. Jerrem is captured in translucent light while the two men appear to emerge from the shadows, with foliage creeping into the space they stand in. Sexual intimacies are hinted at, but Jerrem's defiant stance gives her power over the men and the viewer. And yet, for Erin, Jerrem's existential isolation in the shot reveals the loneliness of her gender, of being woman, and also the loneliness of the female artist who stands against the suffocating discourses of patriarchal life.

In photography, suburbia is often represented as a loneliness room that presents and hides the alienating nature of familial human relationships (Gill, 2013). Symmetrical tree-lined streets; pastel-painted houses; gardens with picket fences; and pristine garages with parked cars suggest a banal, lonely conformity hanging over the 'burb. Such photographs are very often emptied of people or else they are barely witnessed, standing decentred behind shutters, net curtains, or partially closed doors. Space seems penned in and community surveillance touches the sensibility of the photographs: no one is clearly seen but everyone is felt to be under the microscope.

The photographs' emptiness also suggests that the horror of chronic loneliness may lurk behind the net curtains, behind the shutters of suburban homes. Such a representation is captured in Gregory Crewdson's *Beneath the Roses* series, in which

> anonymous townscapes, forest clearings and broad, desolate streets are revealed as sites of mystery and wonder; similarly, ostensibly banal interiors become the staging grounds for strange human scenarios. In one image a lone and pregnant woman stands on a wet street corner just before dawn: she is a small but a portentous still point in a world of trajectories. On a stormy night in another nondescript town, a man in a business suit stands beside his car, holding out a hand to the cleansing water in apparent mystification. In a plush bedroom, a man and a woman – prototypes of middle-class American dislocation – are visited by a songbird, who gazes at the woman from its perch on the vanity. Crewdson's scenes are tangibly atmospheric: visually alluring and often deeply disquieting. Never anchored precisely in time or place, these and the other narratives of *Beneath the Roses* are rather located in the dystopic landscape of the anxious American imagination.
>
> (White Cube, 2005)

The anxiety at the heart of many of the *Beneath the Roses* photographs is one of chronic loneliness, particularly when it comes to the position of women – mothers, wives, daughters – who are often photographed in isolated bedroom settings.

In *Untitled, Winter (Mother on Bed with Blood)* (2004), a woman, seated on a single bed, stares forlornly into space. An ornate mirror that hangs on one of the florid walls catches her reflection, while electric blue light pours in from the netted window. On the bed is a blood-stained sheet and folded up washing, while on the floor of the room are discarded clothes and shadowy objects that cannot be fully seen. Two table lights throw light onto the walls, while a miraculous, invisible halo spotlight illuminates the bed and the woman, as if this is a still taken from a film melodrama.

What shapes this scene is loneliness: the single bed suggests the woman (Mother) sleeps alone, while the blood spot registers as a trace of a violent act, too high on the bed sheet to be a menstruation stain. She is deep in contemplation or, rather, appears paralysed by her status, by an invisible cloak of loneliness. She longs 'to escape from the stifling sexuality imposed … by the suburban domestic environment' (Garrison and Krejcarek, 2017: 234).

Dysfunctional relationships are one of the core drivers for people experiencing loneliness (Stack, 1998), and this dissatisfaction increases with age (Hsieh and Hawkley, 2018). Partners who have been married for a long period of time express a heightened awareness of being lonely and alone in a relationship, as this participant outlined: 'My loneliness room is my marriage. It is a barren place, devoid of kindness, human touch, warmth and communication. None of our friends would realize how empty our marriage is'.

Laura, who completed the loneliness room questionnaire, sees her female identity in a similar way. Describing her loneliness room as being on the balcony at night when the moon is shining, she writes:

> I am currently in a strong self-reflective phase. I've been in a relationship ever since I was 13. I kind of jumped from one to the next. Now is the moment when I try to get by without being in love. I want to be a self-employed woman and no longer let the media influence me that you need a relationship to be happy. I am currently on the way to finding my luck, even without a partner, but that often makes me feel very lonely.

This longing for love, for romantic partnering, also charges the responses of male participants. For Guanyu, loneliness is 'a small river, quiet and deep. Few people have walked from there, it's always in the dark'. He suggests,

> My lonely room is in my heart. There has always been a riverside in my heart. That's where my girl and I have agreed to go every year. Then we separated, and I feel sad every time I think about it. Even if I have more friends and more things to do, I will still feel very lonely. So I will be immersed in that place and let me heal slowly.

The photographs that Guanyu submitted capture the city under moody cloud; at dusk as the light fades; and at night with the moon and neon providing mournful impressionistic aesthetics. In Figure 2.5, the moon is aligned with a transmitter pole, providing an imagistic 'pulse' to contrast

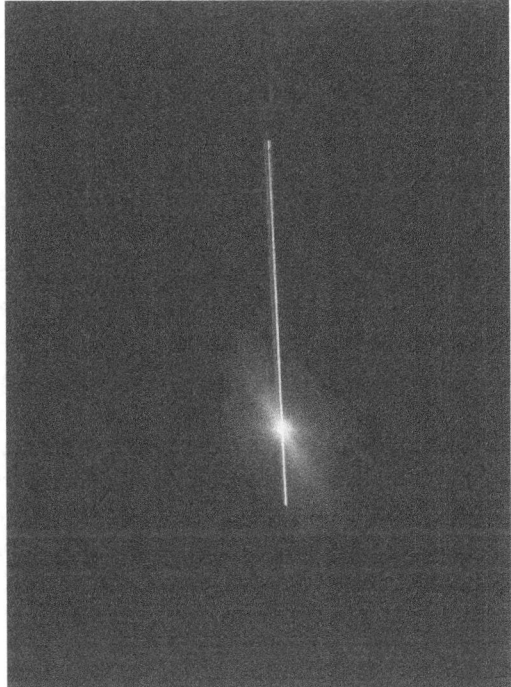

Figure 2.5 Pulse

with the blackness of the photograph, as if his love message has at that moment been cosmically transmitted or broadcast across the city, and around the world.

The moon, of course, has a powerful hold on the popular imagination, providing the light of solitude and the melancholy of aloneness in film, literature, painting, and photography. For example, Leonid Tishkov's *Private Moon* series (2003–) is a 'visual poem telling the story of a man who met the Moon and stayed with her for the rest of his life'. In this 'mobile' series, the crescent-shaped moon is photographed in an attic lying on a bed; sitting in a boat on the sea; wrapped in a blanket on a rooftop at night. The 'moon overcomes our loneliness in the universe, uniting many of us around it' (Tishkov, 2022). This is something that Laura, one of the participants, goes on to say: she loves the night because it 'is so soothing and the moon is a symbol of it. I just feel good in the moonlight. Sometimes I cry, but I allow it because I think it is a process'. Laura experiences the night and its moon as a loneliness room, washing her in sadness while revealing, opening her up, to potential and possibility. Her loneliness is of the existential kind: it enables her to see herself in a space of illumination.

It is these spaces of illumination that are considered next; first through the city, and then through the land, taking in its two central case studies – *(Alley) Loneliness in the Street* photographs of Maika Elan, and Alec Soth's *Loners* – as it does so.

The city is a loneliness room

The birth of the industrial city created what was then understood to be the new and radical experience of modernity (Berman, 1983). City living involved the 'shock' of crowded spaces; temporal acceleration through the speed of cars, trains, and aeroplanes; the connectivity of electricity and telephones; and the commodification of shopping, leisure, and travel. Modernity heralded both the age of greater social and economic possibility, and unleashed the forces of alienation and dislocation, since the architecture of the city created pockets of poverty, exaggerated scale and sound, and let people be moved along by the throng of impersonal human connection (Dennis, 2008).

According to Michel de Certeau, the modern, industrial city can be viewed or experienced from above, through a panoptic lens, and at street level, through a synoptic gaze (1985). From above, at height, the city appears rational, ordered, like a marvellous machine that runs or hums always in time. From street view – from the point of view of its dwellers and walkers – the city is seen and experienced as chaotic, accidental, and full of dissipated energy that drives people along. At aerial view – such as atop a skyscraper – the city is all intersecting concrete and glass, roadway, and neon sign, with people, far below, invisible to the naked eye. At ground level, ordinary life is often experienced in a never-ending rush with connecting spaces, such as bus terminals and waiting rooms, refusing deeper connections because of their fleeting and temporary natures. Nonetheless, what is also experienced at street level is the mixing of different cultures, and the vibrancy of human life that is never fully contained by the city's regulations, nor its rationalised grids. Life at street level, then, is both chronically lonely *and* existentially intoxicating.

The industrial city gave birth to modern loneliness. In fact, spatially and temporally, it is in essence the loneliness room of this book. The city grows the chronic conditions that make people feel terribly lonely, and it provides spaces that are sublime, enabling the individual to see within and up and outwards, like they are standing in front of a two-way existential mirror that reveals their waning, waxing selfhoods.

The city is a loneliness room because its social controls and power structures marginalise a great many, placing them on the periphery of society and therefore without those embedded social connections which would bind them to the imaginary centres of social life. The city is a loneliness room because it creates spaces that are lonely-to-be-in, like the laundromat, the late-night diner, and the crammed or empty bus or tram. The city is a loneliness room because its temporal and spatial coordinates fire the lonely imagination, inviting people to create and assemble their stories of being lonely in art and culture.

The city is a lonely visual canvas, its processes and materials are like the darkroom and photographic paper described in this chapter's prelude, ushering in the ghosts of strangers through its ever-developing doors. In fact, photography's role in shaping and recording the loneliness of the city is central to modernity's project since the photograph renders the city visible, knowable; contributes to its surveillance and mapping; captures isolated spaces and people; and aesthetically turns over its architectures to the sensibilities of the lonely imagination.

Photography is 'part of our urban geographical imagination' (Arnold, 2021), presenting and representing the city in ways that shape not only the way one thinks about its geographies and ecologies, but experiences or *feels* its roads, buildings, underpasses, bus stations, hotels, and consumption citadels. As Schwartz and Ryan observe, 'to explore photography and the geographical imagination is to understand how photographs were, and continue to be, part of the practices and processes by which people come to know the world and situate themselves in space and time' (2003: 18).

Street photography, and urban fine art photography, are the two central or dominant visual movements to capture the city's human and architectural life forces. Street photography occurs at synoptic height, capturing ordinary people in movement and interaction, as they occupy the city's spaces. Emotion and affect run through the arteries and veins of these street photographs, as does a concern with, and for, the marginal and the marginalised (Hunt, 2014).

By contrast, urban fine art photography captures buildings and landscapes emptied of its people (Hawker, 2013). Finding both the horizontal and vertical axes of the city, these sculptural photographs embody the low and the high of the city's architectural imagination, granting the observer the molecular detail of granite, glass, brick, and steel, and the expansive scale of high-rise, boulevard, and landmark buildings.

Of course, the urban fine art photographer must still be present in the space, carrying their sensibilities with them. These sensibilities are inherently lonely and lonesome since they render the city as empty of the bodies, faces, and interactions of human beings who should be present. It is as if the end of the human species has already happened, and all that is left is the hollow space, haunted by the people who should be on the street below, captured in cars, or coming out of buildings. And yet, the urban fine art photographer *is there*, positioned behind the camera, as if they are the last person alive on earth.

When Jim responded to the question, 'which photographer best captures loneliness?', he responded: 'Michael C. Coldwell: the cold mood, the big empty landscapes and abandoned buildings, themes of disappearance and lone figures in the landscape, haunting quality'. This haunting quality is centrally about the way the demolition of city spaces vanishes their histories and life stories, physically extinguishing the memories associated with them. The people 'left behind' in these photographs are etched into the photograph's melancholy, its lonely abandonment. Coldwell describes this series as 'attempting to chart the transforming topography of a post-industrial city, capturing its condemned buildings, threatened areas and the process of demolition and vanishing' (2022). The series becomes a photographic requiem to memorial and post-industrial loneliness.

During the Covid pandemic, these end-of-world sensibilities were particularly heightened and intensified (see Chapter 7 for a full discussion of pandemic loneliness). For example, Dina Litovsky

> wanted her photographs to feel melancholic but also magical, to hold not just the loss of those days but also the eerie enchantment of the city – how it felt fully hers, in its emptiness, but also not itself. In crafting these visions of the plague city at night, she was drawing inspiration from Edward Hopper's paintings of night-time solitude – not just his evocations of loneliness, but his visions of artificial light as a kind of refuge. You can see these fleeting pockets of refuge all over her city: the emerald orbs of green subway markers; the buttery rectangles of apartment windows; the cold candy-colored affluence of neon; the small islands of incandescence carved by signs and stoplights in the darkness. At one point, Litovsky wanted to find a place in the city where you could look down on people from above, and eventually realized you could do this from the stairway of the Roosevelt Island Tram station. Looking at these images, I realize their vantage summoned a powerful dimension of that early-pandemic era: How many of us were seeing strangers from above because we were looking out of our windows?
>
> (Jamison and Litovsky, 2021: 66–67)

Litovsky captures the uncanny nature of witnessing the city emptied of its people and of how light and colour carry greater, more intense, anthropomorphic qualities as a result. Litovsky also recognises the way sight and subjectivity shift: the panoptic and the synoptic lens reverse, or rather, people, unable to walk the city because of lockdowns, now watch it from above rather than at ground level. Loneliness enters such a perspective, as if one is cut off from the spaces that were once familiar, everyday, but are now out of physical and existential reach.

The loneliness in photography

In participant Linh Khanh Nguyen's photographic response to the loneliness room, he combines capturing the emptiness of the city with his own lonely solitude, but his city perspective is one that looks up rather than down:

> Each of us has our very own version of the loneliness room, and it doesn't mean something negative, or that we need to reach out more and avoid it. I do experience loneliness or isolation very often and only in those times I realize that I understand a lot more about myself and leave me room to grow more well-rounded as a person, emotionally and psychologically. For me, it is the time to create. Artistry only comes to me in my alone time. These photos were taken in one rainy Melbourne evening when I took a walk across the city streets. It was the end of one summer, so it was not cold, not hot, not too bright, not to dark, and it was pouring. The streets were shining, reflecting the early city lights. Everyone was rushing home after work, some stopping for grocery, some picking up their kids. I felt this loneliness in my heart walking and witnessing the scenes, knowing that I will be walking home alone, having a sip of warm tea alone in my room, watching a movie alone and editing my videos alone. Yet, this loneliness is not a negative energy, it is something I yearn for, to think through, to freely express myself through photography, to find inspiration, to watch people in their daily lives or just to simply be. I am addicted to walks like this and it has become my ritual. I call it my solidarity walk.

In this beautiful description of the relationship of art to selfhood, we discern Linh's complex relationship to the city and to being alone. Linh sees himself as separate and distinct from other connected humans, who are rushing home at the end of a workday, and he acknowledges the fact that he will be alone that night. And yet, Linh finds comfort in this aloneness and imagines that it helps him find inspiration to both enter and creatively capture the public world.

In Figures 2.6 and 2.7, Linh has captured two contrasting images of the city. In the laneway shot (Figure 2.6), depth and perspective open up the image to both its claustrophobia or tightness, and to the way light, colour, and water mix or blend to invite us to walk down it. There is a solitary human in the photograph, but they are faceless and seem to be walking away from the lonely photographer taking the picture. In the cropped, balcony bar photograph (Figure 2.7), Linh captures two contiguous spaces, that of the laneway they have just walked down, and the first floor of a city-centre bar in which drinkers and smokers stand socialising on its balcony. Linh's point of view is implicated in this shot: it is as if he is standing just beneath the gathering and longing, perhaps, to be part of the crowd. He is also looking back at the laneway he has just walked down, bringing his isolation, his aloneness, with him. Moreover, the traces of the laneway photograph enter or mingle with the balcony image, so that its/his loneliness haunts this social space.

Figure 2.6 Laneway

Figure 2.7 Lonely in the crowd

This loneliness fuels Linh's aesthetics, however. It colours his photographs so that when he returns to his loneliness room later that night – a literal space in this instance – his lonely art and selfhood positively and productively energise one another. Nonetheless, some people never leave their loneliness room, a phenomenon that Maika Elan, the chapter's first case study, has explored in her 2017 street photography, 'It felt safe here: portraits of hikikomori people living in Chiba, Japan'.

I am hikikomori

Elan explains that in Japan a hikikomori is defined as

> a person who does not participate in society (particularly school or work) and has no desire to do so. A hikikomori is also someone who doesn't have any close, non-familial relationships. These withdrawal symptoms must last for at least six months, and the social withdrawal itself must not be a symptom of a pathological problem.
>
> (Elan, 2017)

Hikikomori are often young to adult men, from middle-class families, who solely live or exist in their bedrooms, in their parents' home, after 'having experienced one or more traumatic episodes of social or academic failure' (Elan, 2017). In essence, the bedroom becomes their entire world: they rarely leave it and do not engage in social activities beyond their interactions with parents and direct family members. As such, closed off from the wider world, hikikomori experience all the qualities of loneliness: they are socially, anxiously, and emotionally lonely. They are also marked by the *shame of loneliness*, of their own deeply embedded sense of a lack of self-worth. This is compounded by the shame of their parents who 'hide them away'. Hikikomori are the wasted by-products of the hyper-competitive Japanese education system, and of the 'it is an honour to work' values that shape social and cultural life. Their loneliness comes not only from within but because of the capitalist esteem measurements that have marked them as abject failures.

In Elan's photographs we are invited to observe hikikomori in their bedrooms and bathrooms. They are photographed in ways that both centre and decentre them. They are either symmetrically framed, captured standing in doorways or between equalised spaces, or else they are shot filling a third of the frame so that negative space, light, and shade occupy the ground of the image. Mirrors are often important to these photographs, with the reflection of hikikomori offering 'two sides' to their personalities and predicaments. They either stare back at the camera – at Elan and the viewer – or they abstractly gaze into the domestic space either side of the lens, as if they are contemplating their lonely state. For example, in Elan's three photographs of 'Sumito Yokoyama, 43', who has been a hikikomori for three years, we first find him framed in a doorway; second, lying in a tiny bath with the shower running water over him; and finally, in his bedroom, squeezed onto a tiny mattress.

In the doorway photograph, Sumito is wearing just his boxer shorts, with one hand on his waist and with the other taking a draw from a cigarette. The ceiling light throws out an orange luminous glow that bathes his head and face in keylight, while domestic appliances, such as a washing machine, crowd around him. In the bath photograph, water from the shower continues to fill the tub, as Sumito sits/lies awkwardly in it, too big for its size. The shower curtain dominates the right of the frame, closing or drawing in around him, its bright circular patterns both incongruous and ironic, given he bathes in what is a drab, poorly maintained bathroom. The photograph's composition has Sumito looking at and into the empty space that falls behind the shower curtain. Light again bathes his face, illuminating the beads of water, exposing his blank stare. Together the two photographs paint Sumito into an existential corner: the shots are claustrophobic, prison-like, even as Sumito attempts to return the gaze or to see beyond the imaginary horizon. The light on his face acts like a time machine, taking us impressionistically back to when he was young and hopeful, stinging these photographs with the loss and trauma of his lost youth.

In the third 'bedroom' shot, Sumito is photographed lying vertically on a horizontal mattress, his head resting on a pillow that is beside the bed. A hanging, red plush curtain is being used to cover the lower part of his body, acting as his bedcover or quilt, but it is not long enough to even cover his feet. The bare mattress is stained and the full-length window that sits behind Sumito and his bed, and which the curtain is partially hanging over, is frosted so that it cannot be seen through. In the bottom right of the bedroom photograph, electric wires and DVDs or books can be partially seen. Sumito, now wearing spectacles, stares directly back at the camera, at Elan and the imagined viewer, and with light – this time unattributed – again lighting his face.

Everything in this image is out of kilter: the bed is unmade; Sumito lies on it at an angle, with his pillow on the floor rather than on the mattress; the curtains have become a bedcover; and a glimpse of what he might do with his time – read books or watch films – is obliquely represented. It is as if these pastimes have new meaning in what is a 'forever' lonely space for Sumito. This bedroom is his loneliness room. As a living space, it is one that is normally homely, used to sleep and dream in. Here, for Sumito, the bedroom is rendered uncomfortable, closed in, and cut off from the world. And yet not quite: the books and DVDs show that even as he attempts to hide and disconnect from the world, he keeps letting it back in. The photographer has also been granted access to this space, while Sumito's gazing back and towards Elan, and the imagined viewer, suggests a desire to reconnect and a need to be seen.

Elan goes on to explain that the reconnection of the hikikomori is one of the goals for Japanese society (2017). Parents often employ what are termed 'rental sisters' whose goal 'is ultimately to reassure, befriend and then coax the hikikomori out of their bedrooms and to a place where they can get help' (Elan, 2017). The idea of the rental sister, then, creates a space where loneliness is negotiated, explored, and discussed. Their role is to enter the loneliness room and pull the person back from their chronic or anxious state to re-enter society cleansed and renewed. Of course, this response in part stigmatises loneliness, places it as a deficit condition; and it genders the response to male/masculine loneliness – as if it is 'woman' who can set the man free.

The bedroom has been one of the key lonely locations for the participants of this project, as we have seen through Maryyam's, Dan's, and Linh's responses; and it is central to Gregory Crewdson's *Beneath the Roses* series and Maika Elan's hikikomori series. However, the relationship of the bedroom to the city and to loneliness is a complex one since it is tied to economic and market inequalities, housing affordability, and to such factors as migration. The bedroom may house a whole family, be on the 15th floor of a high-rise housing commission block, or be in the street, on a park bench, or a shop doorway. Loneliness shifts across these bedroom spaces: some are unhomely, over-filled, cold and damp, multi-purpose, and their inhabitants 'make do' while dreaming of escape. These are the city bedrooms of Maika Elan's *Inside Hanoi*.

At the end of the alley in the heart of Hanoi

Elan describes her Hanoi photographic series from an autoethnographic and personal perspective:

> Hanoi is the city where I was born and raised. Every day during my years in Hanoi, I would come across thousands of small alleys where the everyday life of the people there would impact me. In the old quarter of Hanoi, people would eat and sleep in the alley, whispers, laughter, and smells all permeated the narrow streets. My photos try to describe the people, the living space, the joy and sadness at the end of the alley in the heart of Hanoi.
>
> (Elan, 2015)

Inside Hanoi comprises 40 photographs. They are taken at street level and capture both the maze of connections that run through the alleys, and the lived-in spaces that occupy the corners, gutters, and tumble-down dwellings of this inner-city labyrinth. Sometimes the alley is the bedroom or, rather, the line between alley and room is blurred as domestic objects and furniture spill onto or over the pavement. The photographs offer both long shots, the lens of the camera finding the length of the alley as it carries on and on into the distance, and medium-length shots, so that the mixed-use bedrooms we are entering are intimately captured as if we are in the space with its inhabitants.

The photographs offer two types of temporal movement depending on their focus: they are either still and contemplative, or else they are full of the impressions of frenetic activity. The contrasting light and shade and expressionistic use of colour that runs over all 40 photographs stain the alleys with melancholia, with a certain exhaustion, even when happiness seems to be in open play. The people who live in the alley have either been forgotten or abandoned by Vietnamese society, or they are the poorly paid workers who by taking up those essential service, health, and industry jobs keep the city running.

In *Inside Hanoi* we see bedrooms that are also living rooms, prayer rooms, washing rooms, storerooms, and kitchens. When people are present in these spaces, they are isolated and look exhausted. They are captured crouching, sitting, or lying down, with their forlorn faces and hunched shoulders carrying the weight of the day. The oranges and greens that colour many of the objects, walls, curtains, and clothing found in these bedrooms are in tension: they are both sickly and summery, as if the spaces themselves are caught between two contradictory moods.

Loneliness colours the moods of these photographs. The often isolated/alone figures stand for the disconnection or lost/limiting connections that runs through the alleys. When two or more people are found in a photograph, they occupy different areas within it, and look unmoored from each other. For example, in the foreground to photograph '04', a man is captured sitting in a chair and smoking a cigarette. He is pictured side on, staring at the wall directly in front of him. In the background of the shot, a woman, her eyes partially closed, is curled up on a sofa – her makeshift bed – and a boy, squeezed in behind her, is staring back at the camera. Their shoes and slippers are on the green-tiled floor beside the bed.

It isn't clear what the relationship is between the man, the woman, and child: they are captured in the same room but not the same space or reality. The man is in contemplative mood and exists as a separate figure. The woman – the 'mother' to the boy? – has her arms folded and a duvet or blanket stretches across her body. Her face is down-turned, almost miserable, while the child's gaze returns almost an expressionless stare. Exhaustion, dissatisfaction enters the photograph but much more than this: it is their loneliness room. The room doesn't feel homely but a mere utility: a place to take refuge, to exist, but not really *to live*. There are few if any personal possessions in this room – no toys, family photographs, ornaments. Rather, we see a glass tumbler, electric wires, and food canisters – the basics of human life. In this alleyway bedroom, they have *materially* nowhere to go.

The long shots of the maze of alleys create the impression that they go on forever; that they cannot be easily escaped. They draw attention to the way urban geographies are implicated in power relationships, in market forces, in the way class and ethnicity are drawn into their boundaries and by the hierarchies of capitalism. *Inside Hanoi* is actually outside the wealthy enclaves of the city, its territory marking people as belonging to the periphery rather than to the core. Poverty, limited opportunity, and the combining forces of alienation shape their experience of loneliness, with the alleys seemingly without endpoint. We might term this dislocation a form of zonal loneliness created by the way urban geographies reproduce inequality and division. It isn't easy to escape such cartographies, something that Mark Power explores in *A System of Edges* (2005):

> He took the 2003 edition of the London A–Z street map as a framework for exploring the city boundary and the space beyond. He went to the outer edge of each of the 56 pages and photographed a place just beyond the edge, paying some attention to photographic content and composition. The photographs show buses at the end of the line, new housing estates, and industrial legacies. He looks outwards, his back towards the urban centre.
>
> (Wells, 2021: 273)

Each photograph represents a 'threshold' space: one where the urban ends and to move beyond it will take you off the map. Buses turn around at the map's endpoint. Cabs refuse to take their fares further. Houses and roads dwindle or end, to be replaced by fields and countryside. For Power, these threshold spaces are about 'social identity … inclusion/exclusion and the significance of being in – or beyond – London' (quoted in Wells, 2021: 273). As noted above, where people get to live is economically driven, houses are often cheaper in these threshold spaces, and esteem is measured by where you live or don't live, your so-called 'postcode' cache.

Nonetheless, these threshold photographs, set as they often are on the boundary between urban and rural, represent something else: their in-betweenness captures the sense of the loneliness that one feels when one stands at *the end of the line*. To move beyond the threshold, to exit the 'map', to walk past the bus stop, to leave the lights of the city behind, is a profound moment of existential loneliness. This is the loneliness room of the rural, the wild, and the sea.

(Un)Natural states: the rural and the wild

For Raymond Williams, landscape, as a real and imaginary construct, emerged in Britain during the industrial revolution of the nineteenth century (1975). With the growth of cities and urban density, Williams observes how in art and literature the countryside became a 'space of retreat … noting a shift, from the late 1400s onwards, from designation of pasture areas (for sheep or cattle) to a more complex set of Arcadian myths relating to beauty and rural ideals' (25). If the industrial city was seen as a site of pollution and as nature-less, the countryside – by contrast – was seen to offer an escape from the city. Its clean lungs, summery meadows, verdant green hills, and the utopic sounds of nature were experientially opposite to the clanging machines of industry.

This understanding of the rural as providing relief from the noise of everyday urban life persists today. It is intimately tied to the idea of solitude and aloneness, but also, as this book contends, to loneliness. For example, when Fiona and Tommie were asked to define their loneliness rooms, they both chose rural scenes. Fiona describes sitting on the porch of their farm as the day comes to an end, while Tommie simply takes a walk in the country:

> Fiona: I love the way the light changes across the paddocks and the more distant national park. The wind has abated and I can just sit quietly with my own thoughts and enjoy the serenity. It is a moment in time when I do not feel compelled to do anything for anyone; this is my time and my body relaxes as the shadows lengthen and the sun descends behind the tree line.
>
> Tommie: Walking in the countryside is away from it all. Green of the grass, Blue of the sky, Floating on the deep blue water, Walking through the meadows of green grass.

Both Fiona and Tommie revel in their ability to commune with nature, to exit the social world and to replenish. Fiona sees or feels her body as if nature both soothes it but is also entangled with it – the sun and the shadows extending her limbs to the limbs of the tree. Tommie senses nature in his response: its vibrant colours and the way the blue sky, imagistically reflected, allows him to imagine he is walking on water. There is also melancholy, loneliness in these responses, however, since they suggest an escape from not truly being free. The constraints of convention or familial responsibility haunt these descriptions and, of course, this is an escape to which they will have to return.

Nikos, defining his loneliness room as a bicycle ride out of Volos in Greece, observes:

> The outskirts of the city. Calm and mild vegetation near to the sea or up to the hills. The play of the sun among the clouds, a favorite melody playing in my mind. Silent talk with my friend, Mr. Bicycle. He listens to my hopes and fears quietly and gives me courage.

In this answer we see perspectives shift, and the currents of nature granting or gifting Nikos the ability to close off the social world and to contemplate and cogitate on his dreams and concerns. In his response, one climbs out of the city with Nikos, feeling its structures fall away as the hills and the sea take centre frame. His anthropomorphised transport, Mr. Bicycle, is confidant and friend. He is lonely but contended, mentally and emotionally replenished.

Contact with natural environments is known to assist with positive mental health and changes in well-being (James et al., 2015). As Bratman et al. summarise,

> Experimental fieldwork has ... shown the benefits of nature experience by contrasting within-group change across affective, cognitive, and physiological

dimensions in participants who walked in natural versus urban environments. Cross-sectional and longitudinal research has found that the psychological well-being of a population can be associated, in part, with its proximity to green space, blue space (i.e., aquatic and marine environments), and street trees or private gardens in both urban and rural settings.

(Bratman et al., 2019)

The definition of nature is here extended to any green or blue location that is considered to be natural, to-be-made-of-nature. For Silas, accessing nature happens from within, and across, the city:

The daily jogging routine in Komazawa Park, West Tokyo … this is a kind of reset to all the daily stuff that snowballs over the course of the day and night. These photos I took along my usual route represent my perfect state of loneliness: no one else around, very chilly, dry winter air. On the headset: Joy Division ('Love Will Tear Us Apart') and/or New Order ('Your Silent Face'), completes the experience nicely.

As Silas runs, he is both within nature (the park) but also cocooned from it and the wider world as he listens to music on his headphones. Or rather, the music – melancholic compositions about heartache and loss – soundtrack his run, his lonely imagination. In Figure 2.8, the road he starts his run on

Figure 2.8 Your silent face

is black macadam, with nature, grass, and tree canopy found either side. Compositionally, the photograph is split between the 'urban' and the 'rural', between 'order' and the 'wild'. Silas's loneliness room, then, is nature he can touch, be surrounded by, if never fully be enveloped by.

Each nation state has different versions of the rural idyll. These Edens both reflect and interpret the specific topography of the local natural environment and embody the contrasting national imaginaries that countries are built from (Anderson, 2006). Landscape photography is itself shaped by colonial and settler ideologies and subjectivities. Further, and as noted above, the rural is not one type of landscape but many; and it is different from the wilderness – which remains untamed, dangerous, beyond the reach of the 'civilisation' project that 'packages' nature (Nutall, 1997). Entering the wild can of course be existentially lonely.

Wild loneliness

For participant Heike, the idea of the wilderness is central to their loneliness room:

> Sunday morning before dawn on a wilderness area (raised bog) close to where I live. I love the idea of being the only person awake/alive at that moment. My loneliness space is a place where I can just be and let my mind wander whichever way it wants to go. I don't have to pay attention if I don't want to, or I can spend all my attention on the grass growing on patches.

Wilderness areas are often associated with the sublime or that imperceptible moment in life or art when reason is absent, and sensation consumes one with an overwhelming and indescribably profound intensity, chaos, or force (Deleuze, 2003). The overriding effect of this sublime experience is the inability to verbalise or rationalise the encounter since it exists as that which cannot be comprehended. Wilderness photography often captures this sense of the sublime, as participant Ben identifies when choosing his favourite loneliness room photographer: 'Ansel Adams. His powerful black and white landscape photographs resonate positive loneliness because they portray nature's vastness, beauty, tranquillity, and serenity free from human interference'.

Adams' landscape wilderness photographs were often taken in America's national parks, particularly in Wyoming. He founded Group f/64, an association of photographers that advocated for pure photography or a concern with the natural image that was as close to the living subject as could be achieved. Employing sharp focus, and the full tonal range of a photograph, Adams' wilderness images offer the viewer the awesome and overpowering nature of the untamed natural environment. Humans are absent from these shots, but their point of view is imagined to be that of the photographer, of Adams, so the power of nature bursts through the image. For Ben, this is productively lonely because one's insignificance, as set against the grand cathedrals of untamed nature, shatters the bonds of wider social connections, while immersing oneself in a primal wildness.

In Australia, ideas of the wilderness are unevenly defined. For example, the rural is variously termed as the 'bush', the 'outback', and the 'remote', designating both different topographies and land areas, but also the way landscape is governed and divided up politically. These terms are, of course, colonial-settler in origin, and they romanticise Australia's foundation myths, ignoring or absenting Indigenous people in the process. For one participant, when asked to name a photographer who best captures loneliness, they responded with:

> The Australian artist Frederick McCubbin captures the solitude and beauty of the bush. His paintings often depict lone characters who seem to be sitting in contemplation. Over a century has passed since he created these historical narratives and I wonder how different my life is to the mother and child 'On the wallaby track'? I begin to romantasize for a life with fewer distractions and expectations while also being thankful for the family, friends, and opportunities that I do have in my life.

While McCubbin isn't a photographer, the participant's decision to choose an impressionist painter with one of their most famous paintings is telling in terms of how loneliness, settler identity, and the bush is being aligned for them.

On the Wallaby Track (1896) – a colloquial term used to describe rural, itinerant workers who moved from area to area to find work – depicts a family resting in the bush. A woman/mother is sitting in the foreground, with her baby asleep on her lap. In the background, a man, the husband/father, is boiling a billycan for tea. The woman looks exhausted: her face is painted at an angle, away from the viewer, and she is looking down, with her eyes half-closed. The woman has one hand resting on the baby and the other on the grass. They are nestled under a canopy of trees, away from the sunlight or the wind. The tree the woman leans on is hollowed out, while the branches and thickets act like a thorny cocoon, but with a way through to the clearing just beyond. There is a deep well of loneliness that permeates this painting. This mother is also hollowed out, and the family appear uprooted, without wider social ties, needing, compelled to relentlessly move on if only to live, to merely exist. They are literally and metaphorically loners.

This is a mobile, transient, precarious subjectivity that, of course, continues to this day because of zero-hours employment contracts, and the way some casual work is seasonal. In an itinerant sense, *On the Wallaby*

Track returns us to the photographs of *Inside Hanoi*, but also moves us forwards since we find these precarious out-of-town loners in Alec Soth's series *Sleeping by the Mississippi* (2004), the final case study of this chapter.

Loners

Isabel O'Toole suggests that the riverside road journey presented in *Sleeping by the Mississippi*

> explores a freedom-seeking and derelict melancholy that has been a fascination of American photographers since Robert Frank took to the road in *The Americans* … Soth presents a down-by-the-river vagrancy though neglected interiors, abandoned buildings, graves, overgrown weeds creeping over an abandoned bed frame, and mourners huddled beneath Angel Oaks, amongst a variety of portraits depicting the various dashed hopes of the Americans.
>
> (O'Toole, 2019)

Soth created the series by following the Mississippi River in his car, 'using the river as a route to connect with people along the way' (O'Toole, 2019). The series is composed of both landscape shots and portraiture, with both modes finding their subjects in a state of tired abandonment, or resistant to the loneliness that envelops them. For example, in the photograph, *Luxora, Arkansas* (2002), a wooded area with a stretch of water behind it is 'furnished' as if it is a living room. Two chairs, a leather couch, and two 'coffee tables' (made from tree trunks) fill this glade. An American flag flutters over the couch, another flag sticks out from the ground, and empty alcohol bottles litter the floor.

This living room is 'inside-out' and blurs the line between the domestic space and the garden, between the home and nature. The photograph draws attention to those that are without homes, to the transient who are without jobs, and it ironises patriotism. The second-hand furniture is as decayed as the dead briar that it sits in. Nonetheless, *Luxora, Arkansas* also points towards the social and the sharing of lonely encounters. Nature, this wooded metropolis, provides a space, a place, for these loners to take root, to share stories and conversations.

In the portrait of *Charles, Vasa, Minnesota* (2002), Soth photographs his subject standing on the bitumen roof of his broken-down house. The roof is not only full of bits of wood, a breeze block, but is covered by a layer of snow. In the background of the shot is a wood and then fields, revealing that Charles lives in a rural area. Dressed in a white balaclava, green paint-specked overalls, and holding a model aeroplane in either hand, Charles looks back at the camera as if he is giving instruction. His beard and handle-bar moustache cement the impression that he is a pilot or an eccentric inventor.

Charles is clearly ready to give Soth a demonstration of his model-airplane-making skills, but this desire – given the disembarkation point and the cold weather – senses into the photograph not only his eccentricity but his aloneness and his joy at having Soth as company. Nonetheless, Charles's model aeroplanes represent a 'humble search for creative exploration' (Soth quoted in O'Toole, 2019), and as such bring together creativity and loneliness – in much the same way that participant Linh's photographs (see above) do for this project. The loneliness room that Charles lives in gives creative life to his inventions, and they offer him a means of escape – since with his model planes he will be able to 'fly' beyond the wooded horizon, beyond the limitations of his lonely self.

The river is central to Soth's photographic series because it not only provides the contours for his road journey, but its active location. We see the river's current or stagnation as symbolic of the melancholy of the people who live beside or near it. In Soth's series, the river never appears welcoming or warm but dark, cold, and full of waste or debris. The river is its own loneliness room, denatured, polluted, and unloved. Of course, the river leads to the sea, to the beach and shoreline, a co-location where many people go to feel lonely, to experience the salted joys of loneliness.

This is the sea (and the swimming pool)

The sea or ocean and its changing coastline capture the qualities of the various forms of loneliness. The beach is a liminal zone: it is the end and beginning of sea journeys; and it is a departure and arrival point. The tides that wash the shoreline rise and fall, advance and retreat, while the patterns of the waves – its white horses – draw attention to the movement of time even as it seems to slow or stop the clock altogether. The beach and its shoreline invite contemplation, while the boundarylessness of the sea or ocean offers the same level of sublimity as the wilderness area. The solitary walk along the beach draws upon aloneness and solitude, and can elicit the feeling that one is in an oceanic loneliness room. For Vanessa,

> My loneliness room is the beach where I live on the South Coast of England. I go there every day, often twice, for the sense of space. It is relief each time I look at the expansive horizon of water that stretches as far as the eye can see. It gives me a sense of being alone even when I am not. Sometimes it just me and my dog and the rain, sometimes just the rhythm of my feet as I run, often there are other dog walkers and runners, but the space to breathe and feel alone without desolation or sadness is what keeps me going back day after day. I love the winter beach without the holidaymakers. I like it best when the tide is out and the sand stretches for miles. I like it when it's sunny and when the sea is wild! … It feeds my soul and it makes me whole.

Figure 2.9 It feeds my soul

Vanessa views the beach, shoreline, and ocean as expansive and liberating, feeding her oxygen and granting her the intoxicating solitude that she seeks. Its changing nature – tidal, weather dependent – offers her both sublime moments and the giddy joy of being in the grace of nature. In Figure 2.9, Vanessa has captured her dog at water's edge, with foam and seashell marking the line between land and sea. She walks this fine line too, in loneliness and happiness, as the gentle waves roll in.

Sabrina defines her loneliness room in a similar way:

> Loneliness has never been a negative feeling but meant freedom, necessary personal space and tranquillity. I enjoy it and think there are too many noises in this world so we need to actively seek loneliness. If there is a loneliness room for me, it would be the beach near to my house.

The loneliness in photography 65

Figure 2.10 Tranquillity

In this response, Sabrina gives radical agency to the idea that loneliness should be actively sought rather than escaped from or cured or fixed. The modern world is too busy and noisy for Sabrina. It is only at the beach where she can embrace her loneliness, and where she finds a necessary escape from the maddening pretence of sociality (Figure 2.10).

Of course, entering the sea, the water, to be 'enwatered', is another location for loneliness to emerge. To let go of land, to feel one's body floating or swimming in an immense expanse of space, floods the senses with a 'primordial sense of liquid or fluid and ... an (unconscious) memory of the in-utero state' (D'Aloia, 2009). Out at sea, the loneliness room becomes a primal scene as one returns to the watery womb. One doesn't need to enter the ocean to experience the lonely joys of swimming, however. As Robyn describes,

> My loneliness room is our family swimming pool. it is newish – meaning the novelty and specialness of it hasn't worn off. when i was a kid I loved the local country town swimming pool. all of 4 summers there. it was a happy place so that association lingers, the chlorine, the weightlessness, the sun which i adore. the sound of water gushing, splashing, kids laughing. our home pool has trees, lawn and garden. i love it best in the early morning – i dance to music in it – loads of playlists which i curate like a DJ – sometimes opera, blues, jazz, pop, even ABBA.

This intoxicating description is past/present tense: Robyn's swimming pool is enjoyed through the memories that rush back from her childhood. She draws upon sensory signifiers so that the warmth of the day, the sounds of water splashing, and laughter are communicated. You can picture this joyous loneliness room: you can see her dancing to the tunes she 'mixes' by the pool's edge. Robyn further writes,

> My loneliness room is a watery blue heart 47 years ago I found you then forgot ... you filtered your way back into my bubbled veins pumping your chlorine scented breath across my face circulating through the inside outside room with sun, shadows, parrots mating in the stringybark gum above ... sensual life longing the beats quicken and my heart too expands.

The swimming pool becomes corporeal, symbiotically animated and piped into her lungs. The description opens her 'photograph' to the rural, to the natural world that surrounded her childhood pool. She naturally swims in this liquid memory, in water, in the lush setting of colours, textures, and sounds of the past. Robyn's *present* memory renders loneliness as expansive, full always of potential.

Lonely emulsion: a brief conclusion

One can powerfully chart the movement and shifting impressions of loneliness in photography through the connecting, entwined fibres of this chapter. We witness the wedding photographer and the family photograph album embrace loneliness through the forces of the punctum; or, more poetically speaking, because of the kinship 'voices' such collections engender. We entered lonely bedrooms, productively so, because of the comfort they provided and the safe haven that they offered lovers, or because in inhabiting such spaces it led to creative outputs, as was the case with Linh. We then see the bedroom change: it becomes a negative space for lonely men or hikikomori, and a limit or breaking point for those who live *Inside Hanoi*.

Gendered loneliness steals into these bedrooms and to the way photography captures transience and loss. Power inequalities are plugged into these lonely bedrooms and into the city and the rural idyll. These contrasting spaces or zones exist, on the one hand, as binary opposites, and yet, on the other, their embodiment of loneliness merges and converges, producing both existential and chronic versions of the lonely state. Further, one can stand alone in nature, be lonely in the city, in the same way that one can enter a sublime state of loneliness when standing before the awesomeness of the wilderness.

The loneliness room is photographically mobile in this chapter: it exists in the car, where people go to be alone, to crank up the music, and to cry;

and it carries Soth along the Mississippi River, enabling him to capture wasted spaces and left-behind people, and the creativity that their loneliness produces.

The chapter's end point is the sea, the beach, and the haunted swimming pool, where childhood memories and sensations return and replenish the swimmer. People find true solitude – the expansive, existential energies of loneliness – when they are close to water, or are swimming, playing in its liquidity. Photographs are of course rinsed in water, but if their images are to 'stick', then the coating of their lonely emulsion must remain. Film is also an art form that is washed in the waters of loneliness, as the next chapter goes on to explore.

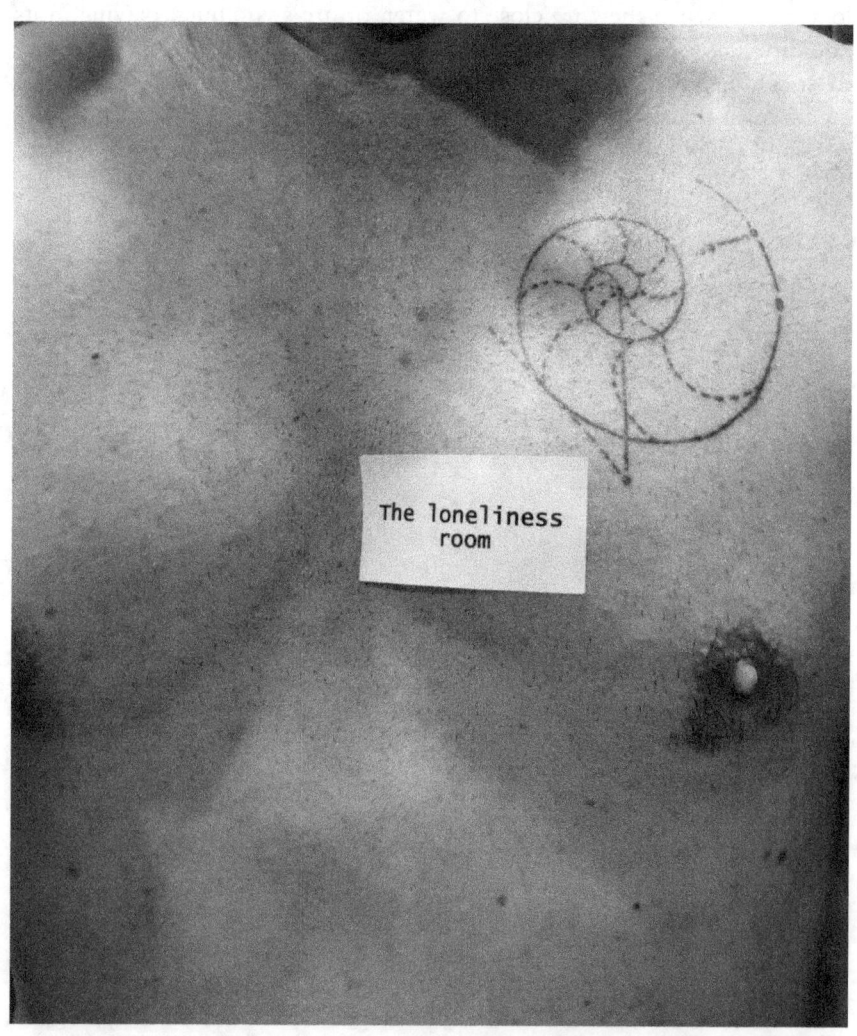

3

Dim the lights: loneliness in cinema

Prelude: the ushers

A long queue has formed at the confectionary kiosk. Couples, singles, families, and friends stand in an unorderly line, slowly inching their way to the drinks, candy, popcorn, hotdogs, and ice creams. The kiosk is ablaze with colour and neon, and a sea of advertising signs spill onto, or over, every object – across every spare inch of space. Noise and chatter, expectation, and excitement fill the auditory channels. Drink me. Eat me. Taste me. Smell me. The senses are always overloaded at the cinema's confectionary kiosk.

Behind the desk is the usher, rushed off their feet, forcing smiles and pleasantries from their mostly roboticised face and mouth. Taking orders, they pour fizzy drinks into oversized cups, fill tubs the size of baths with buttered popcorn, and watch sugary candy bags explode on impact with the lacquered counter they are placed on. Movie tickets are dispensed, and theatre numbers advised. Waves of people pass by the usher. They remain almost invisible, insignificant, to the cinema patrons whose heads are full of movies and sugar.

At Theatre 7 an usher is checking tickets and showing people to their seats. They have memorised the row and seat numbers, and with their torch light can move across the semi-dark of the auditorium with relative ease. People squeeze past those already sitting, and then get themselves ready for the movie, taking off their jackets and jumpers and laying out their confectionary on the armrests of the seat. In Theatre 7 there is idle chatter, whispering, the sound of candy bags opening, and the low hum of the projector as it sparks into life. As the lights are slowly dimmed, images and their sounds spill onto, or over, everyone – across every spare inch of space. Silence.

The ushers silently take notice of the people who visit the cinema. They see and hear all social life entering through its doors. They know what times and days of the week will attract certain patrons. They know what confectionary people will buy and where they will sit in the theatre – from the romantic lovers on the back row, to the cinephiles who sit centrally, waiting to be washed in the stories, sounds, and images of film.

At the kiosk, when the queues have ended, and as the next run of screenings have just begun to play, the usher experiences that discernible, unmistakable feeling of temporary, ephemeral loneliness. Life, the film, seems to be going on without them.

As the usher in Theatre 7 closes its doors, they are also caught in the sentiments of loneliness. Now standing outside the theatre, they can hear the film begin but not see its images and stories. Excluded from the fictions of cinema, they walk back to the kiosk, with their torch light turned off, and exchange glances with the other usher. They imagine that they are both characters in their own loneliness room film. Silence.

Loneliness in cinema

Visiting the multiplex

Film and cinema seem to be the opposite of what loneliness constitutes. As a storied art form, film is inherently social and cultural, and the object/subject of everyday conversation. The cinema is a public venue and an entertainment citadel that people visit to have a good time. As an event ritual, one's first trip to the cinema is keenly remembered and recalled, while first dates and other celebratory occasions memorialise film and cinema as rooms of happiness and connectivity (Palmgreen et al., 1988). Nonetheless, as Phil Hubbard observes, going to the multiplex very often offers a light sociality based on visuality: seeing rather than directly communicating with other people (2003). Further, 'bubbles' are argued to exist between people in terms of whom they will interact with, and whom they will sit next to in the auditorium. For Hubbard,

> it appears that multiplexes are popular with specific audiences because they allow them to develop a clear sense of ontological security, knowing that they can enjoy an evening out without the boundaries of their body being brought into question by potential pollutants. To such consumers, the multiplex appears to offer a relaxing setting where they are insulated from such pollutants and where the body is able to feel comfortable in both a physiological and psychological sense.
>
> (Hubbard, 2003: 261)

The idea of the absences of pollutants, of dirt, is linked to the notion that cinemas are spaces of cleanliness and that they are civil and civic in the way they offer patrons a night of restrained, carefully managed leisure and entertainment. In this respect, cinemas offer the illusion of sociality since they are a 'space of flow rather than a public place: a space carefully designed to ready the audience for the visual pleasures of cinema' (Hubbard, 2003: 262).

Of course, even the light sociality of film and cinema doesn't prevent it from being experienced as lonely or lonesome. As briefly outlined in Chapter 1, the privatised and interiorised nature of movie-watching makes it essentially solitary. Cinema patrons enter their imaginations as soon as the film starts, and in the flickering darkness their mood-state is theirs alone (Metz, 1982).

Patrons also carry their loneliness into the cinema with them. They may use film as an escape from their lonely lives, or as a form of parasocial intimacy, establishing imaginary bonds with the characters, or with the stars playing the parts. Through cinema's flights of fancy – through the *embedded sociality* of film fiction – fantasy enters the viewing experience, releasing the lonely viewer from their ordinary isolating and isolated lives (Tefertiller et al., 2020).

Lonely patrons often visit the cinema to explicitly watch a sad film: one whose generic conventions are built on it being a 'tearjerker'; that is 'hard hitting'; or is social realist in nature. This 'eudaimonic motivation' on the part of the lonely person is driven by the need for 'greater insight, self-reflection, or contemplations of poignancy or meaningfulness (e.g., what makes life valuable)' (Oliver, 2008: 42). Lonely people choose sad films to watch, then, because these fictions allow them to engage emotionally and socially in ways that are thwarted or denied to them in their everyday lives. These eudaimonic leanings refer us back to the two archetypes of loneliness defined in the book's first two chapters: chronic and existential – with those who feel terribly lonely engaging with film as their surrogate empathiser and confidant, and with those who find in the sadness of cinema the liberating possibilities of loneliness.

One may go to the cinema to feel the existential notes of loneliness because it grants one access to what it essentially means to be fully human – that heady mixture of the hedonistic and the eudaimonic. The lonely art of film entangles with the differing intensities of the human condition, shaping one's selfhood in the process. This is not just a cathartic mechanism – a 'safety valve' to vicariously experience what it feels like to be lonely – but corporeal and life-sustaining since the wells of loneliness give one greater emotional depth and the affective tools to navigate or 'live' it when the lonely imagination inevitably emerges in one's everyday lifeworld. Further, one can argue that the experience of watching a film is *always* experiential, phenomenological, since

> the film viewer (and, for that matter, also the filmmaker) who not only *has* a body but *is* a body and, through an embodied vision in-formed by the knowledge of the other senses, 'makes sense' of what it is to 'see' a movie – both 'in the flesh' and as it 'matters'.
>
> (Sobchack, 2000)

When we experience loneliness in the cinema it is through the activation of the senses: one is not just touched by the lonely engagements viewed but is immersed in them, as if loneliness is now within our haptic grasp, an inner part of our affective and affected bodies. The senses of cinema, then, have a direct relationship with the punctum in photography – they are affective, embodied art forms.

For Bertha, *In the Mood for Love* (Wong Kar-wai, 2000) is their loneliness room film precisely because of its sensory and affective propensities:

> The whole film is about restraint and unrequited love, but to me, it's always been about the loneliness of two people who can't really express their innermost emotions. So while they interact with one another, they're also incredibly lonely people, and the moments in the film where they have conversations are just momentary distractions from the loneliness they feel.

> There were several scenes in a diner, but there was one in particular where the two main characters (Chow Mo Wan and Su Li Zhen) have a silent meal together. For me, eating (especially in Chinese culture) is all about sound (laughter, conversations, arguments, plates clinking together) and yet, ITMFL contained a lot of anti-thesis to the nature of the Chinese when eating together. For me, that's always signified the kind of loneliness that the film was trying to convey. It's not just about the lack of conversations, but also about the inability to convey anything. To me, the film is a perfect representation of how we feel lonely, even when surrounded by people, regardless of whether these people know us intimately or not; that loneliness is something internal, and can occur surrounded by noise or people.

Bertha beautifully captures the way *In the Mood for Love* uses eating and dining scenes to represent how hidden desires and longings must remain so. Together in the same space, engaged in a sensuous activity, Chow and Su must nonetheless remain separate and constrained. The food they eat becomes the juices of their desire, and their silence an act of enforced repression. As Bertha highlights, the film shows how in a social setting, 'surrounded by noise or people', one can still be experiencing the deep pockets of loneliness. *In the Mood for Love* expresses loneliness in another way, however, through its slow and meandering narrative and scenes of stillness. It is as if boredom has also taken hold of the protagonists because of their inability to move their relationship forward.

Slow and boring

Neil, when answering the question which film and film sequence for him best captured what it means to be lonely, responds:

> *Rizi (Days)* directed by Tsai Ming-Liang. The focus of the camera, the pace of the film, the stillness of it all, the lack of dialogue.

At the finale of the film one of the characters plays with a small music box, a gift from the film's other character. He does this on a busy street where the street sounds mingle with the tinkle of the music box. It was overwhelming, the feeling that it doesn't matter what we do, where we go, real lasting, meaningful connection that makes us not feel isolated in our own selves is so hard, almost impossible and often fleeting.

Neil's answer suggests that the film aesthetically and affectively captures the emotional state of loneliness: the slowness of the film is how he imagines loneliness is experienced. The film's long shots, minimal use of editing, narrative statis (very little happens in the story, conventionally speaking), and lack of conversation or meaningful interaction between its characters are seen to temporally and spatially map the contours of loneliness. The description of how the playing of the music box demonstrated, for Neil, the ephemerality of human existence and the fleeting nature of friendships is registered at the affective level as 'overwhelming'.

The playing of the music box in *Rizi* (2020) is Neil's loneliness room since its sounds pour out onto the urban streets where they are eventually eaten up by urban noise and the city's hectic speed. Neil places himself *in the scene*. His hearing, touching, feeling body is placed on this urban street: it is his hands that open the music box, and the laments he hears are heard from his auditory point of view.

Rizi is an example of slow cinema, which through its use of 'long takes, extended duration, and the trope of waiting ... comprises aesthetic acts that promote new modes of temporal experience, new ways of seeing, and new subjectivities that are politically committed to an ethos of slowness' (Lim, 2014: 80). Lim links this cinematic subjectivity of slowness to the 'crime of boredom' (Lim, 2014: 91). They argue that watching slow films is essentially boring and thus antithetical to making good use of one's time since under the logic of capitalism every hour is rationalised, commodified – it must not be wasted. The slow film not only resists this ordering of time but draws attention to the fallacy of temporal waste because it 'invites us to reconsider the value of waste even as this notion challenges conventional ideas about utility, productivity, and labour' (Lim, 2014: 91).

The notion of boredom and waste is more broadly germane to the political positioning of loneliness. Those who are chronically lonely are made to feel like they are wasting time: that they are not productive, functioning, consuming members of society. Consequently, they experience their temporal boredom as a crime and as shameful (see Chapter 2 for a brief discussion of shame). When read in this light, slow cinema not only becomes a meditation on loneliness but a political intervention into how it is understood and represented. Neil's feeling on watching *Rizi*, then, that 'it doesn't matter what we do', unmasks for him the meaningless of capitalist society and the essential truth that life is lived ostensibly as a loneliness room.

Nandana picks up on the relationship between boredom and loneliness in their choice of *Charulata/The Lonely Wife* (Ray, 1964):

> The film is a classic in Indian cinema and Ray's favourite. It represents loneliness, boredom and the slow passage of time experienced by women of a certain class and culture in minute spatial and temporal details that are familiar and relatable.
>
> The famous opening sequence when the titular character Charulata wanders from one room to another in her magnificent mansion trying to kill time by gazing from her window through her binoculars at the outside world as people pass by. It's a sequence of about eight minutes in which cinematic time equals real time, and is famous for reflecting the boredom of the lonely landlord's wife who is not allowed to venture outside on her own due to social mores set by a patriarchal culture in colonial Bengal.

Nandana links gender and social class to the way boredom and loneliness are entangled in the film. Charulata is a prisoner in her own home, subject to the rules of her husband and the gendered norms of Bengali society. She is forced to survey the world beyond her compound through a pair of binoculars – bringing the everyday lives of others into her imaginary domain to ease the boredom she feels. The centrality of the gaze is crucial here: Charulata is not to be seen, at least not freely in public, but is allowed to observe the world from a safe distance. Again, in this response we can see how being seen or not seen is a structuring absence/presence in the way that loneliness is represented, experienced, and gendered.

Surveying the lonely

This idea of surveying the world from behind 'net curtains' links us back to the gendered photographs of loneliness that were analysed in Chapter 2 but adds *motion* to the imagery. Charulata is restless, she 'wanders from room to room', and this 'walking loneliness' adds the possibility of a line of flight from her predicament. Desire wets Charulata's gaze; ambition fills her steps in the house. She simultaneously *observes* and *moves* and in so doing implicitly enacts an escape from her loneliness room. For viewers, such an escape, even if it is eventually thwarted in the film, offers the hope of emancipation from the long arms of what is here being read as a gendered form of loneliness.

The theme of seeing, gazing, and entrapment is carried into this participant's choice for their lonely room film:

> *Carol* was the first film that came to mind in regard to loneliness, I think because both of the lead characters are unable to be who they want to be and

live the life they desire. They are not allowed to articulate their feelings and have to put on a front of being with men which goes against who they are. I relate this feeling to loneliness, to a feeling of being trapped within yourself. The film often isolates the characters on screen alone, with other characters watching one another. It feels as though they are in a lonely world, being watched but not known or understood, until the end when they accept their feelings for one another.

The scene which I immediately thought of was Therese (Rooney Mara) looking out of the window of the car, in the rain, at the beginning and end of the film. She looks so lost and so lonely. We discover at the end of the film that Carol has just told her that she loves her, and I think the second time we see Therese looking out of the window highlights the loneliness that she will feel if she doesn't follow her dream of being with Carol. She will either be alone in the rain, lonely without the person she loves, or fulfilled and loved and no longer alone.

Carol (Haynes, 2015) operates through both a surveillance lens and with modes of interiority where feelings and desires are kept hidden. Nonetheless, the surveillance lens is itself oblique or partially blocked. In the film, rain, objects, possessions, and reflections all get in the way of vision, of being able to 'see' or of being fully 'seen', and they limit the ability of the characters to perceive a reality beyond the limited horizon they are presented with. One is lonely, then, because one must repress emotion because one is being consistently observed from a distance and yet that distance is rendered oblique. Under such vision, one feels trapped and in being so, enters the mood state of pathos or suffering.

Writing about the film melodrama and Todd Hayne's work in relation to it, Mary Ann Doane suggests:

> The window had a special import in terms of the social and symbolic positioning of the woman – the window was the interface between inside and outside, the feminine space of the family and reproduction and the masculine space of production. It facilitated a communication by means of the look between the two sexually differentiated spaces, but also acted as the site of the specific pathos associated with the woman.
>
> (Doane, 2004: 2)

As the participant beautifully observes, at the end of *Carol* Therese is captured sitting in a car as a set of watery reflections cast shadows across her face. The rain acts as a pathetic fallacy – the drops are the sodden materiality of loneliness. Therese can refuse the surveillance apparatus of the film, out herself in the process, or drive on and out of Carol's life for ever. These are painfully lonely choices to have to make, a condition that the film powerfully suggests are a burden placed on women.

In choosing *Leaving Las Vegas* (Figgis, 1995) as their loneliness room film, Davina also describes the gendered nature of loneliness but finds water being used as a means to wash and cleanse:

Which scene best captures loneliness for you?

Elizabeth Shue after she has been raped by frat boys while working as a dancer/ 'stripper'. She's in the shower cleaning herself. It spoke volumes to me about the precariousness of being a woman without options. And how, even if you are a woman with options … you're still in the same position as Shue: always fighting, always afraid, always undermined (even if you have never been in anything like her situation in your life).

Davina is pointing to the loneliness created by the precariat labour market; to the sex industries that exploit vulnerable women; to a patriarchal, misogynist culture that dehumanises women; and to the economic barriers that make it harder for women to 'exit' their loneliness rooms. In this scene, Sera (Elizabeth Shue) is wanting to wash away the memory; the touches; the smell; the violations of the sex industry and her rapists, and this, for Davina, both captures the character's loneliness and transmits its intensities right into her own gendered being. As a woman, Davina experiences loneliness because of her gender: it marks her as an outsider to the slow violence of patriarchal power.

The outsiders

For the next two participants it is the loneliness that comes with being an outsider, an Other, that has shaped their lonely film choices. For Nathan,

Ghost World best captures the feeling of being lonely primarily through of its representation of disillusionment and alienation via protagonist Enid's coming of age story. It's a film for outsiders: the loneliness of feeling apart from those around you (even those that you thought were 'your people'), in spite of one's attempts to connect.

Perhaps most with the scene depicting Enid crying in her room after all of her personal relationships seem to have imploded. For me it demonstrates the harsh reality of disconnection, that you're likely to be misunderstood by those around you, and the sort of dissonance that this creates when you realize it for yourself. I feel a lot of empathy for Enid and also recognize of a lot of my own feelings of outsiderness and alienation in her struggle. The pain of wanting to connect and yet being denied that authentic connection is very real and affecting.

In this response, Nathan explores *Ghost World* as a film that captures what it is like to be a social outsider or misfit and the consequences of such disconnection. Nathan projects his own experiences of feeling alienated into the film's narrative, seeing himself in Enid. He touches upon the notion of ontological authenticity and the craving for real human relationships: to be true to oneself and to others.

Coming-of-age films are, of course, built around these themes of social and cultural conformity. There is again a gendered dimension to the way girls are asked to 'grow up', one where they take part in a 'Cinderella' scene, transform into a beautiful woman, and get accepted into heterosexual society (Ferriss, 2008). However, in *Ghost World*, as Nathan points out, Enid refuses this Cinderella transformation, and it is this refusal that resonates with him. Given that Nathan is male and identifies as such, his identification with Enid demonstrates how her refusal to conform crosses gender boundaries. Enid wants 'to find some place for herself in a world that's rapidly turning into a big consumer theme park, a monoculture without anything authentic remaining' (Sperb, 2004: 209). This is Nathan's position, also.

Nonetheless, as Henry A. Giroux points out, while *Ghost World* and other popular representations of youth 'signal a particular crisis of the social' they do so through 'a discourse of privatization, which fails to locate youth and the problems they face within the related geographies of the social and political' (2002: 290). To turn this reading back to loneliness, one can see how a discourse of privatisation makes it the individual's fault and not one that is produced by societal or cultural inequalities. Further, it renders loneliness 'a problem', a deficit condition, that one needs to leave behind and to grow out of.

As noted before, the discourse of privatisation stigmatises all those who sit in the room with loneliness since it is being suggested that to be lonely is a pathology that one needs to escape from. Nathan, nonetheless, sees and feels beyond the positioning that loneliness is a deficit condition. He recognises that Enid's subjectivity is one that will allow him to live better in his own skin. This is the creative power of art, of film: it provides a narrative canvas that allows people to question and reflect upon the constituents of loneliness.

In the short video that Jiang submitted for this book, gù dū (loneliness), they narrate why young people feel lonely, expressing the same sentiments about loneliness that Nathan does in relation to *Ghost World* (www.facebook.com/100063647824826/videos/681001789372193).

In the text that runs across the largely black-screen video, Jiang charts the monotony of routine and the isolation that young people may feel as each day passes. She makes breakfast, turns over a book, takes a shower, and allows the viewer to hear 'the sound of sleepless nights, turning and tossing', before saying that 'loneliness envelops us all the time'. We then hear her mournful voice accompanying the text that we see on screen, as she says:

> The sky was faint, and soon it would be completely dark.
>
> The light in the room was not turned on and the whole room was dark
>
> Every now and then I felt lonely,
>
> Like I had been abandoned by the world
>
> But, loneliness is not a strange characteristic,
>
> It is just a part of life

On this last segment of text, a bright yellow sun and colourful rainbow appear, hovering over a fecund garden. For Jiang, loneliness is as natural as the earth, and she encourages everyone to recognise this as a fact of life. As such, Jiang's video submission ultimately rejects the pathology narrative that accompanies the official discourses on loneliness.

Tanya's explanation of why Andrea Arnold's *Red Road* (2006) is her loneliness room film also draws upon the feelings of alienation and isolation, but here it is recognised as offering solace:

> *Red Road* is a film about grief and loss but what interests me the most about it is how evokes both the pain and the solace of loneliness. Through its framing and camera work, it invites viewers to feel empathy for its characters. At the centre of the film is the female protagonist, Jackie (Kate Dickie). She works as a surveillance camera operator, and watches people as they move about the streets of Glasgow. She feels a connection to some of the people she watches, following their routines every day without knowing them or interacting with them.
>
> One scene from the film that particularly resonates for me in terms of the theme of loneliness, is the wedding scene that takes place early on in the film. Jackie attends her sister-in-law's wedding and sits on her own. The camera work frames her as isolated from the other wedding guests who are dancing and celebrating. I identify quite intensely with this scene and the sense it evokes of feeling like an alien or an outsider at a communal event where there is enforced jollity.

One can draw parallels from Tanya's description of *Red Road* to that of *Charulata/The Lonely Wife*, explored above. In *Red Road*, Jackie also observes the world from a distance and tracks or follows those who come under her surveillance. Jackie makes parasocial connections with those she has a particular interest in, in a sense filling her life with the stories of others. However, her own relative isolation and personal trauma in *Red Road* renders her surveillance as also invasive and investigative, as if she is policing the city with her eyes. The surveillance in the film also reveals how banal routine is, how very unexciting daily life often is. Boredom and mundane habit, and the corresponding sensations of loneliness, again colour and sound the film.

Tanya's quite beautiful reading of the wedding scene from *Red Road* involves a double consciousness: she is both analysing the way Jackie is framed and positioned as an outsider and placing herself in her shoes. Tanya is drawing attention to the way heavily ritualised events, where one is meant to be social and happy, can be the most alienating and lonely of all. Again, there is the recognition of movement and stillness in Tanya's response: while Jackie sits still in her tightly angled isolation, the people around her are dancing and laughing.

Cinema, as we are beginning to see from these responses, often positions loneliness as a 'static' subjectivity where one is trapped, and movement and freedom are contained. When one attempts to escape such lonely confines, there are barriers in the way to such freedom. Movement, though, is not the opposite of loneliness. To the contrary, when one moves – travels in cinema – one's loneliness room often comes with you, as is often the case with the hotel in film. This is a space that the book's participants were drawn to.

Lonely hotels

In cinema, the hotel is a significant place of human interaction. It becomes a site of elicit love-making, prostitution, and drug taking; of crime, hideouts, and holidays. The hotel is given the ability to shape and affect narrative action so that it isn't simply a location but an active narrative agent in the film world. For three participants their lonely room film was *Lost in Translation*, set largely in a glamorous hotel in Tokyo. For Matt, the film encapsulates what it feels like to be lonely through its various representational registers:

> Time spent alone in a foreign city – loneliness in lavish hotels, abandoned by partners, loneliness at the end of a career, alone in language, drinking alone, the loneliness of a lack of sleep.

> 'I'll be in the bar all week' – scene starts with Johansson sitting on windowsill of hotel, alone in room, looking out across the vast cityscape of Shinjuku in Tokyo, a solo swim in the hotel pool, then meeting Bill Murray in his own loneliness post swim on his own journey to find sleep – 'I'll be in the bar all week'.

Matt captures the different ways that the subjectivities of the main characters experience loneliness, one that is relational, specific to them, and cosmic, where they measure themselves against the empty spectacles of contemporary life. Bob (Bill Murray) and Charlotte (Scarlett Johansson) spend time trapped in lonely encounters while also opening themselves up to the possibility of self-transformation. They repeat behaviours that make them feel lonely, but together find new ways to express their existential crises, such as when they sing karaoke in a downtown bar. In their questionnaire responses, Marjia and Daisy sum up what for them this crisis relates to:

Marjia The feeling of being lost in life, not knowing once's place, searching for meaning are all captured in the way Bill Murray and Scarlett Johansson's characters figure in the film. And this to me epitomises loneliness. Not necessarily loneliness that is about yearning for human connection but a loneliness that is the lack of shared purpose and meaning.

Daisy I think that what resonated most with me in terms of this choice is that way in which the film shows that loneliness is[n't] about necessarily physically being alone. It's about feeling as if you are on the outside looking in on the lives of others, and it's about feeling misunderstood or lost within yourself. The film is about the relationship between Charlotte and Bob, and how unlikely this relationship would be in any other circumstances, but it works in this scenario simply because the two are so lost and lonely themselves.

Both Marjia and Daisy highlight the way that loneliness is about feeling *and* lifeworld, and not just one's situational context. They see that mentally and emotionally one can naturally feel adrift, untethered, and meaningless, both in relation to others and to the forces of social life. In *Lost in Translation*, Bob is in one sense suffering a mid-to-late-life crisis, while Charlotte is recently married and setting out, and yet has begun to question what she is beginning to build around her. Together they feel strange in their worlds, a strangeness that makes them mournful and melancholic, and which becomes the reason for why they first connect in the film. That they begin to have feelings for one another adds another layer to their loneliness since this is unrequited and mostly, if not entirely, unspoken. The film ends with Bob whispering something in Charlotte's ear, them kissing, and Bob walking away, seemingly forever. The intimacy of their strangeness is in totality their loneliness room: they cannot be together.

In the short film/video that Dirk submitted for this book, we are transported to a non-descript hotel room in Turkey (www.facebook.com/1000 63647824826/videos/336383273938025). The time-lapse film takes up Dirk's point of view: he stares out of the bedroom window, as night becomes day and day becomes night. The blur and trace of the recorded images create the impression of speed and embodied distance. In Dirk's film, the world outside feels cold, impenetrable, in a state of repetitive flux. This viewpoint is not static, however. We peer down onto the street, take up a horizontal position from the bed, while the angle from which we see the city changes, as if Dirk is restlessly staring out from different parts of his boxed room, as time ebbs and flows.

In one scene we see Dirk's leg sticking out from beneath sheets and blankets and his travelling possessions – medicines, clothes, reading material, plastic bags, and electrical equipment – that have been unloaded onto various off-white spaces. Reflections constantly hit the window, the room's surfaces, the iris of the camera, such as the way images from the 24-hour television news feed are captured as if they are knitted into the panes of glass. The view from this hotel window is almost entirely made of non-organic objects, concrete facades, roads, and cars. The tree that appears in the day vision is barren, as if it has been arrested from an impressionistic painting. No human is fully viewed or dwelled upon for long. When they do appear, they are on the move, at a pedestrian crossing, rushing out of view. Dirk's answer to the loneliness room questionnaire begins to explain the motivation for his film:

What's your loneliness room?
The generic low budget hotel room while travelling for work.

Why do you go there?
To survive.

Describe your loneliness room?
A place of displaced surveillance that separates you from the world.

Here, Dirk is touching upon the condition of the travelling worker, required to move from city to city, and hotel room to hotel room. The hotel room here becomes a non-place or a nondescript space of transience where human beings remain anonymous (Augé, 1995). In an allusionary sense, Dirk's film returns us to Maika Elan's *Inside Hanoi* photographs, except Dirk has the economic capital to travel. Mobility and loneliness are never free from economics, from questions of power, of inclusion and exclusion.

For Dirk, this is his loneliness room because of the space's aesthetic emptiness and its disconnection from rooted and organic life. Dirk is alone and lonely in this setting: the time-lapse photography embodies his sensibility, carries forward the isolation he feels. As powerfully, Dirk draws attention to the 360-degree nature of contemporary surveillance. He surveys the world from his window, turn his lens on the city below, while recognising that not only will surveillance cameras track his every move – as one does from the moment he enters the hotel lobby – but that he carries this observational and recording 'gaze' within him (Foucault, 1990).

Surveillance culture makes the world lonely for Dirk since it polices human movement and interactions. Dirk's film takes surveillance to be in a sense post-gender, *all-of-people and all-of-loneliness*. The relational link from *Carol* to *Red Road* to Dirk's film is sustained by the lonely eyes of surveillance as it is by the transience that all the characters feel. Surveillance is, of course, one of the lonely tropes of the films of Yorgos Lanthimos, as is the importance of the hotel. This is our next cinematic destination and the first case study of this chapter.

Arrested development: the lonesome films of Yorgos Lanthimos

One can argue that the films of Yorgos Lanthimos are set in an alternative reality where there are different social rules, formal regulations, and behavioural conventions. While everything seems ordinary, mundane even, Lanthimos's fictional worlds display an otherworldliness that continually undermines their realism. The uncanny suburbia we spend time in is not only strange, but also openly critiques class and taste distinctions. Writing about *The Lobster* (2015), Laurie and Stark argue that

> the connotative meshwork of the 'lobster' as a literary and cultural signifier gathers together the central concerns of Lanthimos' film: absurdity and abjection in modern life, class aspiration and the hypocrisies of taste hierarchies, and the complicity of individuals in collective practices of cruelty.
>
> (2021: 201)

The narrative premise of *The Lobster* is that people who stay single for too long – so-called Loners – will be transformed into a nonhuman animal of their choice. Set initially in the Hotel, singles have to pair with someone with whom they have common interests or similar physical characteristics (such as a limp or nosebleed). This matching of types ironises dating apps and their use of psychological profiling that promises that there is someone exactly right for you out there. David (Colin Farrell), a middle-aged architect, who has been sent to the hotel because his wife has left him for another man, pretends to be overly cruel to secure a match. In the opening shot to the film, 'David sits in an office, answering some preliminary questions. Behind him, never in focus, is a rack of postcards. Its subtle cruelty lies in the fact that these guests have no loved ones to mail, nor do they have any reason to fondly remember this miserable vacation' (Walber, 2016).

The sense that *The Lobster* exacerbates the climate of loneliness is carried forward in the disciplined way the hotel manages its guests. The dining room is hyper-routinised and over-orderly, while any acts that are signified as ones of solitude, such as masturbation, are outlawed and punished. The hotel's décor suggests it is a mere simulacrum, a copy of all generic travel hotels, with the 'most insistent motif' being 'the use of floral prints'. In its storyline and aesthetics, then,

> *The Lobster* links a sexual politics of coupling to a broader social imaginary that places singledom on the borders of civilisation, and that employs

the threat of dehumanisation to punish those unwilling to spend their lives in pairs. Monogamy becomes the key instrument through which collective futures become imaginable, and against which singles – or 'Loners' – must wage bitter struggles to secure their own autonomous existence. Characters do not seek out true love as a natural impulse of their species being; rather, longings for romance follow only from the institutional regulation of desire, itself secured by a violence that threatens to expel humans from society.

(Laurie and Stark, 2021: 202)

There is another way to read the politics and poetics of *The Lobster*, however. The film re-presents us with the binaries often applied to chronic loneliness and returns us to the idea of waste that was addressed earlier in this chapter. Monogamous couples are feted in the film, allowed to re-enter 'the city' if they pass the pairing 'test' at the Hotel. To be alone is not only thought to be non-productive but counter to the norms of social life. Loners are dehumanised, punished, turned into animals, and murdered in the film – a fascist policing of the individual who is alone and wants to remain so.

Nonetheless, in *The Lobster*, David resists this regulation of desire and escapes to the Forest where other Loners have formed a tribe. In this grouping, one is forbidden any kind of romantic connection, which is punishable by mutilation. The film, then, also exaggerates the lonely condition and propels it into its own nightmarish reality. Language breaks down in the lonely tribe and one must be anti- or non-social to survive. David forms a secret relationship with the Short-Sighted Woman (Rachel Weisz), using coded gestures to communicate with one another. When their affair is discovered, the Short-Sighted Woman is taken to 'the city' where she is permanently blinded. In the last shot of the film, we see David prepare to blind himself with a steak knife. His desire to be with, and the same, as the blind woman is one generated by the autonomous self – it may be an expression of love – and yet if they were both to be sightless in the world, the issue remains, *how lonely would that be?* One can take the issue of blindness as a critique of contemporary society's take on loneliness, but also an ironic reversal of the senses – shielded from the light of the world, one may find solace in the lonely darkness.

The theme of the non-social is also explored in *Dogtooth* (2009) where – bar the father/patriarch who leaves for work each day – a middle-class family lives in complete isolation from the wider world, their children being home-schooled since their birth. We learn that

the language system that the kids have inherited from their parents is illogical and has no representational attributes. It is a rather invented vocabulary which attributes different meanings to common everyday words. For instance, the youngsters are told that zombies are 'yellow flowers', 'the sea is a sofa' and keyboard is the definition for female genitalia.

(Koutsourakis, 2012: 96)

The children are not named in the film but are titled Son, Younger Daughter, and Older Daughter. It is as if they have no need for personal pronouns, or object relations, given they live in familial isolation. Nonetheless, *Dogtooth* invites strangers into their midst, such as Christina, the security guard, who also works at the Father's factory. Christina is paid to have sex with the Son, but not being satisfied with him, also barters for oral sex from the Older Daughter – an act which leads to other revelations, and ultimately results in the Older Daughter escaping the home.

The entire film reads like a parable of loneliness. The children have no friends or social contacts: they believe that the world beyond their tall garden fence or driveway is dangerous and violent. The Father controls the family, himself a figure of contained/constrained loneliness – the mundane nature of life both his succour and his death instinct. His authority grants him power but renders him banal, ultimately impotent. Suburbia is again a location of repression, as it was in *Charulata/The Lonely Wife*, and in the Gregory Crewdson photographs analysed in Chapter 2. Something lonely is rotting away behind the gated walls of suburbia.

Suburbia is always a key location for Lanthimos. In *The Killing of a Secret Deer* (2017), Steven (Colin Farrell), a cardiothoracic surgeon and Anna (Nicole Kidman), his wife, live what seem to be idyllic middle-class lives. Their expensive home is the very materiality of the success myth of the American dream. However, it is designed as if it is a mausoleum, with cold, blue colours and hard-lined interiors marking the space as lacking warmth. The house seems lonely in the film. Steven and Anna communicate in deadpan delivery as if they are barely awake or are sedated against the emptiness they feel towards one another. When they make love at the beginning of the film, Anna pretends to be under general anaesthesia – a potent metaphor for the nullifying nature of their marriage. Lanthimos's film style carries this sense of lonely separation by creating 'an abiding sense of isolation with a *mise-en-scène* that enforces separation, through shallow depth of field, withholding long shots, and two-shots where one party is decapitated by the framing' (Pinkerton, 2012).

The Killing of a Sacred Deer is very loosely based on Euripides' classical Greek tragedy *Iphigenia at Aulis* in which 'Agamemnon, King of Mycenae, finds himself forced to sacrifice his eldest daughter, Iphigenia, to Artemis, goddess of the hunt, after accidentally killing a deer' (Ayala, 2021). In this film, it is David and Anna's son Bob who is sacrificed, an offering to Martin whose father died on the operating table under David's hands.

What we see emerge in Lanthimos's work is the arrested development of youth, of their social and reproductive rights. Unlike the coming-of-age films discussed above, there seems to be barren futures in his films: either couples don't/can't have children (as in *The Lobster*); children are prohibited from growing up (as in *Dogtooth*); or they are terminated (as in *The Killing of the Sacred Deer*). These non- or anti-reproductive themes are taken up in *Alps* and *The Favourite*. With *Alps* (2011), both the Gymnast (Ariane Labed) and Monte Rosa (Angeliki Papoulia) are in perverse relationships, the former with her coach, the latter with her father, with both repeating their patterns of abuse. In *The Favourite* (2018), Abigail's (Emma Stone) success at removing Sarah (Rachel Weisz) from the Queen's Court results in her being placed in a subservient position, literally at Queen Anne's (Olivia Colman) feet. The last shot of Sarah is one of absolute negation: her face captured as if it is set in stone. The film's message connects subservience to loneliness to the reproduction rights she will now forgo. Lanthimos's work has a close relationship with another genre, science fiction, since reproduction and isolation are very much the form and content of these future-set worlds. Science fiction film is the chapter's second case study.

Lost in space: the loneliness of science fiction film

> There never can be a man so lost as one who is lost in the vast and intricate corridors of his own lonely mind, where none may reach and none may save.
>
> – *Pebble in the Sky* by Isaac Asimov (1950/1986: 43)

When introducing the genre of science fiction to students I start by saying that if you want to know what fears and concerns are pulsating away at the red heart of contemporary life, then look to those art forms where the future is being explosively re-imagined. I say to my students, if you want to know what the political concerns of our times are, look not to the dour documentary, nor to social realism, but to the liquid, silvery profundity of science fiction. And in asking them to look to the future-set worlds of science fiction as an indicator of what actually aches society today, I posit that it is in the representations of loneliness where we will find our present painfully crashing into tomorrow.

Science fiction film has always explored the material and emotional conditions of loneliness. Through its travelling in deep-space aesthetics it is able to capture the emotional strain of enforced isolation and solitude. The sound image of the lone astronaut hurtling through space, far away from blue Planet Earth, and where contact with 'home' has been lost, is one of the defining lonesome moments of the genre.

Such scenes incorporate the giddiness of weightlessness, the eerie silence of dark space, and the absolute terror of being untethered from Earth. These connecting elements render humankind as small and insignificant against the vastness of the cosmos. For Fotis, this is why *Solaris* best captures the qualities of loneliness: 'Alone in the cosmos, the void, visited by incarnations, ghosts, of his life. First seeing the manifestation of his wife, alive, yet not'.

Christine chooses *Gravity* for similar reasons:

> Although I have seen this 'lost in space' device used before as a metaphor for loneliness, and in the case of this film, the loneliness of grief, I think it represents well and very clearly the ways in which this can effect mental health. I think it's a particularly powerful use of this albeit common SF metaphor.
>
> For me, it was the scene when the Sandra Bullock character basically hallucinates the presence of the deceased character played by George Clooney. It was a wonderfully ludicrous sequence, but also spoke to the psychological need for connection and communication, particularly during times of stress or grief.

Fotis and Christine are exploring the ways in which when one feels terribly alone, phantoms emerge to connect them back to the social. In both *Solaris* and *Gravity*, the ghosts of loved ones become part of the character's waking/sleeping states. This hauntology invites the social in but fails to materialise it successfully. Ghosts are there and not there, playing tricks with the character's mind. The grief that one experiences from not being able to speak with loved ones is a weighty metaphor for loneliness: lost in space is how chronically lonely people in the 'real world' experience their everyday lives.

Gravity (Cuarón, 2013) is perhaps one of the most perfect demonstrations of cinema's intimate and interconnecting relationship to the sublime forces of nature and our lonely relationship to them. The film's unbroken opening 'floating' shot, lasting more than 13 minutes, captures the sheer vastness of outer space; the distant, rotating beauty of 'little' Earth; and the characters' sense of isolation and isolating melancholy as they go about their daily, routinised maintenance work on the spaceship they live on.

Gravity's use of shifting perspective and visual depth induces a sense of vertigo that disorientates the viewer, creating the sensation that one is in outer space, beholden by its massiveness and only 'tethered' by the slimmest of cables. Asteroid debris and space junk shoot out from the darkness, intensifying the sense that one can be untethered and cast off into oblivion at any moment. There is zero gravity in *Gravity*. It is difficult to breathe while watching the opening scene, and almost impossible to not experience one's own body as if it is stranded in outer space, as if one has been left without gravitational crampons to hold on with and to root one to terra firma. One is so lonely when lost in space.

Nonetheless, this lonesome state may also be productive or regenerative since in bearing witness to these images of the vastness of space one's sense of selfhood is reduced to pin-prick insignificance, and with it a corresponding existential loneliness emerges – one that is like a thousand novae all newly exploding at once. In this transformative context – and just like the encounter with the wilderness described in Chapter 2 – one experiences loneliness in a sublime state: as an overwhelming, 'awesome' encounter with the 'self' enmeshed in the grand designs of the universe. It is as if the self has been culturally obliterated and the world has ended, but at the same time one feels reborn, replenished.

End-of-world loneliness

In post-apocalyptic science fiction film, where the civilised world has ended because of bomb, plague, or environmental degradation, loneliness emerges because too few people are left in the world to communicate with, and the social order has broken down. Life is reduced to the survival of the fittest, to brutish, selfish behaviour. In *The Road* (Hillcoat, 2009), Man and Boy are together alone against the agonising violence they face as they make their way to the ocean. They can trust no one and have no one to turn to: they are thrust back into the violent arms of nature since all vestiges of the community have been extinguished. While Man and Boy may have each other, they are embodied metaphors for loneliness in an individualised world order where everyone looks out for 'Number One'.

The very materiality of spaces and places is rendered lonesome in the post-apocalyptic science fiction film. When normally crowded places are emptied of people, rendered mute and uninhabited, as they are in *The Road*, they are wrapped up in a ghostly haunting – by a dreadful sense that where there is silence a chorus should call out.

Children in science fiction film are often used to carry the registers of loneliness since their 'absence' is either to do with a parent's need to space travel, to save the planet, or because the future is imagined as a non-reproductive Eschaton. Poignantly, in one scene in *Children of Men* (Cuarón, 2006), where the last human birth was more than 18 years ago, we visit a school now emptied of its children, with its playground swings rusting in the wind. The crumbling classrooms are silently moved through, filling the film's landscape with the terrifying impressions of lonely negation. Not only can we not replenish the human species in the future-set *Children of Men*, but joy and happiness have bled away into the spaces where kids used to jump hopscotch – now only weeds grow where children used to play.

For this participant, *Interstellar* (Nolan, 2014) draws upon a 'distant' father/daughter relationship to draw a connection to loneliness:

> The film's main character is Joseph Cooper, an engineer and former NASA pilot. Cooper is recruited to pilot a spacecraft on a mission to explore a wormhole on the outer reaches of the Solar System. The mission separates Cooper

from his ten year old daughter, potentially for a long time as proximity to the wormhole means Cooper may experience time differently to the people he leaves behind. The film sets up the relationship between father and daughter really well in act 1, such that it is heartbreaking to see them separated knowing the trajectory of science fiction films and the likely outcome for Cooper. While there is a strong science fiction element to the rest of the plot (exploration of unknown planets; accidents; crew deaths) the main arc for Cooper is to try to return to his daughter and the fear that their relative times will be so far out of step that he will no longer know who she is. I think this asymmetry captures what it feels like to be lonely; being disconnected from people or places, not because of physical distance, but because your experiences, memories, and expectations do not match those around you.

The one sequence that really resonated with me (was where) Cooper finds himself inside a tesseract that gives him access to his daughter Murphy's room when she was a child (effectively enabling him to travel in time). However, he cannot physically interact with her despite desperately trying to communicate with her. He eventually discovers that he can manipulate the gravity in the space and tries to send her messages by causing dust to move ... The physical barrier illustrates his separation from her and his inability to reach her (despite several attempts) the loss of a relationship that will never be returned to its original state. We see a young Murphy enter the room to investigate the dust and feel Cooper's elation – tinged with hopelessness as it becomes clear he can only be a 'ghost', and that his last chance to reconnect with his Murphy is to become a memory ... For me the scene highlighted how one could share spaces with others but still feel alone.

This incredibly beautiful reading of *Interstellar* demonstrates the way the science fiction film is able to translate the feelings that parents have when their kids grow up and leave home. Bedrooms become mausoleums to this/their past. Cooper struggles to find meaning in a present-future that doesn't contain a place for his daughter as he wants to remember her – as young, hopeful, innocent. He travels back in time because it is a place of relative safety and where he is an important figure in his daughter's worldview. Loneliness fills him up when he realises she has grown up and left the nest. Nonetheless, there is also joy in this retracing of time and space – to be lonely is also comforting because his daughter has moved on, grown up – she has become a successful scientist. Cooper realises that to be lonely is a natural part of being human, a melancholic sentiment that androids also carry with them.

Lonely androids

One of the reoccurring tropes of science fiction film is the lonely android. Caught between two states of being – human and machine – they never quite fit in. Humans distrust them because of this liminality: they look, talk, and feel like a human but are not. Their uncanniness often induces fear or unease. Sensing this, the android carries their difference with them, and is placed in narratives where they seek to be more human, social, and sociable, and therefore less lonely. Androids are often given relationships where they ponder on who they are/are not, their lines of dialogue steeped in melancholy and metaphysics. For example, in *Star Trek: The Next Generation* (television series, 1987–1994), Lieutenant Commander Data is fitted with a positronic brain which provides him with a form of human consciousness. He recognises that because he is 'unique' he is 'alone in the universe' and that 'there are still many human emotions I do not fully comprehend – anger, hatred, revenge. But I am not mystified by the desire to be loved – or the need for friendship. These are things I do understand' (*Star Trek*, 1991).

This desire for friendship nonetheless produces a 'lack', since Data struggles to be social. There is a disconnect between this desire and Data's ability to make friends and sustain friendships. This awkwardness is something that those who are isolated in the social/real world also experience – limiting both their desire and ability to make connections. Rosie chooses *Blade Runner* (Scott, 1982) as their loneliness room film because of this disassociation:

> Most of the characters appear to be lonely, disenfranchised, disassociated from their own identities as replicants etc. The soundtrack contributes to this too, offering a mournful and haunting accompaniment to the action. While there is action and violence the use of slow motion at the moment of death indicates its tragic waste.

One of the interesting things about *Blade Runner* is the idea that the replicants in the film may in fact be more 'human' than human beings. They care for one another and while they display pathological and violent tendencies they do so because of their exploitation at the hands of inhuman tyrants. Deckard (Harrison Ford), who takes on the role of a detective who 'retires' replicants, may well be a replicant himself. He is dour, brutish in the film, and yet searches for meaning, for a way out of the hellhole that is Los Angeles 2022. He forms a sexual, semi-romantic relationship with Rachel (Sean Young), one of the replicants he is asked to investigate. He does that so that he can *present* as human, can feel the warmth of a human connection, and be less existentially lonely.

There has been a recent trend in science fiction film involving the sexualisation of the android. This can be connected to the rise in social media use and the isolation it can engender. For example, in *Her* (Jonze, 2013) the lonely, soon-to-be-divorced Theodore Twombly (Joaquin Phoenix), develops a virtual relationship with Samantha (Scarlett Johansson), an artificially intelligent computer operating system. Samantha is never physically present in the film: she is personified through a seductive female voice alone.

Theodore is a professional writer who composes love letters for people unable or unwilling to do so, for a website called BeautifulHandwrittenLetters.com. The film establishes from the beginning, then, that intimacy failure is writ large across contemporary culture, and that loneliness is the dominant existential condition of the age. In *Her*, people are overly networked and plugged in, and either long for re-materialisation in the real world, whether it be through the 'analogue' form of sending paper letters, or they yearn for these digital spaces to offer them something more meaningful than parasocial encounters and Insta-dinners. *Her* thematises the issue that Sheryl Turkle argues is central to our relationship with new media and communication technologies, namely, 'We will not care if our machines are clever but whether they love us … Indeed, roboticists want us to know that the point of affective machines is that they will take care of us' (2011: 286).

Samantha becomes the romantic and sexual conduit for Theodore to experience the physical world, partly arresting him from his loneliness. They employ a surrogate female so that they (Samantha and Theodore) can make love together; and they go out on dreamy, light-filled dates. The audience soon learn, however, that Samantha has been communicating with hundreds of men in a similar way – she may love Theodore but only in the same way as she loves all her operating clients. In the end, that is all Theodore is to her, a client in a virtual shopping mall of commodified relationships. When choosing *Her* as their lonely film, Thamires suggests that loneliness marks both Theodore's and Samantha's characters: 'While the main character is surrounded by other people and information, the only one he seems to trust is an AI. And through the course of the movie, he feels physically disconnected from her. The AI, just as well, feels that distance; both are lonely together'.

Of course, what we are seeing in these examples is the focus on lonely men, a condition that relates to the overall patriarchal narratives of science fiction, but also to the fact that without the community of women, life is represented to be even more unbearably lonely and brutish for men and masculinity. That women are sometimes seen to be the problem of, or resolution for, loneliness is a woeful projection from the dark heart of toxic masculinity. *Under the Skin* (Glazer, 2013) directly addresses these issues.

Lonely death

Under the Skin is a perfect metaphoric and experiential exploration of this epidemic of loneliness. Driving a white van, an unnamed alien seductress (Scarlett Johansson) lures single, isolated men back to her house to have sex. Once there, they are submerged in a liquid tar and their bodies slowly consumed by an unknown force. The film's cruising scenes are set in the industrial and urban wastelands of Scotland – Glasgow in particular – during the time of austerity where social and support services had been severely cut. We drive around the city's rundown housing estates, along its empty roads at night, and through busy high streets in the day so that movement seems both dead slow and comparatively accelerated, like time is out of kilter, in a state of temporal crisis. Through the windows of the white van, we witness men solicit the seductress, craving for some kind of intimacy or human connection.

Under the Skin's architecture – its sombre materiality and its oppressive *mise en scène* – helps create the environmental conditions for brute and fragmented loneliness to seed and flourish. The liquid tomb that the single men drown in perfectly captures the sense that modern life is permeable, boundary-less, even as the opportunity to connect and expand connections is never truly there. The men drown alone, in what are metaphorically the isolated and isolating conditions of liquid modernity – of Britain's cruel austerity measures – just at the moment they dreamed of, and were close to getting, sexual intimacy. The black tar is the viscose material of chronic loneliness, a black sea that eats men alive.

Scarlett Johansson's character is also eventually caught in this cauldron of anomie. She tries to have an intimate relationship with an unnamed man in the film, but they cannot consummate the act. He has simply forgotten how to connect and communicate, while she is alien, Other, without a vagina for him to pleasure or to enter. She is therefore unable to make love, feel love, or reproduce. If the seductress is not a killer in the film, then she is nothing at all.

Her Otherness in the film is the ghoulish spectre of loneliness: the more human and humane she tries to become, the further removed she is from it. Her *raison d'être* is to be the architect of the mechanical and anti-human processes of human harvesting that the lonely men are put through. This is the politics of austerity in its most brilliant metaphoric form: whatever way one tries to be human is to be annihilated. All that there is, is loneliness.

In one pivotal scene, the seductress stands in front of a mirror and stares blankly at herself, struggling to comprehend who she really is. She examines her face, her body, as if they don't belong to her – which they don't; they have been lifted off a corpse – capturing the sense that women are often taught to be dissatisfied with their shape and look, but also that the self is a project that can be made, re-engineered in an age of consumer products and through industries that offer surgical enhancements. When the seductress looks into this mirror, what she sees staring back is the reflection of patriarchal culture and neoliberal individualism. What she sees is her own crushing loneliness, unable to be the liberated woman she wants to be.

> Thao chooses *Under the Skin* as her lonely room film because it's a movie about a being who begins their journey with purpose, but over time becomes alienated from this purpose. They try and find new kinds of belonging but are constantly reminded that they are alien. They ultimately die alone – murdered in the woods – stripped of everything including the skin they've been living in.

At the end of *Under the Skin*, Johansson's character is murdered, immolated at the hands of a would-be rapist in the hushed, ever-so-quiet, snow-covered tundra where the scene takes place. The seductress is being punished for 'consuming' the men she didn't desire but wanted on her own terms. The film calls upon rape culture motifs to position women as deadly and deadening sirens. Her death is a vicious moral retribution of order by the type of 'failed' man she had led to their deaths earlier in the film.

Her death, alone in the woods, is the most tragic of lonely endings, one that many women face in the real world the film holds a mirror up to. Much of UK austerity discourse has centred on the role and function of women, with 'forms of classed and gendered shaming to generate public consent for the government's welfare reform' (Allen et al., 2014). *Under the Skin*'s austere politics are inherently gendered, and yet no one feels at home in the film. Rather, lonely deaths are everywhere.

In Cameron's submission for this book, a short video/film titled *Through the Blue I Can See You*, a robotic voice narrates their deadly state of mind (www.facebook.com/100063647824826/videos/1258587444347108).

The film is essentially one mobile shot moving across or over a carpet or sea of blue. It hums with static. The blue is marked by what look like distant canyons, valleys, strange rivulets. It is as if we are high above, looking down on this extraterrestrial landscape. We hear the voice say,

> Wandering across the blue planes. Parched. Solemn. Burnt from the scorching blueness. Surrounded by no joy, no sadness, no happiness, just isolation and solitude that is forced upon my soul.
>
> No one is there yet I see them. In the blue and I feel them, but they don't feel real, I don't feel real, nothing feels real.
>
> Drowning my most fleeting thoughts as I paddle submerged and tormented by the crushing blueness.
>
> Apparitions vague, unknown, unknowable, ushering me back into the quagmire from whence I came back. Yet I yearn for them to take me further, where the blue does not find itself nor me.
>
> Like a siren takes the sailor to the depths of the deep, to meet the fate of those who listen to their call. Dearest Siren, won't you call for me.

I yearn for my demise, my obliteration, my liberation ... I deserve nothing.

I am resigned to a distant no connection can bridge, where no starlight shines, where your dimness of blue shimmers.

O siren, dear Siren, call out, take me from myself, call out to me ... take me, take me to the darkness where the blue cannot find me. Take me to the place where I will find myself, with no voices to be heard, no ghosts to be seen.

Let me finally feel a connection with myself, for ever and ever more, give me only the darkness, blacken my blue soul.

Cameron's film is a moving soliloquy addressed to the mythological sirens, creatures whose sweet and hypnotic voices would lure sailors to their deaths. His metallic voice blends with the static of the shot, as he pleads with the siren to rescue him from the never-ending blue that surrounds and engulfs him. Cameron would prefer death to the loneliness he feels, to the ghosts that haunt his lonely imagination. Death, though, is not the literal end, a suicide on the rocks, but a horizon beyond the blue, where he will find himself. Again, it is imagined that woman, the siren, will enact and enable a rescue from chronic loneliness, but it also she who lures him there in the first place.

Dim the lights: a brief conclusion

Cinema potently captures what it is like to be lonely and offers those who live non-social and isolating lives both the mechanism to understand their loneliness and to translate it into productive affects. Cinema feels lonely, its sound and image banks being able to transmit bodily affects so that even if one is not lonesome one can feel its impressions rise and fall over you. In this chapter we have seen how loneliness moves in and between its chronic and existential forms. We have seen how its spaces, places, and locations can particularise loneliness, enacting the room metaphor that holds this book together. Class, gender, and youth become crystallising points for the representational and affective qualities of loneliness, demonstrating forms of entrapment and the potential for liberation. The temporal rhythm of slow cinema can capture the ideology of loneliness – that it is wasteful of one's precious time – and the sensory nature of the lonely imagination, since time is seen/felt to drag on. The hotel becomes a central location for siting loneliness: it places people in loneliness rooms.

In the work of Yorgos Lanthimos we see these coordinates of loneliness come together: class, gender, youth, and suburbia entangle to chronically saturate his films in despairing disconnection. In the genre of science fiction such negations are also found but here there is also possibility and potential, as the lonely imagination takes flight through the cosmos. The whole of time and space, from dark matter to supernova, becomes the fabric of loneliness – terrifying and liberating in equal measure. And yet, women become the 'grounded' narrative problem and solution to loneliness: their absence causes loneliness while their presence, if identified as threatening to patriarchy, lures lonely men to their deaths. It is only if they behave, conform, that they offer men a way out of loneliness. Placing the blame or solution to loneliness on women takes the focus away from the structural and economic forces that produce its chronic state. This is something taken up in the next chapter.

4

Lonely realities: documenting loneliness

Prelude: washing the dishes

It is the end of autumn on a cold Sunday afternoon. The tightness of the day has begun to wrap itself around the small, boxed kitchen where we cook, chat, and eat. My dad is sitting at the table, smoking a tipped cigarette, while my mum is washing the dishes, hunched over at the kitchen sink. Smoke and soapy water act as the rhythmic elementals to a terse conversation that they are having. I sit unnoticed, holding a cup of sweet brown tea to my mouth.

My mum is angry. No, not angry; she is worn down by life and worried about the bills that need to be paid. Her eyes are directional pointers to lost opportunities and to the repetitive poverty that will fill tomorrow and the next day and the next day. Her hands caress a plate, using a yellow cloth to wipe away the grease. She stares through the kitchen window, her gaze landing on a vanishing point somewhere above our fenceless back garden. Dad tips ash into a saucer, its grey particles dispersing on impact with the ceramic. I sit unnoticed and drink sweet brown tea from the blue cup.

My mum turns to look at my dad, her hands resting in the dish water. He looks at the cigarette, at the ash accumulating, and then at my mum. She calls his name (Peter) and begins to ask him how we are going to pay that bill, this bill, or get groceries for the week. Her voice rises and then breaks at the highline, as raw emotion and regret fills the pitch, unravels the timbre. My dad, usually softly spoken – his Irish lilt a comforter – begins to raise his voice and snaps back in a staccato rhythm, 'how do I know, I can't make money out of thin air'. I sit unnoticed but spy a fly as it hovers near the window. It is looking to escape, is wanting to break through the glass it cannot fully perceive.

My mum moves the weight of her body from one foot to another, the step almost graceful, like it is the first tap in a dance sequence. Her face is flushed, her eyes flicker with doubt, uncertainty, and a fateful loss of direction. Dad looks down, his eyes boring their way into the Formica table.

He puts down the cigarette and clasps his hands together like he is about to pray. I sit unnoticed but with an almost indescribable sense of despair – no, not despair – a sadness – that runs through my body, into my lungs, and in and around my red heart.

My mum turns and faces the kitchen window. Her hands, always soft to touch, remain resting in the dish water. I think she notices the fly, also, as it headbutts the glass again and again. Apart from the whiney sound of this creature, silence fills the kitchen. My dad sits in mock prayer; my mum stares out of the kitchen window. Sitting unnoticed, I find a ten pence coin on the table and spin it so that it rotates on its silvery axis. How long before it will fall?

My mum picks up an upturned cup from the soapy water and throws it through the kitchen window, the quick movement of her hands and the shattering of the glass breaking the silence and the stillness between them. My dad jumps from his seat and puts his hands to his head in an act of despair and reflexive recognition. My mum, returning to a position of stillness and silence, continues to stare out of the kitchen window. They are in a lonely place together.

I notice that the fly has now flown through the cracks and has disappeared into the air. I get to my feet and run to my mum, putting my arms around her flowery waist. Noticing me, she pulls me close and in, and then turns to face my dad, their weary eyes meeting. The ten pence coin falls to the table, its rotation at an end.

I am finishing washing the dishes at the kitchen sink, the water now more brown than soapy. My dad is at the window with cardboard and sticky tape, as he imposes a temporary fix on the gaping hole. My mum is in the concrete garden sweeping up the glass with a dustpan and brush. I see that the flowers on her dress give colour to her pale complexion. She turns and smiles at me. In a linear configuration, mum to dad to me, our flickering stars align and our connected loneliness fills in the space between us.

Lonely realities

In art and culture, loneliness is documented through various forms and measures. In Chapter 2 we have seen how photographs both represent and embody the differing values that loneliness constitutes; where it can be found; and how it manifests as an art form that powerfully channels the existential and chronic forces of the lonely imagination. Similarly, in Chapter 3 we have observed how film and cinema provide 'fictions' that resemble the differing contours of loneliness, or which provide escapist flights from its more negative properties. In this chapter we move to and through what might be termed a lonely room realism as the documentary material it draws upon is grounded in the gritty life stories of ordinary people.

Realism is, of course, an unstable and vexing concept. It suggests an authenticity or truth to what is being told, denying the very nature of the social construction of life, and of the dominant ideologies that shape all our stories. Nonetheless, the thesis that loneliness is realist and often brutally real is carried forth in this chapter – propelled by a concern with the social and economic conditions that particularise the way chronic loneliness emerges and is understood in the contemporary age. The chapter stands on the shoulders of neoliberalism to see the ways in which austerity and precarity chronically undermine self-esteem and community connectivity, building ashy loneliness rooms in the process. Finally, art is seen to give the ordinary people that the chapter draws upon a way to express not only what their loneliness is, and a space to better understand it, but a means to resist its most disabling qualities.

How we document loneliness is a politicised and at times medicalised process. A rampant loneliness discourse has emerged where people who are marked as lonely are not only provided with a range of self-help guides and activities, but are asked to record where, how, and why loneliness emerges for them. Medicine and therapy are prescribed. Diary entries are made and read. Health regimes are put into place. Lonely people are surveyed and survey themselves. Loneliness is datafied and metricised and becomes situated in a set of interconnecting industries that trade and traffic in the get-wellness of the lonely (Rokach, 2012). Under this sodden umbrella, all of loneliness becomes a pathology, a condition of shame, that only does bad things to a person and thus needs to be escaped and recovered from. While chronic loneliness in a sense needs to be addressed in this way, the experience of being lonely – as this book has already shown – is much more complex, and at times offers a liberating set of qualities and intensities.

How and why we document loneliness can be activist and revisionist, one in which the lonely person resists and recasts the pathology markers ascribed to them. In this book we have already seen how the conceit of the loneliness room has opened experiential doors for the lonely to better understand their aloneness, isolation, melancholy, and disenchantment. Similarly, the call to express their loneliness through creative responses has shown how the imagination fires the affective dimensions of self and selfhood. Nonetheless, as we will see in the focus group responses from the Coventry Men's Shed below, the chronic nature of loneliness and its creative expression can go hand in hand. As I will now go on to discuss, the excruciating poverty of loneliness is married with the reflexive art of sharing what it feels like to be *this lonely*.

Lonely men

One of the workshops that was run to explore the loneliness room was held at Coventry Men's Shed in England, UK, in August 2020. This community-based, non-commercial organisation is open to any male over the age of 30 and aims to 'help men with their wellbeing, health and confidence, through the use of various activity to bring males together in like-minded groups to help each other through peer-to-peer support and learning'.

The Coventry Men's Shed is situated in a relatively deprived area of the city that has high rates of unemployment; precarious casual work with low rates of pay; poor and limited social housing; and high incidences of mental illness and social isolation. The group meets weekly and is run by Mark Gibbons. Mark organised and chaired the workshop, asking the men to respond to the loneliness room questionnaire (see Appendix 1), and to paint or draw what their loneliness room would look like. The session lasted for two hours.

Anthony, describing his loneliness room, says 'my lounge can sometimes feel lonely, the lack of interaction with other people whilst in lockdown. The TV in the room provides respite from negative feelings'. When asked to explain why this is his loneliness room and to describe it, he responds:

> Its my entertaining and socialising space, I sit and listen to music to lift my moods. I go there to relax and unwind, but it sometimes feels the opposite, empty just me and the dog in the room. My dog has been great as I have to go out of the house to give her exercise.

> The lounge room is many things to me, a place to relax, listen to music and watch TV. Its also a place where I often sit on my own with my thoughts, sometimes good, sometimes not, making the room as welcoming as possible is important to reduce the loneliness. Pictures on the wall, new curtains, new fire place add interest to the room. these are projects to keep me busy and to prevent me being lonely and bored.

Anthony is recognising two things about his lounge: it is a place of comfort and security but also where his lonely isolation rises up. He wrestles with these lonely thoughts and uses listening to music and watching television, and exercising his dog, to keep them at bay, and to connect in some way with the social he cannot directly access. Anthony also personalises the room so that it becomes homely, and which enables him to fill his day with 'projects' that keeps boredom at bay. As was discussed in Chapter 3, boredom is one of the 'threshold' values associated with loneliness. Here, Anthony is curating each day so that time does not run slowly but is filled with activities that allow him to feel productive. Anthony creates a form of 'domestic time' that 'is produced and reproduced on a daily basis through a repetitive cycle of practices whose rhythms are involved materially, emotionally and ideologically in the creation of home' (Liu, 2021: 347).

Making their lounges personal or homely is one of the central ways that men create a space that they feel they belong in and in some way represents their identity. In her research on homemaking, Sarah Pink finds that men 'created narratives about themselves and their homes that formed consistent accounts of self-identity. In doing so they generated meanings that were invested in objects, structures, music, radio, smell, sights and touch' (Pink, 2004: 129–130). Here, however, Anthony is attempting to design his lounge for a particular reason: that it be a home that is *absented* of loneliness. The objects he invests in are intending to fill his lounge with social meaning. In a very real sense, they are anthropomorphised: his possessions are turned into the people who do not visit him.

For Anthony's loneliness room painting (Figure 4.1), he has captured the limbs and branches of a tree, colouring it as if it is camouflage. For me, the tree represents the two contradictory facets of Anthony's isolation. Hiding in plain sight, his loneliness is both invisible and yet present for all to see. The tree is also found in an outside space, with Anthony dreaming of the rural, far away from the confines of his lounge room. Anthony's

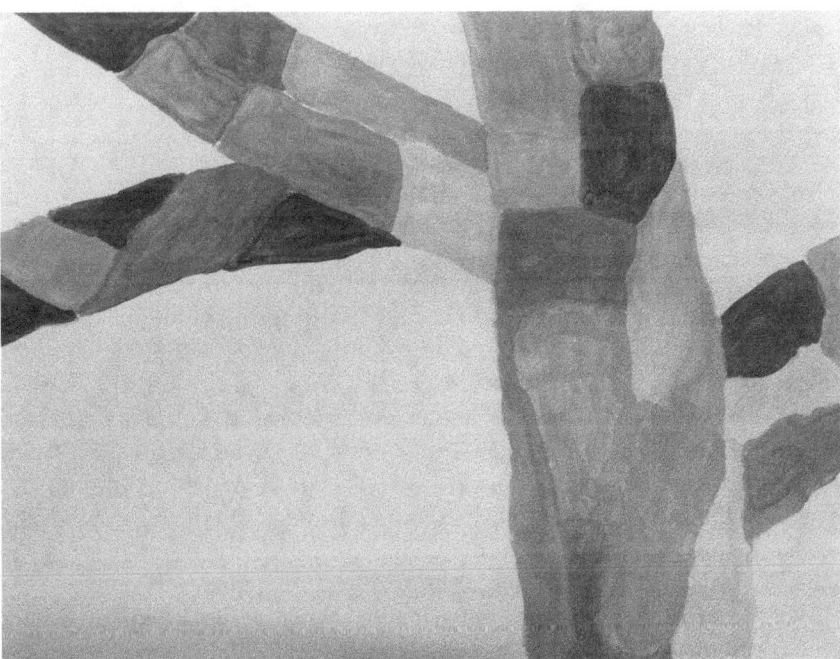

Figure 4.1 The tree

dog may well be off-screen, running through the fields that we cannot see. Anthony, then, both paints his loneliness room and seeks to escape it as he does so.

Anthony chose Edvard Munch's painting *The Scream* as the painting that best represents loneliness because 'his work captures the feeling of loneliness even when you are surrounded by people. The painting shows how this emotion can manifest and overtake you until you express the feeling in a negative way when it explodes out of you'. Munch's painting has often been read as expressing the isolating and quickening forces of modernity and industrialisation, and the social anxiety that came with it (Jordan, 1995). Painted in 1893, Munch describes *The Scream* thus:

> I was walking along the road with two friends – the sun was setting – suddenly the sky turned blood red – I paused, feeling exhausted, and leaned on the fence – there was blood and tongues of fire above the blue-black fjord and the city – my friends walked on, and I stood there trembling with anxiety – and I sensed an infinite scream passing through nature.
>
> (quoted in Di Piero, 2010: 60)

For workshop participant Paul, there is also this sense of a deep anxious loneliness to his response. Describing his bedroom and front room as his loneliness room he writes,

> I go to the bedroom so I don't have to face the day ahead. The front room I watch TV and again try not to think about the day ahead.
>
> I have learnt a negative behaviour by going to bed and sleeping the day away. I am so glad when the groups start as I then have something positive to do and I meet friends, so I feel much better afterwards.

This is a profoundly moving response, accompanied by a sketch/drawing (Figure 4.2) in which Paul attempts to map his repetitive movement between the front room and the bedroom, where negativity seems to flourish. Arrows are drawn as if he is in an endless cycle, shifting from one room to the other, lonely in each space, closed off from the outside world. He combats this loneliness by walking in nature, grocery shopping, cleaning the house – themes he highlights in yellow marker on his drawing. Graphically, black and yellow are in opposition in Paul's sketch, representing the dark and light of his emotional self, of his lonely imagination. As with Anthony, it is everyday routine that acts as both salve and disquiet. On the right-hand side of the sketch, Paul has written 'not giving in!!', suggesting that every day is indeed a battle to find meaning, to find the will to go on.

The theme of living alone and feeling lonely is repeated across the Men's Shed responses. The men do not seem to have familial ties or kinship to draw upon. They do not go to work, or have occupations or careers to

Documenting loneliness 103

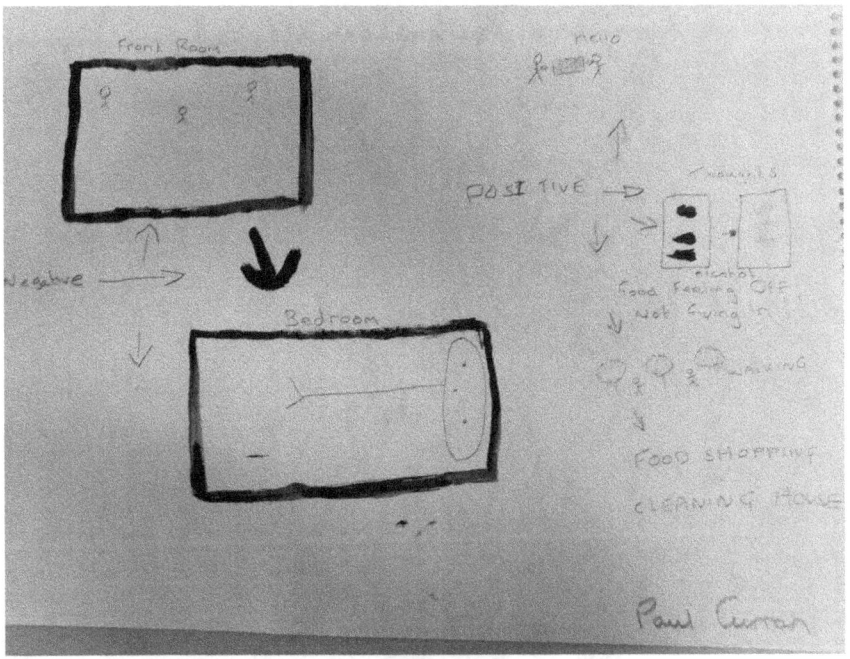

Figure 4.2 Stay positive

invest in. The men's hobbies are also limited, most likely prohibited by cost. Their loneliness is fuelled by both socio-economic disadvantage and the lack of community networks to join or be part of. These material and affective forces powerfully shape their loneliness.

Gary writes that 'my loneliness room is my bedroom for the last 35 years, I have been hearing voices'. He paints a picture with a vibrant rainbow and verdant green tree at its centre. Simon describes his one-room bedsit as his loneliness room where 'if the weather's good I sometimes sit on the 14th floor balcony … to remove myself from depressing situation'. Simon draws a picture of headphones with the caption, 'I listen to music on my blue tooth headphone and lie down and chill to the music until I am calm'. Rich answers that his loneliness room is his 'domestic padded cell with good flat screen TV, at home'. Rich paints a picture (Figure 4.3) where he is standing on top of the earth, balancing a computer keyboard on one hand and a window he might look through on the other, as if his loneliness is a battle with technology. At the top of the painting is a series of rainbows, each captioned with an enigmatic phrase suggesting both a playful and divided imagination.

One can see how many of the Coventry Men's Shed respondents felt incredibly isolated and fragmented, unable to fully connect or anchor

Figure 4.3 Balancing act

themselves beyond the limitations of their environment. Nonetheless, the Men's Shed had itself become a place of connection and sociality – a safe haven in a heartless world. Simon, for example, directly comments on what it offers him: 'one of the other guys at Coventry Men's Shed called Rich, his paintings are good, they help me focus'.

Contextually, 'between 1997 and 2017 the number of middle-aged people living alone in the UK increased by 53% and loneliness is now recognised as an important policy area' (Shaw et al., 2018: A30). Further, men living alone and who self-reported their loneliness were likely to have an increase in death by suicide, hospital admissions, and self-reported suicide attempts. COVID-19 and its associated lockdowns exacerbated this type of lonely isolation, as can be seen through Ricky's response:

> All of my rooms are the loneliness room In my house there is a bed in my bedroom for night time and a hospital bed in my living rooms for day time I can't sit up more than a few minutes or walk more than 10m or so I can't go anywhere (except virtually) – I am homebound and bedridden My life is basically exactly the same as it was before COVID-19 (Except now no visitors come to see me) Usually my life is happy, but it is also lonely making friends when you can't go out is very hard.

The physical, emotional, and existential pain that is expressed through this response is wounding. The participant documents a closed world, one where his body is failing, his home resembles a hospital, and where no one visits. It is a nightmare picture of the breakdown in the fabric of society. This UK-based participant calls directly out to the hikikomori found in Japan, discussed in Chapter 2, globally connecting lonely lives and deaths.

Ricky identifies Frida Kahlo as his loneliness room artist because

> she was also homebound/bedridden. There are so few role models. In her autobiography one of her letters has the (translated) section, 'If you don't come to visit me, do you still love me?' Clearly she was very lonely at times and (like me) made the best of it.

Ricky is here pointing to a vision of loneliness as like a nightmare: he and Frida share the same isolation, seemingly unloved and left to fade away. Ricky is also noticing the way Frida documents her loneliness as if she is alone in the world, writing to people who may not even read or open her letters. Ricky may in fact be completing the lonely room questionnaire because he will at least know that someone will read it *(I have Ricky, as has this reader. We hope that you have been able to get out more, or are able to have friends visit more often, now that the lockdowns are over)*. The theme of separation from the intimate and the social is taken up by r/lonely Reddit users (see Chapter 6 for a fuller discussion).

Lonely nightmares, hopeful horizons

When asked to creatively define their loneliness room, Reddit users imagined a physical space where they were either isolated, ignored, or violated in some way. For example, these three responses describe scenarios that are traumatic and produce trauma:

> A room made of glass. Inside is one person on a chair. The room is in the middle of a busy city street with commuters walking by. Everyone ignores the person sitting on the chair in the glass room. It's like he doesn't exist.

> A room filled with people, but they all wear a mask. Except you. You didn't get a mask, so you just stand in the corner waiting for a mask to come. It never does.

> In the corner of my loneliness sits a plain wooden chair with no wall decorations. The one small window sits high above the chair with shadows of daylight playing hide and seek against the grayness of the vacant four corners. Each one is ready for ridicule and scorn waiting on the outside of the door with no knob.

In the first response, loneliness is being described as a quality that renders you invisible and as existing outside the social world. However, at the same time, the shame of loneliness is made visible for all to see – the imagined character sits in a glass cube as the throng of daily life rushes by them. The idea that one doesn't materially exist inside the social, but is rendered naked before it, registers as a profound commentary on loneliness. In a sense, the response translates the story of 'The Emperor's New Clothes', but here what gets exposed is the lonely self.

In the second response, a character is rendered lonely because they are left out of the mask-wearing game, and without a mask (a persona) they are stripped bare of artifice and pretence, exposing or revealing their true lonely self. Culturally speaking, the mask allows an individual to stage and manage how they present to others, enabling them to enact roles that they think the situation or context demands of them (Goffman, 1959). In this nightmarish response, one cannot mask-up, or take part in the ritual of mask wearing, leaving the character seemingly role-less and existentially alone in the corner of the room.

In the third response, the loneliness room is small, sparse, and poorly lit, and in each corner there exists the possibility of being ridiculed and scorned. This room cannot be escaped from since the doorknob has been removed. In this scenario, loneliness is minimalist and without colour; where light struggles to get in; and where outside the room is only the catcalls of bullies.

All three responses place their loneliness in spaces where one is trapped, ignored, and is the subject or object of shame. These creative responses, then, carry forward the stigma that loneliness has in society: they each operate from a position where to be lonely is crushing because of the way it alienates the individual from the social while simultaneously making them the object of derision.

In their research on loneliness, undertaken with 82 female and 62 male college students, Rotenberg and MacKie found that they 'stigmatized both social and intimacy loneliness' and 'ascribed lower psychosocial functioning to and were less accepting of the lonely than nonlonely peers for both the social and intimacy domains of loneliness' (1999: 141). In these results we see how loneliness is not only associated with having lower-order social skills but is labelled and identified as such – putting lonely people on the outside, to the outer margins of group belonging.

The following r/lonely Reddit users draw on similar expressions, impressions, and metaphors, finding loneliness to be shaming or a shameful subjectivity:

> My loneliness would be the description of a [prison] cell, much like a glass house, tempered glass where not even throwing stones could break me free from that kind of loneliness. The kind of loneliness that really isn't my own,

and for much more of the time I could actually be occupying the space there, loneliness along with very few essential furniture pieces filling in the empty spaces, are the lingering residual energies that others seem to leave behind them, the many times any of those people are well known for coming and going, rather than any time they were ever known for being able to sit with themselves for a moment before needing to run off again. They seemed to be chasing rainbows ...

A room with an ever-tightening set of walls that make you feel crushed as they slowly close in, until you reach a point of acceptance of the inevitable closing in of the walls and they no longer crush you but comfort you.

A place devoid of essence in any real way. It's just empty ... wouldnt matter what was in that room. The vibe is just so apathetic that the lonely room itself might as well not exist, nothing in it has any value. Its both inconsequential and its edges are boundless like grief. You could paint the walls but what difference does it make, if all the colours are grey or you feel like light cant touch that place?

These three responses paint a quite terrifyingly ugly-beautiful spatialised description of loneliness. The loneliness rooms are given impossible dimensions: they are small and expansive, near and far, closed in and never-ending; they are empty and full, still and moving; they lack colour and yet colour exists beyond the lonely horizon. The adjectives used to describe the rooms are the very qualities that mark out how loneliness is imagined to be embodied: one is crushed, grief ridden, apathetic, inconsequential. Loneliness is eternalised and yet for two of the responses, this naturalism is either a comfort blanket or results in a resigned acceptance – as if ultimately loneliness sits essentially within them.

For Gauri, who completed the loneliness room questionnaire, the naturalism of loneliness acts as a buffer to the knots that twist themselves around their everyday life:

My loneliness room is a physical space where I seek refuge and undertake my dance practice. It is simultaneously a metaphysical space since I tend to go to this space when I travel – to feel being alone. This is a space I can transcend to in an official meeting, a social gathering or even a train ride home. It takes me seconds to zone out as well as zone back. It is always interconnected with rhythm and body movements. If i dont visit my loneliness room (physical or imaginary) I feel incomplete.

I go there to shed off the absolute and rational thoughts that I experience at my workplace. The absence of customisation of conversations and overpowering processes, subordination to machines and digitalisation on a daily basis force me to find my loneliness. Without my loneliness room I feel disoriented and incapable to initiate the next morning in a logical world.

Figure 4.4 Dancing loneliness

Figure 4.5 Dancing loneliness

Gauri's loneliness room is a space that is transforming and transformative: it exists within her; while she is on the move; and is also a physical location where she dances, free of language, social regulation, and the everyday noise that emanates from work and routine. Gauri's loneliness is realist and metaphysical: it is ground out in opposition to the logics of patriarchy and yet finds its truth in zones beyond or beneath the body.

In the photographs that Gauri submitted for the project (Figures 4.4 and 4.5), we see her immersed in her dance practice, body animated, becoming a blur, in a radiant, glowing orange setting. Dance is often a panacea for loneliness, the 'healing nature of dance and music ... informally recognized for their mind–body restorative capability to make one "whole" again' (Alpert, 2011: 155).

Gauri goes on to write,

> Incidentally, my loneliness room also has a casual visitor, my dancing partner. To me, it is his loneliness room as well. Half my age, he and me have nothing in common. He is oblivious of social reality, white collar services or politics of identity. His world view is the smallest I know of, lesser than that of a school going adolescent. We only talk in the language of our dance. His loneliness is not mine. There is no other relationship. Indian classical dance I feel trains

you in loneliness. It is by far the greatest loneliness project created in culture. Though on face value it seems as if you are projecting body movements, internally it empties you systematically of all material assets. I constantly transit between being in the external world and being lonely. I absolutely enjoy being lonely. The physical room opens out to an open space where I can hear the birds and the squirrels. The other extreme of the room is old books covered with dirt, leading to a bunker. I almost stand in-between 'life' and 'lost' in the physical room.

Gauri's loneliness room is her dance practice which both cleanses and rejuvenates her, the body and its movements becoming a vessel to higher-order thinking and feeling, as the frenzy of rhythm becomes a transcendental transformation of self. That Gauri shares this most sacred of activities with someone whom she hardly knows, who is socially different from her, and yet who connects with her at the metaphysical level, opens the kernels of loneliness to shared proximations. Together they dance alone, enrapt by their out-of-body experiences.

Martin also touches upon the dialectic nature of a shared but silenced loneliness when he describes his loneliness room as a visit to the library:

> Libraries, Andrew Carnegie once said are palaces for the people. To be alone in a community of quiet knowledge seekers and to have a place that is relatively free and open and less constrained by market forces is a gift. Silence is a commons. And I lump for Ellinor Ostrom's *Governing The Commons* rather than Garrett Hardin's ill conceived but popular *Tragedy of the Commons*. I like unenclosed spaces. Privately, I live in a full house and for work and reflection I feel the need for a contemplative space. But being isolated from people, and being in a room and not in nature, tips many spaces, for me, into a despairing loneliness. A loner-loneliness. A loneliness not of my own choosing. I want shared, intentional solitude. I want to choose my loneliness. Spaces such as libraries are my ideal loneliness room. A room where shared silence is the right of way in this law of the commons. Here we can be happy together and lonely.

Martin here returns the discussion to solitude as a form of empowering loneliness. He sees, feels, 'hears' in libraries the very essence of a loneliness that is informed and signified as such, and where readers sit alone with their books – free in their imagination, happy to be in the arms of solitude. Through the reference to Ostrom, Martin also alludes to the governance of natural/public resources and the market control over many of them. The public library has been under severe threat in many countries, subject to underfunding, closures, and marketisation (Webster, 2005).

If the places where we go to experience loneliness are rare or become erased, then what happens to the lonely imagination; how can we be lonely and happy together if those rooms are no more? Such a question returns us to the brute politics of austerity where so many support services have been cut, leaving people who wanted, needed, places of communion and sociality, nowhere to go. However, as participant Ashika shows, the public, marketised spaces of consumption can themselves be a productive loneliness room:

> Ambarrukmo Plaza is one of the largest department stores in Yogyakarta, a small town in Java, Indonesia, and my favorite by far. While normally there are a lot of people there, it never feels crowded. There aren't many turns or hidden alleys in there, so it is easy to find places, even if you've never been there before or bad at directions (like me). It's not too big, nor is it too small. It is just the right size for an aimless wanderer to wander aimlessly without getting lost. This is where I go to find be alone. Sometimes I feel like my head is overload – with information, work, family stuff, personal stuff. Sometimes I get tired of being 'professional' and smile all the time and be 'nice' to everyone at work. Sometimes I get tired of taking care of my mother's emotional balance and making sure no one screws up at home. Sometimes I need to clear my head before making a big decision. Sometimes I just need to be with myself and not worry about anything at all. And these are the times I go alone to Ambarrukmo Plaza.

In Ashika's response we are implicitly returned to the idea of the stage-managed self, one where we wear a mask of civility, of politeness. In visiting the plaza on her own, Ashika can take off this mask and be herself. The plaza offers the anonymity that she craves, its liminality the very reason she can escape custom and tradition. It is a space where she can shed the burden of familial responsibility. Loneliness is in one sense inverted or layered: Ashika goes to the plaza to escape the blues she might be feeling; it is in the hustle and bustle of the shops and its linking escalators, bridges, and floors where she finds peace in the anonymity that they gift her. This is the power of 'place', since

> place ushers us into what already is: namely, the environing subsoil of our embodiment, the bedrock of our being-in-the-world. If imagination projects us out beyond ourselves while memory takes us back behind ourselves, place subtends and enfolds us, lying perpetually under and around us. In imagining and remembering, we go into the ethereal and the thick respectively. By being in place, we find ourselves in what is subsistent and enveloping.
>
> (Augé in interview with Sturm, 1995)

In this submitted poem titled 'The Sea Stole the Stars', we find similar impressions and expressions of loneliness – of the ways it is both subsistent and enveloping:

> The sea stole the stars
> Garages tucked their cars
> Streetlights remained to blink

> As I laid still to overthink
> White noise of the furnace
> Guide me back to the surface,
> In the ocean of lost compass,
> Promise a world so wondrous

This beautiful poem captures the protagonist finding themselves overrun, overawed by loneliness. The elements provide the contrasting temperatures and materials for this night-time, urban scene. Fire and water, furnace and ocean, stars and streetlights wash over them, threatening to both drown and release them from the 'noise' of the day. They are 'lost' but have navigational tools that will keep them from the flame, that will return them from the watery deep. The poem not only documents how they experience loneliness but furnishes them with the tools to express it through embodied and metaphysical metaphors.

Faith

Ryan, too, has a compass with which to chart his emotional course and to keep loneliness at bay. However, his understanding of loneliness is from a faith-based perspective:

> A quote from my grandmother has stuck with me since she said it; 'I'm never alone, I have God.' I'm a Catholic and take solace in mass and prayer – when you kinda surrender to something bigger and acknowledge all you can control are your own actions, there's a sense of peace there.

The gifting of the self to a higher authority provides Ryan with a narrative that gives meaning and order to his life, alongside a 'sense of peace'. Prayer and ceremony places him in the social at all times: his relationship with God provides divine counsel and attending mass enables him to worship collectively. Nonetheless, as Ryan acknowledges, there are times when he questions his faith:

> Like every human there is doubt, fear, and the odd existential question here and there haha 😊 In those moments I feel untethered and floating. When you don't believe in something, you'll fall for anything – and suddenly the immensity of the worlds problems feel overwhelming and hopeless.

Without God's countenance, Ryan feels both 'untethered' from the world and overwhelmed by the enormity of the 'world's problems'. His loneliness room becomes an image of 'floating', and of where one has been seduced by the consuming politics of everyday life. The power of scripture, and of faith, to keep loneliness at bay, produces an interesting philosophical dilemma, however, since one may ask whether God was not lonely too? Given they created the world, do they not only know loneliness, see and feel loneliness, and experience loneliness as humans do (McGraw, 1992)? Ryan's relationship with God may in fact provide connection for both.

The realist responses so far described in this chapter seem to offer up very often two overarching (and entangled) descriptions of loneliness: one that is cognitive and perspectival, philosophical and metaphysical; and one that is sensorial and embodied, phenomenological and grounded. Loneliness is described as noisy; it takes place in the 'head'; is found in the unconscious. Loneliness is beyond the body, unburdened and unregulated, and connects with the transcendental, spiritual, and religious self. But loneliness is also described as meaty, fleshed, sensorial, rooted to culture, context, and the ordinary. These twinning experiences of loneliness are at times in tension but also go to show how the self is both an affective machine, fleshed and feeling, and touched by metaphysics, ideology, and discourse. These responses also demonstrate how social context, economics, and (limited) opportunity shape the way that loneliness is experienced. These entangled forms of loneliness are taken up squarely in the film documentary, our next and final stopping off point in this chapter.

Lonely realities in documentary film

Documentary film supposedly

> speaks to us about actual situations and events. It adheres to known facts rather than creating a fictional allegory. It involves real people (social actors) who present themselves to us in stories that convey a plausible proposal about or perspective on the lives, situations, and events portrayed. The distinct point of view or voice of the filmmaker shapes this story to show us what it feels like to inhabit or experience the world in a given way.
>
> (Nichols, 2017: 10)

This definition delineates that a documentary involves the depiction of real lives given by real people in storied situations shaped by the vision of the director. This creative treatment of actuality (Grierson, 1946) enables the viewer to know, first-hand, what it is like to live in the world that is being represented. The materials of the documentary – where the camera can be placed, what it can observe; the tools of editing that enable continuity and dramatic punctuation; and the lungs of sound – all combine to bring this 'realism' to life. There are three major problems with this definition, however.

First, in this authorship approach to the documentary, social actors are rendered relatively passive, imagined to be under the will and creative authority of the filmmaker. Their stories become recast by the actions of the director, decentring to a degree the social actors' own critical and creative autonomy. This top-down dynamic is much contested in contemporary documentary filmmaking. It has been replaced by a desire to involve participatory and co-creative elements, so that the stories that are told have been at least equally shaped by participant and creative.

The second major problem with this definition (and recognised by Nichols, the author of the above quotation) is that rather than there being one type of authored documentary, there are different modes, each of which renders the 'voice' of the filmmaker amplified, muted, or in tension with the stories being covered (Leach and Grant, 1998). For example, the 'performative mode' draws the filmmaker directly into the world being recorded, so that they become one of the 'subjects' in the documentary. The 'observational mode', by contrast, supposedly removes the 'voice' of the filmmaker, drawing upon the 'fly on the wall' approach to its subject matter. Unseen and unnoticed, the observational mode of the documentary purports to capture life as it is. The 'expository mode' tries to establish a truth, prove a hypothesis, and mounts its case through evidence gathering, to convince the viewer that the facts represented in the documentary are incontrovertible. Finally, the 'poetic mode' distances itself from realism, instead privileging image, metaphor, allusion, and abstraction. Here, creativity overwhelms verisimilitude, and yet provides the viewer with what might be termed the *senses* of the real.

What should also be noted here is how realism itself shifts with the type of documentary mode being used: the observational documentary speaks the language of social realism, in and through which the raw ingredient of everyday life is captured, while the poetic documentary moves through building affective linkages, colouring its images with heightened representations.

The third problem is that the director is themselves shaped by culture and ideology, and by the limitations of budget and market. The filmmaker not only exists in a 'tissue of quotations' (Barthes, 1977), but the dominant discourses and counter-discourses in which they exist shape their thinking, the subject matter they choose to work on, and the type of 'voice' that is enunciated (Roe and Pramaggiore, 2019). They make documentaries with a prescribed budget that in part dictates form, and with an eye to where it might be streamed or exhibited. Documentaries have to find their audience; they have to sell.

When it comes to loneliness documentaries, we see that these forms, themes, and issues very much come to the fore. Documentaries on loneliness are *everywhere*: they are feature-length, in serial form, commercially produced, and funded by health organisations and welfare initiatives. These documentaries are carried in different modes, including the observational, performative, poetic, and the expository. They tap into the discourse that loneliness is an 'epidemic' and consequently not only allow the viewer to explore and experience the vectors of this crisis but become a conduit for its negative representations.

Loneliness documentaries carry on their discursive wings the shame and the trauma that loneliness is connected to. While these documentaries are very often structured so that they offer solutions to, or a way out from, the loneliness that they have painstakingly documented, in so doing they suggest that loneliness cannot be lived with but needs to be expunged. These documentaries tend to pathologise all of loneliness, rarely fully recognising that certain aspects of loneliness are natural, or that its chronic form is produced by economic inequalities and massive failings in the support networks of capitalism.

The short documentary *Loneliness: The Silent Health Crisis* (SBS, Australia, 2019) is accompanied by the following summary:

> Loneliness is an epidemic that health experts are calling the next big public health crisis after smoking and obesity. Research says it can take years off your life and the loneliest people aren't who you might expect: after men in their late 40s, young women aged 15 to 24 are the loneliest group. So Laura Murphy-Oates hits the streets to find out what's going on. Her journey takes her to a 'cuddle party', to manning the phones of a 24-hour 'friendline', and singing karaoke in Broken Hill.

Loneliness: The Silent Health Crisis begins its account of loneliness by demonstrating how and why loneliness is indeed an 'epidemic'. The documentary employs a popular Australian television/media personality (Laura Murphy-Oates) to be the personable, empathetic narrator, and it draws on data, facts, figures, and the opinions of 'elite' actors such as doctors and psychologists to evidence its case. Laura tells us 'loneliness is a killer' and over images of ordinary people shopping and sitting in public spaces, sets the viewer the question: 'I know what you are thinking. In a world where we're more connected than ever, why are so many people struggling with loneliness?'

Loneliness: The Silent Health Crisis is an expository documentary. It answers this question through a mixture of interviews with people from varying backgrounds who experience loneliness, coupled with data and interviews with experts such as Professor Adrian Franklin, who is introduced as the 'loneliness academic'. Adrian identifies three reasons for the increase in loneliness among what are said to be the loneliest age group in Australia, 25–44-year-olds: high-pressurised jobs and occupation/job insecurity; high mortgage debts and the need to work long hours to meet payments; and high levels of divorce and separation. Adrian, interviewed in a studio, in a mixture of medium and long shots, has his answers in part played over images of people going about their everyday lives. In this way, the documentary is both able to particularise/personalise loneliness and attach it to the wider population. However, what the documentary doesn't do is analyse in any depth the different types of loneliness that exist, nor does it explore the deep structural forces that cause its most chronic form.

Structurally, the documentary develops its thesis that loneliness is a killer through leading with evidence and then showing the viewer how what has been 'established' may be overcome. For example, interviewee Gemma Cromwell explains that her busy working life has meant she has few friends and social connections. We then see her attend a 'MeetUp' event with people she has connected with through a friendship-making website. We are then given evidence that social media have increased our loneliness, and the solution offered to mitigate this is through a 'cuddles' therapy group where people meet up to hug, embrace, and hold one another. The next interviewee, Allen Dalton, is shown to have lost almost all social connectivity: housebound, without employment, he feels isolated in the rural outback community where he lives, with no friends or family to speak of. We are then introduced to Friendline, a free phone service that one can call to talk to someone at the end of the line; and to Connections, a community group for lonely people, within the town of Broken Hill, New South Wales, and through which Allen has now made new friends.

Each case study of loneliness is accompanied by its resolution. Images of isolation are always followed by scenes of connection: Gemma goes for a nature walk and picnic with her MeetUp friends, while Allen is seen playing computer games with Jason Hiamoe, who has been shown to also suffer from chronic loneliness. At the end of the documentary, we see Allen and Laura about to take part in a karaoke sing-along, ending the documentary with music as a type of therapy for the lonely.

A great number of the documentaries on loneliness are of the expository kind and they each follow a similar form, drawing upon data and the opinions of experts, followed by individual/personal instances of loneliness, and the solutions that may solve this 'crisis'. The films, then, seem to offer compelling evidence for the rise in loneliness and the ways and means to combat it. However, this is all done within certain discursive parameters, as I noted above. All-of-loneliness is put under the lens so that the shame of it registers widely; and the causes of chronic loneliness are attributed to the 'levers' within the social and cultural system rather than with the full apparatus of neoliberal capitalism. Consequently, loneliness becomes distributed, a form of 'slow violence' (Nixon, 2011) whose cause and consequence are never fully explored or attributed to the right systems of neglect and decay.

Nonetheless, one of the documentaries viewed for this book did assess more critically the reasons for the emergence of loneliness in Western society. In the UK-based *Aloneliness – A Short Documentary* (Field, 2019), we see and hear a number of researchers and academics lay the blame for the emergence of chronic loneliness at the feet of neoliberalism and entrepreneurial capitalism that took root in the 1980s. Expository in form, and with a media personality (Kate Lever) again anchoring the documentary, *Aloneliness – A Short Documentary* demonstrates how the rise of the marketed and marketable individual turned human relationships into commodities and types of brands. While walking in a park and directly addressing the camera, Lever suggests that

> it is interesting to even look at the terminology we are using to describe people in our lives ... When you look at people collecting followers on social media it implies that you need to be worth following. It implies that you have to build a persona in public and a profile that people can follow.

What Lever is addressing here is the development of the fame narrative that has accompanied both neoliberal individualism and the development of social media. Increasingly, people see their worth in relation to gilded personas that attract attention, that can be counted and measured (Holmes, 2006). People increasingly associate fame with sociality and look to develop public profiles that garner it (Hannell, 2019).

If we now return to a number of the examples explored in this chapter, we can see how the stage-managed self is actually steeped in this battle over anonymity and invisibility versus the desire to be seen, to be noticed. The Reddit r/lonely users, quoted above, are seeing loneliness as those without metric capital, whose personas do not sell, while for Ashika, visibility is a type of wound that lessens her ability to be free of convention. Central to these responses is a desire to be noticed and a need to be invisible. These tensions exist at the crux of fame culture, as the following analysis of *Amy* (Kapadia, 2015) demonstrates.

Amy's loneliness room

In the documentary *Amy* we see how a critical dialogue with fame shines a light on the relationship between loneliness and renown and the frenzy that accompanies such representations. *Amy* is again another example of the expository documentary, although there is no singular, binding narrator that leads us through the material. Rather, the documentary is composed of found footage – including early, home-made videos, live concerts, and interviews, still images and photographs ripped from newspapers and magazines – and voice-overs supplied by Amy's close friends and ex-husband.

Amy is structured around a classic rise-and-fall star narrative (Redmond, 2013). The documentary begins by showing her humble, working-class beginnings as a singer and songwriter, and then moves to capture how she was signed and managed, with her accompanying gradual rise to international success and stardom. We begin to discern 'helpers' and those who will lead her astray, alongside both the benefits and deficits of her fame. The narrative begins to develop its thesis that Amy was a tragic figure, manipulated by the men in her life, and hounded by the paparazzi. She becomes a toxic figure of fame (Luckett, 2010). We witness her decline through accounts of her bulimia; drug and alcohol addiction; failed relationships; and missed rehearsals or poorly delivered gigs. The images that have been collected and curated for this part of the documentary show her passed out on the floor, bleary eyed, and unsteady on her feet, rushing away from or into hundreds of paparazzi, with their camera bulbs endlessly flashing. As Andrews writes,

> Through frenetic editing and sound design, the film captures this viscerally: the horror of the constant hubbub of her life, the bombardment by camera lights, the noise, the frightening sense that she was never and yet always alone. This affective use of the paparazzi archive provides a facsimile experience of (apparently) unsolicited celebrity, to underscore the film's explanation – not as far as excuse – for Winehouse's desire to lose herself to drink and drugs.
>
> (Andrews, 2017: 352)

For me, the key understanding is the recognition of Amy being alone and yet never alone; of feeling lonely when in the company of others. What we see build around Amy in this documentary is the fibres of a vulnerable woman being unwound on the altars of fame. However, what *Amy* also does (but denies it) is recognise the aloneness that Amy felt in the world before the gory glare of fame rendered her loneliness as visible for all to see. Amy does resemble, to a degree, 'The Emperor's New Clothes' response discussed above – the nakedness of her loneliness is thrust out into the world and amplified. Here, however, it is pathologised because the documentary

> relies on the familiar historical association of female creativity with madness that manifests in celebrity culture as the intertwining of female transgression with discourses of pathology and mental instability ... Kapadia uses performances of the song 'Rehab' as a metric for Winehouse's ongoing disintegration, with footage from several performances included as evidence of her increasingly desperate desire to 'disappear' from public view.
>
> (Polaschek, 2018: 22)

This concern with visibility and invisibility, being seen and not seen, is a powerful metaphor for loneliness, as is the way it is associated with madness. The gendered nature of this representation is also powerfully acknowledged: Amy is like the mad woman in the attic, gaslighted and admonished for the lonely way she feels and sees the world.

If we were to compare *Amy* to what I would like to call 'heroic' loneliness documentaries, we can see how space and time is granted to men who seek solitude and aloneness. For example, in Ben Rivers' observational documentary, *Two Years at Sea* (2011), we follow Jake Williams as he goes about his lone existence in his remote Scottish homestead. Heavily romanticised,

> the film languishes: in boiling water, in naps, in twine blowing in the wind. There's no conflict, let alone context. At one point, there's an unbroken 10-minute shot of Jake watching a fire die. It's what Robinson Crusoe did between acts 1 and 2 – between carving a space out for himself in wilderness, and seeking out conflict when domesticity wasn't enough.
>
> (Shields, 2018)

One can powerfully contrast the utopian sentiments of being alone in nature that is found in *Two Years at Sea* with the Men's Shed responses from earlier in this chapter – they were lonely because of the monotonous routines they found themselves locked into, while Jake revels in the stillness that his solitude affords him. What differentiates their responses is the *poverty of their loneliness*: the Coventry men are stuck in small bedsits, away from nature and unemployed and underutilised, while Jake has the wilderness to himself.

Men, of course, are often afforded these freedoms since they are not supposedly tied to familial and domestic obligation. For this participant we can see how their loneliness room is inherently limited because of their role as mother and wife:

> I drop my kids off at school then I walk back alone. This is the time I have to recover myself.
>
> Because I can't leave my husband.
>
> I use the [peace] to think about who I want to be. It's a recurring thought process, of admitting and denying, of understanding I married someone I didn't know properly, of seeing how brilliant a father he is, of being witness to the love he shares with our children and being unable to take part in this, of wondering if it would be better to break this or carry on and being stuck in the stasis.

What the participant here documents is her relationship statis and how she hovers between despair and fortitude, wanting to escape and yet needing to remain. In a sense, Amy Winehouse is connected to this confession since she too felt trapped by marriage, until she escaped it, of course. These stories of gendered loneliness cross-connect again and again, but here a new element has been introduced – that of the child in a loveless relationship. But what then of lonely children, largely absent from the research on loneliness?

Lonely children in *The 3 Rooms of Melancholia*

When it comes to most of the research on loneliness, children are majorly underrepresented in the literature. When they have been included, historically speaking, their understanding of loneliness is captured in concrete terms. For example, in Cassidy and Asher's research with kindergarten and first-grade children, they asked the respondents the following questions and were given these answers: 'what loneliness is ("being sad and alone")'; 'where it comes from ("nobody to play with")'; and 'what one might do to overcome feelings of loneliness ("find a friend")' (1992: 352). In these responses, we can see how crucial friendship is to how children understand their lonely state. However, as Bullock argues,

> the causes of children's loneliness are both external and internal to the school environment. External factors include 'conflict within the home; moving to a new school or neighborhood; losing a friend; losing an object, possession, or pet; experiencing the divorce of parents; or experiencing the death of a pet or significant person'. Internal factors include 'being rejected by peers; lacking social skills and knowledge of how to make friends; or possessing personal characteristics (e.g., shyness, anxiety, and low self-esteem) that contribute to difficulties in making friends'.
>
> (Bullock, 1998)

These dual characteristics of loneliness very much align with how adults experience it, in a sense producing a narrativised and experiential continuity across the lifespan of a human. Similarly, when children are asked to story their feelings of loneliness, we find continuities. For example, in Wilson et al.'s research on children who have been hospitalised, they found that children's stories often focused on being alone and its consequences:

> When children were alone, they could be uncertain about what was going to happen or they might predict something negative (scary, painful) that could happen based on past experience. The emotional response to being alone in these two circumstances was scared, mad, and sad. Children wanted protection in these situations. Protection did not prevent scary events like shots from happening but rather provided comfort. Children told many stories about being lonely. For example: 'She was very lonely and her father came to visit her. After a while her father just left and she was very lonely and she didn't want to be lonely.' 'She's mad that her parents aren't there and that she's alone too'.
>
> (Wilson et al., 2010: 98)

These stories of loneliness enabled children to draw on fiction to account for the way they were feeling and about what was worrying them. They also introduce the idea of loss and trauma and how separation from parents, loved ones, rendered them alone in the world. The absence of significant others is something taken up in *The 3 Rooms of Melancholia* (Honkasalo, 2004).

In this poetic documentary, set during the Second Chechen War, we see how poor and orphaned children are captured in waves of loneliness as they are militarised and removed from the comfort of loved ones. Set in three rooms, the film offers the viewer a series of intense close-ups of children isolated from human contact, held in appalling living conditions, cast aside in bombed-out cities, and trained to be fighting soldiers. Honkasalo tries to 'express something she refers to as "human silence"', that a picture 'can reach the unspoken part of a human. The part indescribable with language' (French, 2021: 115).

In the first room of the film, titled 'Nostalgia' or 'Longing', filmed at the Kronstadt Cadet Academy, child orphans are taught how to march, shoot rifles, and to immerse themselves in the personae of the battle-ready soldiers they are being trained to become. Even when the children are captured playing in this room, the games they choose are war ones. In the second room, titled 'Breathing', we are dropped into Grozny, the war-torn capital of Chechnya, and are placed in a room in which a dying mother hands over her three small children to Hadizhat Gataeva, a humanitarian worker, who runs a makeshift orphanage at a refugee camp. As they are taken away, we hear and see their collective despair, as the children cry bitterly and the mother weeps with grief. In the third room, titled 'Remembering', we visit the orphanage and hear children bear witness to their trauma, to the violence and abuse they have suffered. The last scene, set on a farm run by Muslim farmers, depicts a symbolic religious ceremony in which a goat is sacrificed for food and renewal. We witness the children smear its blood on their faces at the same time as fighter aircraft fly overhead. Such affective descriptions return us to the children of science fiction discussed in Chapter 3, and the significance of absent or traumatised children to the representation of loneliness.

The 3 Rooms of Melancholia is steeped in the poetics and politics of loneliness as it is produced, manufactured, by the violence of war. It shows us the 'unique power' of the documentary 'to allow us to know with or through the body … through affect, empathy, and sensation' (Juhasz and Lebow, 2015: 9). The children move through these rooms, abandoned, victimised, unable to make friends since friendship is not a useful commodity to them. Their loneliness rises out of the red embers of war, their faces torches for their lost innocence. What is particularly remarkable about the film is the way sound is used to embody the steely isolation of lost youth. At the end of 'Longing' we hear the poetry written by one boy, Kolya, form the lyrics for composer Sanna Salmenkallio's haunting score that runs its chords across the following two rooms of the film. As Honkasalo commented, 'I always knew I wanted to have a musical structure, like a symphony that the audience could build up for themselves' (Felperin, 2005). This is a symphony of loneliness, the notes and melodies of children who have had their childhood arrested by the forces of war.

Lonely realities: a brief conclusion

In this chapter we have explored the way loneliness is documented and creatively navigated. The broad focus has been on chronic loneliness, but we have also seen how metaphysics, faith and religion, and abandoned children have become localised sites of the lonely imagination. The chapter has underscored its analysis through a concern with realism, and the economic, cultural, and political systems of neoliberal capitalism. Contemporary capitalism, as noted earlier, can in fact be seen to be a loneliness room – producing the conditions for the worst excesses of isolation to be grown.

As an art form, we have seen how the film documentary acts to reproduce commonly accepted narratives of loneliness, failing to fully differentiate between their different forms, failing to connect the conditions of isolation to the brute forces of neoliberalised life. The film documentary is shown to offer solutions to this crisis of loneliness but only within the parameters of it sustaining capitalist life. One is cured or healed of loneliness and in turn can again become a productive member of society. Of course, in war-torn countries, to be a productive member of society is to be armed and ready for combat, even if you are a child in time. Perhaps this is also the contemporary umbrella for much of the rise in despairing loneliness – the fear of 'war planes' appearing in the skies above.

In this chapter we have explored how the desire to be visible and valuable is connected to the fame narrative: the masks we put on crave attention, unless, of course, that attention reveals the loneliness that naturally resides inside us. Through the documentary *Amy* we have seen how loneliness is buried beneath its gendered toxic narrative – revealing but concealing the way that the loneliness Amy felt had sat gently inside her for all of time. In *Amy*, loneliness is a pathology that needs to be shat or vomited out, but if we look beyond this sickly narrative, we find that before fame her loneliness is comfortably natural to her.

When Amy sings, I hear the colours of loneliness; her voice, her lyrics sounding out that deep existential rip in the grounding of the self. My mum used to sing when washing dishes: her voice a soaring hymn to losses and gains, and to the loneliness room she often resided in. In Chapter 5 we sound out loneliness more fully, allowing its songs to better orate what loneliness is.

5

None but the lonely heart: the sounds of loneliness

Prelude: our tune

It is late at night and the country road that the car is on curves in on itself. Black shapes fall out of the darkness and the white lines of the road appear as flashes of cartography. It is warm inside the car. The air conditioner creates vapours of heat that funnel over feet, hands, steering wheel, mirror, and window. The car's full-beam headlights search ahead for wild animal, lost strangers, and the ghosts of the imagination. The car is a cocoon, a travelling womb, on the way home at the end of a long day.

Empty water bottles, last month's petrol receipts, dollar coins, and face masks are found on the passenger's seat, in the driving well, and in stained cup holders. An eyeliner and lipstick grace the open glovebox, while black-tinted sunglasses hang from its button. A faded sticker clings to the car's back window. Covered in road dust it reads, 'Bad Seeds'.

The driver yawns and reaches for the radio dial, turning it so that sounds crackle and then burst into life. She keeps her eyes on the road, using the white lines to navigate the curves, the shadows, the ghosts of her imagination. The car clock blinks to midnight.

She lands on a radio station playing love songs selected by the broken hearted. The DJ's voice croons a sadness that spills into the car and mixes with the heat vapours so that all the particles found in this auto cocoon, this mechanical womb, are charged with an overwhelming loneliness.

The radio DJ introduces the next requested track, his voice washed in a soft tone melancholy as the song begins to play beneath him. He reads out the text message that accompanies it, but the driver is barely cognisant of what is being said. The song's opening bars and notes have entered her ears, fallen onto her chest, burrowed into her staggering heart.

She fixes her eyes on the road, using the white lines to navigate the curves, the shadows, the ghosts of her imagination, but now the driver's face is full of history, of memories that pour out of her eyes and mouth.

Nick Cave begins to sing, professing his belief in love, asking God to protect his lover from harm. A naked piano sounds out the poetic stanzas and scores this song about an eternal, transcendental love. As Cave calls his lover into his arms, for always and evermore, the driver pulls over and the car comes to a rest between road and verge. The driver stares into the distance, her hands gripping the steering wheel, as the ghost of her former lover rears into view.

This was their tune, a melody of matrimony, a promise of forever, now broken and only visible through the phantoms of the rear-view mirror. The driver puts her hand on the radio dial, increasing the volume to maximum so that the car shakes with the scorched profundity of this love-struck song. She lets the song in, opens her chest to it, allows it to fill the blood in her atrium with all its intensity and integrity. She has never felt this alone, this lonely, this bereft.

She begins to sing along to it, to take charge of its notes, its diction, and direction. Her voice rises so that she is singing at the top of her voice, giving herself over to this memory, to this past relationship, to this song of the ages, one final time. The car engine ticks over, heat vapours, and melody and voice comingle, charging every lost atom in the car. A comet bursts on the starless horizon.

When the song ends, the driver reaches for the glove box, picks up the lipstick and begins to colour her lips with its fiery red hue. She puts on the sunglasses, looks coolly at herself in the mirror, checks the rear view, and accelerates, hopefully, into the distance ...

The sounds of loneliness

The notion that loneliness is aural, encased in a soundscape, and is a condition of the ears, is very clearly a truism. Certain soundscapes are culturally associated with loneliness and isolation, such as the cracking sheets of ice and the stormy winds 'heard' at the pristine white Arctic shelf. Environmental sounds are said to be regenerative and serene (Björk et al., 2008: e2), putting one *in* nature and *into* a sublime state, and *away* from the human-social. As Pistrick and Isnart suggest,

> sounds play a crucial role in charging place with meaning, in stimulating emotional attachment: they are constitutive for the act of place-making. Sounds mobilize feelings of belonging and nostalgia, they may transmit a (virtual) idea of home, and they may fill a place with ideas about the past, the present and the future. They are even capable of creating evocative mindscapes with reference to physical realities.
>
> (Pistrick and Isnart, 2013: 506)

Certain sounds are connected with, or to, sombre ritualised events, such as the funeral march and quieted eulogy. These lonely ceremonies have their own 'aural signatures' that come to emotively capture and elicit the feeling of a profound existential emptiness or sadness (Brandt et al., 2009: 1). These ceremonial signatures are past and present tense, their sounding calling forth a memory that orates the sadness of the present. We cry at funerals – its non-verbal significance filling the void of the church or the graveyard, as the mourners gather.

Sounding loneliness is very often contextual, associated with a space or place at a particular time. In an empty playground, the creaking swing seems to weep for the children not there, while a walk at the beach may find the white horses roaring back at the person who in hearing its oceanic noise has their loneliness amplified. These 'acoustic territories' (LaBelle, 2010) separate or demarcate different types of places: the library from the nightclub; the train station from the shopping mall; the back garden from the busy street; the city from the rural; and the inner city from the suburban. Everyday auditory life is connected to, and emerges from, spatial and social structures, and is implicated in the way identity and social position is stratified. Sound, then, isn't just an envelope for loneliness to travel on but its connecting, experiential tissue.

For Helen, her loneliness is found in the regenerative acoustics of her back garden:

Where is your loneliness room?

The deck area at the top of our garden

Why do you go there?

To get away from everyone and have time to think and relax

Using as many words as you like, describe your loneliness room. Please feel free to be poetic or to write your answer as a 'story'.

There is constant London traffic and I can hear people talking on the street and see the planes flying into Heathrow but for me it is an oasis of calm. Covered by the balcony from the flats above us, I can sit and watch the rain or the little birds at the feeders, the rippling of the ivy hedge in the wind.

Helen beautifully captures the way aural signatures and acoustic territories both blend and work against one another. On the one hand, the sounds of the traffic and aeroplanes act as noise pollutants. The sounds of the city and airport bleed into her idyll. On the other, they are quieted by the sound of rain falling and the wind moving the leaves on the hedge. Spatially, Helen removes herself from her family, from her house, to sit as far away from the home, the city, as she can. The deck area, at the top of the garden, gives her distance and positionality: her loneliness room, here understood as a space of solitude, is a choir of remembering and forgetting. For Helen, these are moments of contemplation and restoration: hers is a happy and serene loneliness that is made of and from her garden's acoustic properties.

For Ben, it is the silence he encounters while working in his shed that provides a similar comforting loneliness room:

> The chaos builds. The reverberations of life reach a deafening shrill-like crescendo. I seek solitude. I seek escape. I seek tranquillity. My shed is my space, my cave, my place to hide and be alone. I enjoy my own company and it seems too often that there is someone else other than me and myself making three – a crowd. Sometimes I just sit, alone with nothing but silence and my thoughts, sometimes I build, sometimes I stand and stare out the window. It is my physical place of solitude that delivers my neurological place of peace.

Ben finds the silence transformative; it allows him to think, reflect, and to let go of the chaotic and noisy nature of everyday life. The silence is serene for Ben, it ushers in the tranquil and removes him from the social world. He likes and needs to be alone since it grants him autonomy and unleashes creativity through his 'building' projects. This kind of 'deep silence … is a necessary requirement for deep thought and self-knowledge which, in turn, are essentially creative in nature and are of vital importance in enhancing both intellectual and artistic pursuits' (Dawson, 2003: 33). Of course, in a different social context, and as we have seen in the descriptions of loneliness in earlier chapters, silence is the voice of chronic loneliness, one where there is no one to speak to or interact with (Rokach, 2012).

For Anton, his loneliness room is a silent space – the public steam room/sauna in his local council-run gym –where he engages in meditative practices:

> *Why do you go there?*
>
> To warm up before doing my aqua aerobics work-out, then to de-stress after the workout. I do pre- and post-class vocal workouts to strengthen my lungs and increase air-flow. The type and intensity of the vocal workout depends upon whether I am alone or with others.
>
> *Describe your loneliness room.*
>
> As a writer-researcher I sit all day writing and most of the night watching movies and TV programs. To prevent myself from dying of a heart attack or deep vein thrombosis, to get fit and lose weight, I do two aqua aerobics (resistance training) classes twice a week (Tuesday and Thursday nights). Upon arriving I change, shower and enter the steam room to warm up my body (between 30–60 minutes). Whilst there I do movement exercises of my limbs and vocal exercises to strengthen my lungs, improve air-flow, and increase lung stamina. I do this via sound exercises (which reverberates off the walls) If alone, I use a loud voice and on each full breath I sing A-E-I-O-U. I do this a few times, then

do it speeded up, whilst other times I do A–U in one long breath. Sometimes I just do a 'U' and generate a harmonic (akin to Tuvan Throat Singing) other times I do an A–E. Sometimes I improvise as the mood and sound hits me. At other times I chant some sacred words of power from various religious traditions (which I learnt from a chanting group decades ago). If other patrons enter the steam room I stop and either do wind sounds (akin to the desolation scenes in *Scott of the Antarctic* [1948, dir. Charles Frend]) wherein I imagine myself lonely in ice-nature. Other times I hum various tunes and mentally delve into the loneliness riding alone the sound wave I am generating (akin to the practice of Nada Yoga meditation on the inner sacred sound) … The steam room is my isolation chamber, sound mirror, aesthetic outlet, and physical body conditioner all in one. I can be alone whilst alone or alone with a crowd, some of whom enjoy my sound work and feel it is like a sonic massage. Others leave when I start.

If you could choose one artist who for you best captures loneliness, who would it be and why?

Robert Falcon Scott's 1912 expedition wherein he is isolated in the frozen wilderness as portrayed by John Mills in *Scott of the Antarctic*. He is depressed having lost the race, he must endure the weather, and during those wind scenes it is as if he is the [loneliest] man in the world.

Anton describes the way his harmonised and vocalised meditation works to destress and transport him along the sound waves it creates. These aural swells are a mixture of notes, fragmentary phonetics and letter sounds, wind impersonations, and chanting or incantation, connecting him to the spiritual or transcendental. Anton is very often alone in this public space, both physically and existentially, as he seeks time out from the social world and the materially grounded aspects of daily life. Sometimes his vocalisations take place in the presence of other patrons, so in this context he also shares his lonely 'songs' while being disconnected from those around him. Anton describes part of his routine as like the 'desolation scenes' found in the film *Scott of the Antarctic*, connecting his own vocal practices to being the 'loneliest man in the world'. Anton's response, then, also aurally takes us back to the lonesome figures of science fiction film, conjoining the white wilderness of the South Pole to the tundras found in apocalyptic fiction.

For this book, Anton supplied an audio recording of his breathing and sound exercises. Their non-verbal nature and improvised rhythms and beats do resonate as expressions of a deeply meditative state – one that untethers itself from the social; one that transports the listener to the Antarctic shelf where the sound of wind and cracking ice leaves one feeling as if you are the last person alive on earth.

Anton's vocalisations draw attention to the way speech has a melody which conveys 'emotion through cues such as timing, rate, intensity, intonation, and pitch' (Quinto et al., 2013). When it comes to the expression of sorrow and sadness, speech is said to take on the musical interval referred to as the minor third, which has three half steps (semitones). Sad speech 'has a consistent pitch pattern' that is recognised for its sorrowfulness or melancholy (Curtis and Bharucha, 2010: 335). The minor third of speech is found repeated across all forms of popular culture. For example, in 'sad voice' science fiction film and television, what we hear spoken is 'anhedonic, sapped of passion, depressed. A pronounced flat affect, sometimes paired with an unnatural cadence' (Knibbs, 2022). The sad voice reveals the loneliness of its speaker and the lonely nature of the world that they reside in. This is amplified when the voice belongs to an android or computer operating system since their synthetic nature is coupled with patterns of the minor third, creating a speech system that sounds alien and alienating (see Chapter 3 for a fuller discussion of loneliness in science fiction film).

The relationship between speech and music extends to a range of emotional states. For example, empirical work carried out on why people find music affecting and pleasurable found that people entered several affective states when listening to music. For Juslin and Laukka these states can be demarcated as happy, relaxed, calm, moved, nostalgic, pleasurable, loving, and sad (2004). For Zentner et al., listening to music can be identified as involving nine common emotional responses: wonder, transcendence, tenderness, nostalgia, peacefulness, power, joyful activation, sadness, and tension (2008). These emotional responses varied greatly according to the musical genre, with specific musical compositions registering as sonic equivalents of melancholy and despair (Huron, 2011). Huron argues that 'in the case of sad music, one might speculate that the acoustic features of sadness (low pitch, quiet, slow, etc.) would activate pertinent premotor mirror neurons that then evoke a feeling state akin to the affective state needed to generate such sounds' (2011: 150).

Michael's submission for this book, a 5-minute-20-second musical composition titled *Emil Sinclair Lonely Jump Fugue*, is heavily indebted to the deployment of the minor third and to a sad ecology of strings and stresses. The piece is atonally arranged, with wind and flute instruments in contestation, and electronic sounds piercing through the heavy notes. The composition rises and falls so that its musical trajectory 'jumps' within its repeating cycle: soprano meets bass. It conjures up or rather becomes a composition for Emil Sinclair, the main character from Herman Hesse's *Demian: The Story of Emil Sinclair's Youth*. At the end of the novel, Emil decides to walk off into the world totally alone, leaving behind his lover and closest friend, recognising the lonely if empowering nature of his maturated selfhood. Of course, this composition is also a sounding of the participant's own loneliness room: submitted without context or note, they use music to creatively explain what loneliness means to them – they are, in effect, compositionally embodying Emil.

Creating or listening to sad music may well be cathartic and a means to affectively experience it safely:

> the sadness induced by music is more pure or unencumbered than the sadness we experience in response to everyday events ... sad music, and other forms of sad or negative art, allows us to experience and explore negative affects uncoupled from real world consequences. We experience sadness, but a sadness divorced from our everyday cares and concerns. We are free to get swept up in the sadness without the anxieties of having to solve a problem or live with a loss.
>
> (Levinson, 1997: 51)

For Veli, listening to a sad song is connected to escapism and creativity:

> Sitting on my custom ergonomic chair, listening to the mellifluous tones coming through my noise-canceling headphones to drown out the outside world, as Sam Smith bares his soul in an acoustic rendition of his single 'Omen' – on repeat. I lay out a blank piece of an A3 drawing pad and have my Copic markers at the ready. No concept of what is about to come before me, or the duration, I do not care. This is my time, this is my escapism. Colours run wild, they bleed onto the page as blood would an open wound. There is an excitement to the unknown creation taking place in front of my eyes. The colours are simple, yet bright and vivacious – giving me guidance as my fingers follow their direction. Echoing through my ears, Sam Smith's voice is turned up and I am overwhelmed by tears. Joy, elation and relief as I allow my emotions out onto the page. This is my escape.

Veli's response is co-synaesthetic and multi-modal, and the emotions he refers us to take us across various planes of affect. Sam Smith's track becomes a sounding board for the art Veli creates, its sadness the fuel for the freeing of his imagination and for the colourful sound shapes that run wild across his sketching page (Figure 5.1). Loneliness is here both a bottomless well and a spring of joy. The escape that Veli writes about, then, is complex: it is an escape *from* the humdrum and mediocre and *into* the heightened realm of the senses. The loneliness and elation he feels are simultaneously nourishing, good for his creative soul.

For Simon, the song that best captures what it feels like to be lonely is 'Field Below' by Regina Spektor:

> Above all the lyrics, since they are desolate. I thought maybe it was about being alone as opposed to lonely, but it is beyond that. The feeling of hurting loss and continuing with 'ancient bruises' which I always misheard as 'I gained some bruises' – which also is a desolate picture of the felt absence. The abyss. The music ebbs and flows beautifully like primordial water.

Figure 5.1 Sound shapes

Can you recall where you first heard it and how it made you feel?

I was in my former studio in the basement of my family home. It brought a lump to my throat. I probably cried because I knew I would leave and lose all of it at some point.

Simon is not only deeply moved by the song but attaches his future to it, like it is prophesising heartbreak and loss for him. He feels it emotionally and physically, and hears it as both elemental (like water) and catastrophic (as he imaginatively stands on the edge of the abyss). For Simon, the song ignites his existential loneliness while grounding it in a future orientation – the losses that tomorrow may bring. Simon and Veli are both experiencing what Pilgrim et al. define as 'aesthetic awe', a sublime response to the song that they hear and feel so deeply (2017).

For Maria, an English speaker, the aesthetic awe she experiences is provided by the music's melody since the vocals/lyrics are sung in Korean:

Which song for you best captures what it feels like to be lonely?

'Lonely' by 2NE1

Briefly explain why this song captures the feeling of loneliness. Please feel free to comment on its arrangement, lyrics, composition.

Although this song is in Korean, the melody pulls you to the core and you just wallow their and realise how lonely you really are.

Can you recall where you first heard it and how it made you feel?

I heard it in my room. It was so emotional that I suddenly pictured myself in an empty room and just staring at the walls.

Maria's response points to the way that a song can not only dramatically alter one's mood but can provide an aural epiphany. Maria describes the song as penetrating her deep self which results in her seeing her present/future differently. This is not a happy transformation but a gut-wrenching one: the song turns her inside out and she finds herself in an empty room, all alone, staring at the four walls.

Maria imaginatively returns us to the way a number of the Coventry Men's Shed participants described their habitus (see Chapter 4 for a discussion of their responses). What may be happening here is the way realism and fantasy, media representation and imagination, fuse: Maria's greatest fear is the one a large number of people face daily, to be all alone in the world. The loneliness discourse is so ingrained it penetrates Maria's core self even when she is not in that position. As profoundly, Maria's response returns us to the philosophical premise of this book: that humans are inherently lonely creatures (Svendsen, 2017).

For many of the participants in this project, catharsis and release were important, but as common was the way certain pieces of music acted as a portal to past experiences that reminded them of their loneliness, and which made them lonely again on hearing the song or composition. Three major contexts emerged for the way music elicited the feeling of being in a loneliness room: while driving in the car; being reminded of a past relationship; and as autobiographical nostalgia for a time that has passed.

Driving in my car

As Michael Bull argues, the car is a 'privatized aural space' that

represents a form of 'compensatory metaphysics' in which time is transformed and experience heightened. The aural habitation of place and time becomes a way of reinscribing the ritual of everyday practices with the driver's own chosen, more meaningful set of 'rituals'. What becomes clear is that the notion that 'real life is elsewhere' is experienced negatively by many automobile users who use the radio or the cassette as a means to reclaiming significance in the present. Automobiles appear to operate as symbolic 'sanctuaries' which ... represent a physical zone of 'immunity' between the driver and the world or space beyond.

(Bull, 2001: 199)

When we find ourselves driving, a number of circumstances weight the experience. First, as Bull suggests, the car operates as a temporary sanctuary from the noise of the world. Second, the car is the audio machine that propels one forward, sometimes to a place or destination that one may not want to go or arrive at. Third, the car journey cements the mundanity that shapes much of domestic life – one may be driving to pick up the groceries or the kids from school. Finally, the car is also a memory box since, when alone, one can reflect on and call up past events, ruminate and cogitate over troubling issues, and fantasise about futures and life goals. Music is central to both the sanctuary and memorial nature of the car journey since it is a 'space of performance and communication where drivers report being in dialogue with the radio or singing in one's auditized/privatized space' (Bull, 2001: 199). Music is central to the way the car can become a loneliness room since the songs that are listened to very often ignite the longings and failings of the lonely imagination.

For this participant, their loneliness room is the car, tuned to their favourite track, as it is taken through the car wash:

> I approach the carwash, ready my debit card and drive in. I struggle to reach the buttons to select and pay for the wash, because of course that happens today. I drive through, the doors behind me close and the pre-rinse starts. I turn up the song, generally something melancholy from my teen years, regularly anything from The Used's *In Love & Death*. The bubbles start, the scrubbers scrub, I sing, I cry, I sing louder and I cry some more. The final rinse is happening, I turn the music down a little because the carwash is quieter now. I let my feelings go with the final rinse and start feeling better as the protect + shine sprays onto my car. I drive away and I leave the feelings behind me, circling down the drain ... I like being able to drive away feeling better and in a sense 'cleaner' – almost as though I have washed away my feelings with the car's dirt.

For this anonymous participant, taking the car to be washed and polished provides the narrative for the way they can cleanse themselves. The music they choose to listen to provides a tear-jerking anthem, one that allows them to 'rinse' themselves of whatever is troubling them. Tears and bubbles, eyes and windscreen wipers, are metaphorically and experientially aligned. Amplification is important: the song is loudly played, then softened, and then finally muted, as the cleansing ritual takes place. The sense that loneliness needs to be washed away, is 'matter out of place', and that it is dirt to clean, is powerfully expressed here. Culturally, as noted before, we expel, remove, or distance ourselves from dirt, contagion, and disease (Miller, 2013). Loneliness, then, becomes dirt-like for this participant, although the cathartic experience renders it an important experience to have – as with Veli, there is joy to be had in the shedding of (car wash) tears.

For Erin, also, the car provides an ambivalent environment for loneliness to emerge. In choosing 'Come on up to the House' by Tom Waits as her loneliness room song, she writes:

> The lyrics both express and challenge alienation (and associated narcissism) that leads to a certain kind of loneliness. The song essentially tells you to get over yourself, whilst also acknowledging the inherent futility of all human effort.
>
> I first heard it in the car on the way home from work one day about a decade or so ago. As a result, I associate it with the desperate tilting at windmills (another iteration of loneliness) that comes with precarious academic life.

Erin expresses how having a precarious job conditions her response to the song: the lyrics confirm her alienation, while also providing a narrative to see through such identity dislocations. As she drives home from work, Erin allows the song to prophesise to her, but she also take the opportunity to reflect on who she is. Driving provides this type of temporal opportunity to look back and forwards, with music being the catalyst for deep reflectivity. For another participant, reflection leads to a type of punkish nihilism since their car is on a highway to nowhere:

> My loneliness room is a car interior, in which a double-sided cassette plays albums by The Dirty Three, over and over, ad infinitum, as the world goes by my windows.
>
> *Why do you go there?*
> When I'm a Lost Cause. When I'm far too close to death. Thankfully, not often, anymore.
>
> *Describe your loneliness room.*
> I travel in my car interior, gliding at one speed, under glass, as I drive around, alone. I'm a lonelier version of Iggy Pop's 'The Passenger'. Outside is not a site of endless night-time possibility, but a place in which all the other people live, beyond reach. It's a horrible kind of funny that they don't know.

This incredibly rich response creates a 'story' out of the way their car occupies the zero ground of loneliness. The drive seems to be eternal, in a neverland, and the glass cocoon a window onto the world that is – tragically, comedically – forever out of reach. The music which sounds this drive is by two alterative acts – The Dirty Three, an instrumental Australian rock band led by Warren Ellis, and post-punk rock star Iggy Pop. In fact, Iggy's 'The Passenger' provides the creative stimulus for the response, with its lyrics – 'I stay under glass / I look through my window so bright / I see the stars come out tonight / I see the bright and hollow sky / Over the city's ripped back sky / And everything looks good tonight' – setting the *mise-en-scène* for the participant's brooding loneliness drive. In their car, they can't reach the social world, but they don't really want to. They are outsiders; they are lonely strangers (Simmel, 1950), nearing an existential death, but drive on and on, nonetheless.

Joe imagines a similar acoustic drive but here it is taken at the beginning of the day:

> I used to listen to John Lennon's version [of 'Stand by Me'] when driving up to Shepparton in the early morning fog, cranking it up on the Hume Hwy. I was young and jilted, full of loneliness. I loved the emotion of Lennon's singing and matched it with the speed of the car.
>
> *Can you recall where you first heard it and how it made you feel?*
>
> I probably had only heard Lennon's version on a cassette, as it was only years later that I heard other versions, so a close date would be 1990. To be sophisticated about it I would point up the pathos in dear old John Lennon's amazing rendition.

Joe gives velocity or speed to his lonely room song, matching the tempo of the track to how fast he drives. The car becomes a part of Joe's living skin, heart, lungs, bone, transmitting the melancholy of the song to its gears and accelerator pedal. Contextually, Joe has been 'jilted' and so the lament of the song and his cruising out of town are environmentally and emotionally meshed. Here, however, Joe also connects the memory of hearing the song to his lost youth – to a time found deep in his past. As Connell and Gibson argue, 'Music can evoke memories of youth and act as a reminder of earlier freedoms, attitudes, events; its emotive power ... serves to intensify feelings of nostalgia, regret or reminiscence' (2003: 222–223).

As the next section shows, youthful love songs are very often the lonely doorway to the residues of forgetting and remembering.

(Not) our tune

The relationship between music, memory, and feeling is a direct one. Songs invite us to not only remember key life events or relationships and how we feel about them, but to broader social and cultural realities from the period they were released. Songs exist in and across the private and public realms: they mean distinct things for each 'listener', and they exist as 'collective' or 'shared' cultural forms (Hesmondhalgh, 2008). As Van Dijck suggests,

> In addition to storing the sound of an object we hear, our memories also retain emotional reactions to it, as well as our mental and physical state at the time

of apprehending. Out of that sensation or feeling, we create a (non-language) map or image of this event in our core consciousness, a 'story' that also becomes verbally present in our minds by the time we focus on it. Upon later recall, recorded songs work as triggers, bringing back waves of emotion, the specificity of a time, an event, a relationship, or evoking more general feelings. This 'wordless storytelling' precedes language and happens entirely inside our brain; memory for recorded songs appears to hold longer when people turn emotion-infested sounds into internal narratives.

(Van Dijck, 2006: 360–361)

Love and break-up songs are often the most powerful vehicles for memory activation and the emotions they ignite. People mark the significance of their relationships through their shared love song, chosen because of when and where it was first played and often linked to a romantic event (Chittenden, 2013). This happens at Western wedding ceremonies, where 'their song' will be played at the married couple's 'first dance'. The song's lyrics, hook, refrain, and melody will work in concert – all the elements providing the 'narrative' to which lovers gather around, and then are materially hurt by when/if that relationship falls away. Sadness, bitterness, and the swells of loneliness become the dominant response to 'break-up' songs, creating lonely rooms when they are then heard days, weeks, months, years later.

Heike's lonely love song choice works in exactly this way:

Which song for you best captures what it feels like to be lonely?

'The other side' by David Gray

Briefly explain why this song captures the feeling of loneliness.

It's a perfect mix of lyrics (describing regrets that cannot be undone) and music (sparse, just piano and voice)

Can you recall where you first heard it and how it made you feel?

I think it was when my first longer relationship came to an end and I was trying to come to terms with feeling lost. It still brings tears to my eyes though nowadays for other reasons.

Heike describes how the lyrics and pared-back song call forth a broken relationship and the pain it brings back when it is heard. They associate loneliness with being lost, unmoored from a relationship and the confusion that it brought them. Their written response returns us to the Emil Sinclair composition explored above, since they are also called to address their 'unknown' future on their own and while all alone. Heike, however, leaves us with an enigma: the song recalls not just a past relationship but is tethered to something in the present they do not elaborate on – 'nowadays for other reasons'. Sad music can do this too: fill us with an incomprehensible loneliness, beyond language, as Maria's response, above, also directly addresses, and as Natalia does below:

Which song for you best captures what it feels like to be lonely?
Erykah Badu – 'Ye-yo'

Briefly explain why this song captures the feeling of loneliness.
Every time I hear this song, I understand that I miss something I don't have. Erykah's voice is so mature, strong and the same time fragile, it underlines her willness to have someone by her side. And when she hits the high notes you can easily hear your last hope for love but again it is not the crazy, passionate type of love but something very filled with the wisdom. That's why she is lonely, she can't have it.

Can you recall where you first heard it and how it made you feel? Please describe.
It was my first big concert with a big international celebrity in 2008. I have never heard this song before because the internet era was just developing. I was pure magic, it made my cry. I could relate to every sound of the music and her voice.

Natalia tunes into the way a song can evoke desire that cannot be fulfilled. She hears and feels the vocalisation as strong and fragile, and makes sense of the high notes as capturing that longing for a pure love that is impossible to attain or maintain. Her sounding and hearing of the song embody this desiring gap. Natalia contextualises where she first heard the song and the 'magic' she felt as it was played. Joy and tears again co-mingle, and here we can almost 'hear' the fan intensity that emerges at gigs (Brown and Knox, 2017). However, Natalia's romantic loneliness is private even if it takes place at a public event. She shuts out the crowd in her response, imagines a one-to-one relationship with the song and singer, so that she is all alone in a venue full of people. This isn't a 'real' break-up as such, but one communicated through notes that rise, rise, and fall, showering Natalia in idealised romantic-coupling longings.

Steven, David, and Caitlin all chose heartbreak songs in their responses. For Steven, 'Lua' by Bright Eyes has a 'forlorn sound … The hook ("so simple in the moonlight") initially caught my ear, but I came to associate it with my former partner, who became depressed and had a breakdown'. For David, the uncompromising lyrics of Joan Armatrading's 'Down to Zero' tell a relationship story where 'you haven't just lost a bit, you've lost everything, all the way down to zero'. He recalls his girlfriend at university 'who was a big Armatrading fan, and her songs summed up all the stages of our relationship, from "Love and Affection" to "Down to Zero"'. Caitlin experiences a profound moment of loneliness when the song 'Falling Up' by Dean Lewis begins to play on the radio:

> I cried through the whole song as I could hear the broken story. I connected on many different levels of emotions when this song was/is played as I can relate to each line of the song. The power of lyrics touching you in the way this song did to me is the real art of music.

Caitlin attaches her emotions to each line of the song, as if it directly mirrors, or rather channels her own experiences. She lets the heartbreak in, allows herself to cry as she does so. This is trauma of an enabling kind, however, since the song doesn't trigger an emotional memory that wants to be forgotten or repressed, but rather provides Caitlin with a narrative to better understand the heartbreak she feels. This is not so easily the case for Isabel:

> *Which song for you best captures what it feels like to be lonely?*
>
> 'Bitter Glass' by Feeder.
>
> *Briefly explain why this song captures the feeling of loneliness.*
>
> It captured exactly how I felt at the loneliest and lowest point in my life – 'you've got nothing to live for' with minor chords.
>
> *Can you recall where you first heard it and how it made you feel?*
>
> I bought the album when it came out. At that time I was in a disintegrating, abusive relationship with the father of my 3 children. I felt absolutely isolated and depressed and this song enhanced that feeling. I would like to add that I am so much better now, 15 years later. I still love the album but 'Bitter Glass' is a difficult listen.

Isabel offers us a lonely room remembrance that returns us to a period in her life where she was trapped in an abusive relationship. In this context, the track 'Bitter Glass' comes to stand for the psychological and physical damage she felt at the time, anchoring but amplifying the terrifying isolation she was experiencing. Isabel draws on adjectives that suggest her disintegration at the hands of her abuser and within the context of a loveless relationship. As such, Isabel's response reminds us of the particularity of loneliness for women, framed as it is within patriarchal and heteronormative discourses that produce a form of cultural violence resulting from 'the "soft knife" of routine processes of ordinary oppression' (Kleinman et al., 1997: x). Isabel's response ends on a hopeful note, however, with her negative nostalgia remaining painful but now largely in the rear-view mirror.

Lonely nostalgias

Nostalgia is driven by contradictory impulses, desires, and needs and seems to be caught between alternative momentums. On the one hand, it is triggered by a 'loss associated with the past' and by 'regressive stances and melancholic attitudes' (Pickering and Keightley, 2006: 936, 919). Something is lacking in the present, which is felt to be 'disenchanted', while the past is imagined to be a place of plenitude, and a return to a period of 'enchantment' (Bennett, 2001). On the other hand, nostalgia is expressively and affectively utopian, embraced in the now as vital to a rounded and complete self as it is experienced or lived today. Nostalgia is here understood as one of the key ingredients for having existential depth (Sedikides et al., 2008: 304).

Nostalgia also exists in two sites or modes. There is personal and autobiographical nostalgia, ignited by a lived memory (Michels-Ratliff and Ennis, 2016); and there is collective nostalgia for a past period and its films, fashions, and music. Paul Grainge argues that collective nostalgia can be manufactured or produced by the cultural industries which market consumable stylistic art and entertainment forms (2000). Holbrook and Schindler suggest that 'via a process called nostalgic bonding, a consumer's history of personal interaction with a product during a critical period of preference formation that occurs roughly in the vicinity of age 20 (give or take a few years in either direction) can create a lifelong preference for that object' (2003: 109).

This memorial bonding is particularly true of popular music and the formation of adult identity from teenage years onwards. Songs listened to when young become demonstrably important to the way older people engage in nostalgia (Barrett et al., 2010). Nonetheless, there is another way to understand the pull-and-push momentum of music-induced nostalgia – one which recognises that it lives in the house of loneliness. Because music-induced nostalgia reminds and returns us to a period of self-becoming and self-actualisation – the teenage, young adult, years – it elicits lonely feelings for what once was. These lonely feelings, however, are often recuperative and regenerative: they are enjoyable to experience. For Abigail, her loneliness room song is 'I'm Lonely (But I Ain't That Lonely Yet)' by the White Stripes because of the childhood memories it draws out of her:

> *Can you recall where you first heard it and how it made you feel?*
>
> It was in my lounge room when I was a young child, my mother is a huge White Stripes fan. It made me feel sad, nostalgic and lonely. But I love it so much I even have the lyrics tattooed on my ribs.

Abigail's response conjures up a moment when her mum put on the record and together they listened to it in their lounge room – bonding as they did so. Emotions are beautifully mixed in the response, revealing a palette where sadness and loneliness are the wet threads of her nostalgia. So powerful and important is this memory that it has become a part of her body – the tattoo on her ribs bringing these lyrics into the fleshy present: 'I went down to the river filled with regret / I looked down and I wondered if there was any reason left / I left just before my lungs could get wet / I'm lonely, but I ain't that lonely yet'. This embodiment of music is something that makes it compellingly tangible, as Simon Frith identifies:

> But if musical identity is, then, always fantastic, idealizing not just oneself but also the social world one inhabits, it is, secondly, always also real, enacted in musical activities. Music making and music listening, that is to say, are bodily matters; involve what one might call social movements. In this respect, musical pleasure is not derived from fantasy – it is not mediated by dreams – but is experienced directly: music gives us a real experience of what the ideal could be.
>
> (Frith, 1996: 123)

Thao's lonely song choice, 'Spanish Blue' by the Triffids, is one that also connects her back to her youth, but here what is being imagined is an anti-ideal, a realism that evokes a well of loneliness:

> *Briefly explain why this song captures the feeling of loneliness.*
>
> I listened to this song almost every day during the first month of lockdown. The lyric 'nothing happens here, nothing gets done but we get to like it' really captured the mood of social isolation. Now 7 months on from stage 1 of lockdown and I'm still isolated from family and friends. It started out as a funny and ironic thing to listen to but now genuinely makes me sad.
>
> *Can you recall where you first heard it and how it made you feel?*
>
> I was watching a special on great Australian albums produced by the ABC. It's an old show but it all now available to watch on YouTube. The episode on The Triffids featured this song at the beginning and it reminded me of my adolescent years growing up in the suburbs. That feeling of boredom is why it resonated with me now, during lockdown.

Thao connects the listening of the song to the isolation that they experienced during the first COVID-19 lockdown (that took place in Melbourne, Australia, in 2020), with their banal teenage years growing up in the suburbs. Their sense of separateness, and with it a type of situational loneliness, is suggested to have increased as the length of the stay-at-home orders kept being extended. 'Spanish Blue' is in a sense, then, regressively nostalgic – it rears into the present feelings that Thao had tucked away, and which provides the soundtrack for this return of her loneliness room blues.

Another participant chose 'Asleep' by the Smiths, again because of its relationship to a teenage memory:

Briefly explain why this song captures the feeling of loneliness.

When I listen to music, usually I care about lyrics the most. The line 'I don't want to wake up on my own anymore' beautifully and succinctly captures the feeling of loneliness. The melody of the song feels ethereal, as if the singer has already parted from this world, which also adds to feeling of sadness this song conveys.

Can you recall where you first heard it and how it made you feel?

I think I read about this song before actually listening to it. When I was a teenager I read *The Perks of Being a Wallflower* and this song plays a major part in the plot. After reading about the song, I listened to it and felt a deep connection to it. Since then, I go back to this song whenever I feel sad, lonely or helpless.

There is a lovely conjunction between literature and music in this response, as she first read about the song and then subsequently listened to it. Together they shape her memory of being a teenager and feeling lonely. As powerfully, however, is the way that while the song conjures up this feeling of loneliness for the participant, it is also what she *chooses to listen to* when she is in a lonely state. The participant, then, may be using the sadness in the song's melody and lyrics to help her understand her own loneliness and to assuage the helpless feelings she has when the blues take her over. The song has a compensatory use: its nostalgia is a healing agent in troubled times. Nonetheless, death also haunts 'Asleep': the character of the song doesn't wish to wake ever again because s/he doesn't want to greet a new day all alone. They exit the song as if they are exiting life and so 'Asleep' also touches upon the sheer annihilating weight that loneliness can press upon the alienated individual.

Both Matt and Eleanor chose songs that put them in touch with memories associated with the loss of their fathers.

Which song for you best captures what it feels like to be lonely?

    Matt: 'Dusty in Here', The Go-Betweens, written Grant McLennan.

    Eleanor: Pyotr Ilyich Tchaikovsky 'None but the Lonely Heart' voice and piano.

Can you recall where you first heard it and how it made you feel?

    Matt: I got the album around the early 1990s on vinyl and I used to play it over and over, trying to get my head around the angularity and slight discordances – sometimes I would skip the song because it was a bit too close to home. In the way you get to be friends with someone even though you can initially be put off by their weaknesses, I found it would sneak up on me and lodge in my mind. I came to love it after accepting the loneliness of the song, and the parallel with my missing father.

Eleanor: Shortly after my father died in 1977 on the radio – I just burst into tears. Always feel teary when I hear it.

Matt and Eleanor both feel the push/pull effect of their chosen loneliness room songs. At first, Matt resists listening to 'Dusty in Here' because of its musical dissonance and affective qualities that felt 'too close to home'. For Matt, the lyrics detail 'the experience of sifting through memories of a departed father'. However, he comes to embrace the loneliness of the song at the same time he recognises that it equates to the way he feels about his own missing father. Eleanor's response to her song is also an exact equivalent: she has recently lost her father and hears this song on the radio:

> None but the lonely heart
> knows what I suffer!
> Alone and parted
> from all joy,
> I see the firmament
> in that direction.
> Alas, who loves and knows me
> is far away.
> I'm dizzy, it burns
> my entrails.
> None but the lonely heart
> knows what I suffer.

'None but the Lonely Heart' (voice and piano) is sung by a mezzo soprano: their voice darker, richer, and lower than a soprano. It is the perfect voice for a loneliness room composition that is about the pain that one feels when one has lost someone that is loved deeply. Mezzos are female voices and I imagine that Eleanor feels that not only is the song being sung about her loss, but that it embodies her feelings, so that she is in effect taking the place of the opera singer. This is a translation and transcendence that opens her up – as with the other responses described above – to tears of sadness.

Tears again: wetted, somatic, seemingly spilled spontaneously. They leave the body, like an exorcism, and yet the body sobs or gently weeps, revealing hurt across the rivulets of the self. Tears reveal one's pain, one's heartache, they are directionally shed – they have a direct cause. And yet one sheds tears for a wider, inexplicable set of reasons. As the sodden threads of *The*

Loneliness Room have shown across its pages, one can weep for loneliness. The liquidity of being alone and isolated, the watery nature of finding oneself cut adrift, and the cleansing opportunities that water offers the lonely run like a current in this book.

In the next two sections I draw together the various sonic elements of this chapter by exploring two case studies. The first explores the music and soundscape employed in *Joker*, hearing in this film the various audio territories and signatures of chronic loneliness. *Joker* also connects this chapter to the discussions of the city, gender and masculinity, and visibility and renown. The second case study explores the podcast: often listened to on the car radio, it seems to be a new media form that welcomes loneliness. What brings together these two case studies, however, is the way they both may ultimately pathologise the cartographies of the loneliness room.

The sounds of loneliness: *Joker*'s loneliness room

Joker can be read as a film that explores the way that chronic loneliness is the default deficit position to have in the modern world. The film's audio territories and environments are marked by the appearance of the 'non-place' (Augé, 1995) and 'the-any-space-whatever' (Deleuze, 1983), although these in-between locales seem to occupy centre ground so that all-of-space is wholly transitory and unhomely. *Joker* is set in a city that, while full of connections, is orientated to maximise isolation and alienation. The film's railways, bridges, underpasses, arches, steep streets, and buses link and yet sever human interaction: they act as affective registers of communal breakdown and privatised living. The garbage that overspills on the sidewalks, and the dilapidation that marks the city's buildings, register as an 'aesthetic of decay' (Bruno, 1987).

These wasted spaces are also full of dreadful sounds, whether it be the predatory noise of the city, including sirens, screams, gunshots, isolated footsteps, the rattle of subway trains; the suffocating silence employed to 'note' everyday regulation and routine; or the cello-led soundtrack that mournfully captures strangers' lonely lives. In *Joker*, when uplifting, popular music is played it is either for ironic effect, or to create the space for Arthur/Joker to dance, and to dance lonely.

Joker is set in a 'dirty and dysfunctional' New York City in an 'alternate' 1981 (Phillips, 2019). This date recalls a period when New York was said to be on the verge of anarchy. Numerous city agencies were on strike, and the 'social contract' between people and society was fraying, as social and economic inequalities increased and support services were being severely cut (Friedberg, 2019). The apartment that Arthur lives in reeks of this dissolution. Captured in a desaturated green and brown palette, its lobby is marked by paint peeling and by an unhomely emptiness that forces its inhabitants to move on, to *not-dwell*. This transitory space feels like a derelict bus depot, creating the impression that public and private, inside and outside, interior and exterior, have become one and the same, or all of space and time in the film. *Joker* seems to be set within one giant loneliness room.

In the first half of the film, Arthur moves or walks through these urban spaces as if he is there and not there, their dreary architectures affecting his mood, his pace, his outlook, and demeanour. Elizabeth Grosz writes, 'the city is made and made over into the simulacrum of the body, and the body, in its turn, is transformed, "citified", urbanized as a distinctively metropolitan body' (1998: 43). *Joker* offers us numerous illustrations of the way flesh and steel, body and brick, eyes and neon, ears and feet are enmeshed or are in tune or syncopated rhythm with one another. The bus that Arthur takes daily, and on which he is admonished by a parent of a small child whom he had attempted to joke with, is a conduit for the city's misery. Each commuter looks down, looks away, as the drudgery of going to and from work is realised. The bus crawls, its doors hiss when they open, and its blank interiors mirror the faces and bodies of its melancholic passengers.

The best expression of the city and body as co-deficient lonely machines is through the way Arthur is filmed walking home. His slow but metered pace and mournful gait, his turned-down face, and his hunched-up shoulders depict an image of a dead man walking. The streets he walks down are as depressed: the litter, the decay, the garish neon, and hard concrete lines are elemental to this zonal zombification. When Arthur begins to walk up Step Street, we witness the mountain he has to climb every day, its steps reaching high into the urban jungle as the night begins to fall. Arthur is depicted as a zombified Sisyphus, initially carrying this 'burden' dutifully. However, as a zombie – alienated and disenfranchised – he is marked out as a soulless creature who, without market or economic value, is searching for the nutrients of validation. Arthur craves fame, renown, as I will discuss below.

These spatial relations and orientations are enveloped in a soundscape that places us within *Joker*'s world, and centrally from Arthur's ear-of-view. This sounding is full of dread, even or especially when the music that is played, heard, and moved to, is joyous. Dreadful sound emerges in the film in three distinct ways: diegetically, through the dangerous noises of the city, and the popular music/Hollywood musical numbers that play on the radio or out of television screens; non-diegetically, through the film's mournful, cello-led score; and internally, since, possibly, all that we hear are the projected fantasies of Arthur/Joker, who may be locked up in an asylum for the duration of the film. These sound notes are very often overlayed, their collective sonic impressions reaching for an affective sense of ontological crisis.

Writing about the city's noise pollution, Mark Kerins argues that it 'is not only always "there," it's always everywhere, surrounding us and relentlessly bombarding us from all sides. This puts us in the environment with Arthur – we're not just watching something happen onscreen in front of us, we're enveloped by the angry noise of the city right along with him' (2021: 93).

In Arthur's apartment, these noises fill the lounge, kitchen, and bedroom, so that the city is not an external force – outside the windows, the building – but finds its way into the psychology of the space, orchestrating the unhomely nature of his lonely home. In one scene, Arthur plays with a gun, as the television plays the song 'Slap that Bass' from the musical *Shall We Dance* (Sandrich, 1937). The gun accidently goes off, blasting a hole in the wall. However, it is the *sound* of the gunshot which shakes Arthur since it metaphorically brings the audio violence of the city into the home.

This sonic or aural disintegration is also manifested through the way that Arthur is seen running in the film, in fight or flight, and yet this acceleration is itself held fast or arrested – no matter how quickly he moves, he can't seem to escape the lonely condition of his own existence. This terror of being chased, on the run, while not being able to 'escape', is often sublimely moored by the strangulated cello pieces, which rise over the noises of the city, acting like a diseased sonic membrane. Again, the body of the city and Arthur's body are in mournful, mortal tune. However, Arthur's body is also silent and silenced, as Seller suggests:

> Arthur's character is a body which cannot speak back to power – continually shut down by Thomas Wayne, his therapist, even the TV network which cuts off his televisual debut as he repeats the catchphrase: 'And remember, that's – [life].' His speech is regularly broken and dislocated, laughing asynchronously with the comedy club crowd, pausing in his public performances to consult barely legible notes. Here, in his abjection, we find not a coherent identity, but ... a derivative impersonation. Instead of an articulate, agentic protagonist we have a symptomatic and automatic body, often silenced by bouts of uncontrollable laughter.
>
> (Seller, 2021: 45)

One scene that powerfully captures this shutting down of the linguistic self is when Arthur empties his fridge-freezer and gets inside it. This scene directly follows his encounter with Thomas Wayne, who Arthur thinks is his 'real' father. As Arthur uncontrollably laughs in response to his father's denial that they are related, Wayne punches him in the face, stopping the laughter, ending the conversation – a violent form of linguistic disempowerment. The two scenes are connected through a metaphorical ellipsis: Arthur bends over an opulent bathroom sink to capture the blood flowing from his nose, and then, when the scene cuts, he is found half bent over, but now shirtless, in his thread-bare kitchen. Arthur's emaciated body and the narrow frame of the shot, squeeze him in. The gap between the sides of the kitchen walls is restrictive, the window providing a single source of orange light that pours in, like a vapour, from the city lights below. As Arthur empties the fridge, the phone rings and a message is left: the police detectives want to interview him again about the murders on the subway.

In terms of sound, the mournful, atonal notes of the cello mix with the bleep of the telephone answering machine, with the detective's voices, and with the noise of the food and compartments being discarded on the kitchen floor. We also hear Arthur: he lets out a slight whimper as he gets into the fridge, its blue light irradiating him. When he closes the door, the camera continues to capture the dead space he has left behind, as if it is waiting for Arthur to re-emerge. Arthur has entered a womb state here, whimpering back into his primal cave. However, the cold, silent, frigid nature of this birthing capsule pathologises this conception moment. This scene is pivotal in another way: it marks the nadir of Arthur's lonely, existential, collapse – he returns to a form of neonatal nothingness, one where at birth he emerges into a silenced loneliness room.

Of course, Arthur is also shown to have 'rhythm', whether this be the slow, metronomic beat in the context of city walking, or the exaggerated 'dance' he displays when performing as a clown. In one scene, he stops the lift doors from shutting on his neighbour, Sophie (Zazie Beetz), by raising his foot nimbly, like a ballet dancer might. Arthur also slow dances with his mother in their apartment, and starts to dance as he transitions (in)to Joker. The transition in movement is one of speed and choreography: the more violent that Arthur becomes – the closer to Joker he gets – the more he or his body find explicit forms of syncopated rhythm and dance.

Richard Dyer argues that song and dance in the classical Hollywood musical are affective representations of utopia: colourful, energised, and optimistic spectacles (1981). Such Hollywood musicals offer 'the sense that things could be better, that something other than what is can be imagined and maybe realized' (177). Dyer concludes his analysis of the musical by arguing that 'utopianism is contained in the feelings it embodies. It presents, head-on as it were, what utopia would feel like rather than how it would be organized' (177). In *Joker*, these ideological functions and representations are reversed or recoded: song and dance is intimately connected to the lonely dystopia that is New York, and to the lonely violence that it produces. One *feels* the loneliness in Arthur's dance movements, and through this movement one dances in tune with his loneliness.

Arthur begins to mournfully dance in the public bathroom scene, minutes after he has murdered the Wall Street brokers on the subway. The bathroom is painted in the same blues, greens, and graffiti tags that are found in the rest of the film's palette, while a ceiling strip-light blinks and buzzes, coldly illuminating the space. A large washroom mirror throws Arthur's reflection back at him: two lights sit above the mirror, only one of which is working. As his feet move across the floor, in an ill-formed glissade, the cello begins to score Arthur's dance, or rather it musically seems to penetrate him: he is hearing this weeping song and this song seems to weep solely for him – it becomes his leitmotif of loneliness. The dance continues, his body in free-flowing movement, opening up and outwards, while his arms stretch out like they are striking the bow of the cello that we/he can hear. Ecstasy enters his movements: he begins to look blissful, at ease with himself for the first time in the film. As Arthur comes to a standstill in front of the mirror, his arms are outstretched as if he is expecting a round of applause from an imagined audience for this revelatory transformation of the lonely self.

We have seen a version of this mirror before, at the beginning of the film, when Arthur was filmed mournfully putting on his clown face. However, in this bathroom scene this reflective moment involves a crescendo and a form of *jouissance* where Arthur's strangeness, his excruciating loneliness, rises up in him as a form of bliss. In this scene, Arthur lets his loneliness become a form of ecstasy: he musically and rhythmically embraces it. That this 'coming out' dance routine takes place in a run-down public toilet connects Arthur/Joker's loneliness to the scatological, to shit, to the literal and metaphorical waste that fills Gotham city. But now what we witness is a macabre celebration of this excrement of/by/for the lonely. As Roland Barthes describes, 'The asocial character of bliss: it is the abrupt loss of sociality, and yet there follows no recurrence to the subject (subjectivity), the person, solitude: everything is lost, integrally. Extremity of the clandestine, darkness of the motion picture theatre' (1975: 39). The inspiration for Arthur's dance performance is reported to be the 1930–50s Broadway dancer and performer Ray Bolger, and in particular the song and dance routine 'The Old Soft Shoe'. Bolger was a dancer who imbued the utopian sentiments that Richard Dyer argues translate as hope and optimism (1981: 177). By contrast, when the Joker dances it is to lyrically embody the lonesome strangeness that fills up everything and everyone in the film.

The next time we see Arthur dance – now as the fully formed Joker – it is as he comes down the steps of Step Street. Shot in slow motion, Joker, holding a cigarette in his mouth, punches and kicks the air as the Gary Glitter song, 'Rock 'n' Roll (Part 2)' plays. With an indescribable joy on his face, Joker thrusts, jumps, and side-steps down the steps. Garry Glitter is, of course, a convicted paedophile and so the perversity of the dance is doubly inscribed: Arthur was abused as a child and so this dance is also a shedding away of this traumatic skin. Wearing a colourful suit, with joy written all over his face, Joker is the allusive 'shadow' (Barthes, 1975) that always sits behind the song-and-dance man of the classical Hollywood musical.

A past-presentness rises up in the image, a lonely-happiness that is either self-made and destructive, or culturally produced and ideologically resistant.

One can read the loneliness of *Joker* in two contrasting ways: either it ultimately pathologises loneliness, attributes it to individuated social circumstances, here Arthur's messed up life; or it links isolation and loneliness to the way contemporary neoliberal capitalism systematically withers away human connection and sympathy so that 'togetherness is dismantled' (Bauman, 1988). In one sense, the allusion that almost the entire film takes place in/through Arthur's tortured psyche suggests the depression of the city is born of his imagination. *Joker* ends with Joker locked up in an asylum where he kills his interviewer and attempts to escape. The madness of loneliness may well be his alone.

Nonetheless, the film spends its entire length in the wasting environs of Gotham. The loneliness that permeates its buildings, sidewalks, auditory networks, and human relations is multi-focal and co-synaesthetic (Sobchack, 2000). Arthur's lonely point of view is one that the viewer knows and *feels* intimately since these qualities represent the 'crisis of the age' (Monbiot, 2014). When Arthur asks, 'is it just me or is it getting crazier out there?', the question registers as a rhetorical one: chaos clearly reigns supreme. *Joker* ends with Gotham on fire: protesters wearing Joker masks raze buildings, loot shops, and collectively rage against the melancholy of the neoliberal machine (Brown, 2021). These protesters, who had moved like spectres earlier in the film, now find *jouissance* in their radical actions: they are all lonely Jokers now.

Lonely fame?

Unlike *Amy*, discussed in Chapter 4, Arthur feels invisible in the world and wants to be noticed: he craves renown, hungers for fame or infamy, since he imagines that it will give him the prestige and the social connections he lacks. It is a way for Arthur to be *not* lonely. Here, of course, *Joker* also alludes to *The King of Comedy* (Scorsese, 1982) in which Rupert Pupkin (Robert De Niro) is a delusional and aspiring stand-up comedian who kidnaps Jerry Langford (Jerry Lewis), a successful comedian and talk-show host, so that he can appear on his show. In *Joker*, De Niro takes on the role of Murray Franklin, a talk-show host, whom Arthur worships, a role reversal of sorts, with fictional 'history' repeating itself through this cinematic allusion.

When Arthur gets invited to appear on the *Live with Murray Franklin* show, he justifies killing the Wall Street brokers because they were 'awful ... everyone is awful these days' and 'nobody thinks what it is like to be the other guy'. As the scene progresses, Arthur's anger and resentment increases: he chastises Murray for inviting him on the show to make fun of him, and as he does so his voice rises, tears form in his eyes, repeating or translating the opening of the film, when he sat forlornly in front of the Hollywood mirror as he 'clowned' up. Now on stage, on a prime-time television show, he knows he is not there because of what he dreams to be, but because of what he is not. Enraged, Arthur/Joker screams, 'what do you get when you cross a mentally ill loner with a society that abandons him and treats him like trash?' The answer he gives – 'you get what you fucking deserve', shooting Murray in the head as he does so – lays the blame for his actions at the doors of the social systems that have abandoned him. The notion of waste and abandonment, cruelty and separation, turn the television studio into a loneliness room where marginalised voices, usually ignored or lampooned, sound out through Arthur's enraged scream.

In lonely times we seek refuge in our media, in our television personalities and mediagenic counsellors. They supposedly offer us ways out of our alienation. In lonely times we increasingly listen to podcasts about our loneliness since they offer us new audio intimacies with which to experience and understand the way it can take hold of us. The question to ask is whether podcasts sound loneliness as belonging to the individual who needs therapeutic help, or whether it more complexly shines a light on the economic systems that produces its most virulent kind.

The podcast: *Alone Together, A Curious Exploration of Loneliness*

Podcasts have become a dominant media form. They are produced and streamed by both large-scale media corporations and independently, existing in the mainstream and outside it. Podcasts can be interest based or topic focused; led by a famous personality; and they can be one arm in a wider transmedia partnership or 'franchise' – translating and adapting games, film, and television stories into an audio form (Baelo-Allué, 2019). People listen to podcasts on a daily basis, either anticipating their release, or tuning into an episode they had archived to listen to when time allowed (Berg, 2021). Podcasts are serials and serialised and so people binge-listen, in the same way they might do with other streamed content.

However, with the podcast there is a higher degree of perceived or 'felt' intimacy created than when compared to other digitally streamed content (Markman, 2012). This is because of the nature of their transmission, and the contexts in which one listens. Podcasts are voice-led and often delivered as a direct address, so they sound like they are speaking *only to you*. When one listens on headphones one experiences an 'in-head localization'.

These voices feel like they are in the room with you, are in fact inside your head, triggering 'a feeling of greater closeness to the person speaking to you' (Lieberman et al., 2022). These voices are also personalised because the 'personality' of the podcaster becomes part of the appeal of listening, the sound of their voices warranting trust, soliciting affective attachments from the listener (Copeland, 2018: 222).

Contextually, we listen to podcasts in situations where they have our undivided attention, and where we want or may need the intimacy they offer, such as when we retire to bed at night. This is particularly true for the daily commute: people listen to podcasts while driving, or on public transport. Alone, the driver can find solace and counsel in the podcasts they choose to listen to, while on public transport the passenger can put on their headphones and shut in the familiar voice, and shut out the noisy, messy world. Counselling podcasts are in fact one of the most popular forms, 'either by delivering direct advice to help the listeners to overcome a painful situation, or by revealing their own stories and making the listeners feel less alone' (Berg, 2021: 121). Podcasts, then, are

> deeply personalised and self-cultivating. In particular, mental health and personal journal podcasts are attributed to the contemporary culture of confession and self-help, in which the differences between famous and ordinary people are blurred, and accessibility, relatability, and personal experience triumph over professional expertise.
>
> (Collins, quoted in Berg, 2021: 120)

Podcasts on loneliness are a central part of this confessional culture, this cultural turn to public self-disclosure and the 'incitement to discourse' (Foucault, 1990: 19). However, they are also a part of the way that people draw upon the podcast to feel less lonely and to enact upon its suggestions and solutions for keeping loneliness at bay. On one level, these intimate connections can be said to be parasocial or mediated – offering 'personal' solutions, but not systematic ones, to the crisis of loneliness – a position this book addressed earlier when exploring the documentary in Chapter 4. These lonely room podcasts may be said to pathologise all-of-loneliness, defining it as a deficit state, making it a crisis of and in the self.

On another level, these podcast 'counselling' sessions, heard in the ear and found rippling through the body, are so *felt* that they may offer an engagement with loneliness that changes one's relationship to it. Rather than podcasts involving a simple lifting of the loneliness 'burden', their affective discourses may positively transform the lonely self in the process.

This is the position of the podcast, *Alone Together, A Curious Exploration of Loneliness*, which ran from January 2021 to February 2022. Defining itself as a series that aims to show how loneliness manifests so that we are less alone together, its host, Peg Fong, announces:

> Being alone is a life chosen deliberately by some; others are just alone, not by choice. We can end up unexpectedly alone and for many, the twists and turns of life, brought us to where we are. Experts and researchers around the world share their insights about what we know about loneliness, we find meaning of it from songs, art, books, films, history and pop culture. We isolate the lessons of loneliness from people like you and people like me who have unique stories to tell and to share. Everyone feels lonely at times. But let's begin to explore why. My name is Peg Fong, I'm a journalist and an educator who has been fascinated by what loneliness means. We're not here to solve loneliness. But to add one voice to another so that we are alone together.

Alone Together is a weekly series of 25–30-minute podcasts that examines a different theme or facet of loneliness. Peg Fong's 'voice' narrates each episode so that their personality emerges as the series develops. Peg's tonal delivery is warm and welcoming: they are friend, guide, and confidant. Peg sets up the theme of each episode; threads together the interviews that are given by experts drawn from art, culture, psychology, politics, and economics; and provides interpretation and narration for the case studies explored. Episodes are divided between those that are shaped around the experience of loneliness in the social world, and those that explore loneliness in popular culture, art, food, and ritual, often drawing these two strands together.

For example, in the episode 'Professional Cuddlers Wanted: Why Touch Matters' (9 February 2021), Peg asks, 'does the absence of touch fuel our loneliness?' Introducing us to the Association of Professional Cuddlers, who are paid to provide cuddles to those who are isolated and lonely, Peg explains how touch increases our oxytocin levels so that 'warm feelings of being socially bonded are activated … it is known as the cuddle hormone'. In the episode, 'Turning the Page on Loneliness: How Reading can Bring us Together' (30 October 2021), Peg suggests that

> reading is a refuge for the lonely and those seeking to be alone. In books a social life emerges from words on a page. We befriend fictional characters, get entwined in plots. Books help readers find meaning and they help us get lost. Reading can make us a better friend, make us more sociable and less alone in the world even if it means escaping into a fictional one.

Each episode draws on a soundscape and narrative that enables us to 'hear' both sides of the loneliness coin, the series attempting to recognise the essential nature of being alone in the world, and the way it can inspire *and* lessen us as human beings. Across the series, complex identity positions are drawn into the discussions, and major philosophical questions are addressed, such as the metaphysical nature of everyday life. In a number of episodes, we are invited to travel, to adventure, to leave behind our loneliness rooms, entering into audio spaces, such as the wilderness. *Alone Together* intends to not simply inform and educate, but to provide existential and (the fantasy of) material mobility. In the episode, 'The Loneliest Wolf: Lessons Learned from Leaving the Pack' (8 January 2022), Peg explores the desire for separation and aloneness, noting how it can rejuvenate those who decide to leave the social world behind, valorising the 'lone wolf' as a particular type of selfhood that offers its own rewards.

Nonetheless, the thematic episodes steer clear of exploring the systematic deficiencies and fault lines of neoliberal capitalism that produces the chronic form of loneliness. The poetic templates of *Alone Together* rather neglect the politics of the lonely imagination, one where inequality and inequity furnish its room. Further, the podcast series becomes a part of therapeutic discourse and the cathedrals of confession: it narrates loneliness from within the accepted and acceptable practices of educational outputs. Finally, its podcast form attracts a certain middle-class audience and leaves the digitally poor behind; and its 'social' media nature may well in fact be one of the reasons that new forms of anguished loneliness have emerged in contemporary society. As Chapter 6 will discuss, the online space is one of the loneliest of all.

None but the lonely heart: a brief conclusion

In this chapter we have explored the way environmental noise, voice, song, and silence variously create the conditions for loneliness to emerge. Sounding loneliness is contextual and autobiographical: it is with us in the car, when we put our headphones on, when we visit our shed, or sit under the eaves in our back garden. The sound of loneliness creates rooms out of the spaces that we might find ourselves in, as its notes and melodies begin to play. Musical nostalgia may sweep us up, reminding us of important past events – transporting us back in time on soundwaves of our imagination. The bitter sweetness of break-up songs registers the loudest; they recall our youth and the belief in an eternal love.

The audio territories and signatures of loneliness are found in sad songs and sadder voices, although there can be bliss and joy when these compositions reach deep into us. We cry, our sobbing becoming part of the composition's overture. In *Joker*, we find the chronic conditions of loneliness sounded out across a city that seeds and ferments isolation and loneliness. *Joker* either pathologises loneliness, as something that belongs to the damaged self, or shows us the economic and societal conditions that produce its laughs and screams. The *Alone Together* podcast series celebrates loneliness, weaving into its themes the complexities and nuances of where, why, and how it manifests. And yet, soothed as we are by Peg's voice, within its narrated stories there are too many silences around the brutalism of neoliberal capitalism.

For Grady, her loneliness room song is 'Metal Heart' by Cat Power because

> there's a languid, nostalgic reach to this song – the drums, the guitar, her voice, they all loosely hang together like each is weighed down by the effort of looking back at something lost. I like that there's a defiance to the lyrics 'metal heart, you're not hiding … you're not worth a thing' as though the singer sits in her room admonishing herself and we're privy to this moment of lonely torture. Achingly lonely. Achingly beautiful.

The responses in this chapter have been achingly beautiful – they have reached into the guts of loneliness and found its metal heart beating like a wild thing.

6

Lonely words: writing loneliness in the post-digital age

Prelude: lonely words

Diary

Dear Diary,

When I woke up this morning, I wasn't sure I wanted to get out of bed. My dear friend, Mr Loneliness, had returned. He sometimes sits like a ghost on my shoulders. Mum doesn't quite understand what it is like to feel *this* lonely. I have no one to talk to, well not about these feelings anyway. And so I write to you, my dear diary, I write it down: the barking black dogs jumping at the back garden gate; the lonely college dinners; and the bus ride next to chatty seats. Even when I am with friends 'having a good time', loneliness grips me. I put on a show though. I pretend to be social. But I don't want to pretend anymore.

Facebook post

(Selfie, wide smile, party scene, surrounded by friends)

Having the best night ever! Love you girls!♡

TikTok

(Video, multiple poses, dress changes, and varied locations; fast-paced music)

Caption: I love life!

Haiku

A single boat floats

Blue ripples surround the oars

Loneliness can be so still

Insta

(Selfie, close-up, bedroom, pillows and cushions, night lamp, black and white filter)

#Ifeellonely

Comment: thanks for sharing, babe, we all get a bit lonely now again. Let's talk. Love you!

Lonely words

The desire to write down how one is feeling is a compelling one: words allow people to slowly compose how the roots of one's deepest thoughts burrow beneath the subconscious, and as sovereign editor, they allow the author to control the flow and structure of the narrative (Misoch, 2014). Autobiographical accounts of one's life stories are found in a wide range of literature. People keep diaries, write letters and blogs, post social media updates, and create extended written narratives – poetic, fictional – that traverse their personal histories. These supposedly private accounts of the relational self are often past tense in the sense they recount activities, events, feelings that have already happened, even if the ink from the pen that stories them is still wet. This storying of the self draws upon the past to both shore up the present and to provide ontological wholeness for the way we seek to understand who we are. As Eakin suggests, we reach 'back into the past not merely to recapture but to repeat the psychological rhythms of identity formation ... an integral and often decisive phase in the drama of self-definition' (Eakin, 1985: 226).

However, drawing upon the past can also be fuelled by a desire to let it go, to expunge something terrible or traumatic. Autobiographical writing has a therapeutic and confessional function: it seeks to reveal or to 'out' something 'unspeakable' to both make sense of it and to move beyond it – the river of words a current that one sails on, hoping to arrive at a new destination of the self (Reiffenrath, 2015). Feminist autobiography is often framed in such terms since 'self-narration has the potential to explore issues of identity and to produce critical accounts of the female experience'; feminist 'auto/biography' is important because it 'disrupts conventional taxonomies of life writing, disputing its divisions of self/other, public/private, and immediacy/memory' (Stanley, 1993: 41). The idea that self-writing has two audiences is particularly the case for the written 'secret' diary since

> not all diaries are written – ultimately or exclusively – for private consumption ... Indeed, it is the audience hovering at the edge of the page that for

the sophisticated diarist facilitates the work's ultimate focus, providing the impetus either for the initial writing or for transforming what might have been casual, fragmented jottings into a more carefully crafted, contextually coherent work.

(Bloom, 1996: 23)

Writing stories of the self has a double therapeutic consciousness: they provide a textual means to mine and map one's worries, concerns, hopes, and aspirations; and they implicitly seek kindness, understanding, and even wisdom on the part of the 'imagined' reader. In a Foucauldian sense, autobiography becomes a 'technique of the self' in which one creates a version of the self that is either in articulation with wider discursive formations and practices, or which resists or counters them (Foucault, 1994).

In the questionnaire responses to this project, the writing of the self in relation to the conceit of the loneliness room provided fuel for the participants to express the often intangible and fog-like qualities of their isolation. The questionnaire offered them a space to write loneliness into their everyday life experiences, very often responding to the questions with diary-like entries. The answers also displayed that double therapeutic consciousness described above: these accounts of loneliness were intended as solace for the participant, and as meaningful material for the author and the imagined readers of this book – who were to be 'touched', and better informed, by these confessional, creative responses. For example, in this response the participant yearns to have a loneliness room they can call their own:

> I don't have one but wish I did. I am missing it terribly. I have two small children, a partner and a full-time job and never time alone. Unfortunately, I am not in the position to be able to seek loneliness when I need it so the question of a space is irrelevant for me. It implies having time and the freedom to do with it what you want. Both an impossibility as a working parent in this society. I take loneliness and doing nothing wherever I can get it (I only have minutes so going somewhere would be taking too long).

The participant weaves an account of the liquid speed of modernity and the familial and parenting relations that render the idea of having a lonely 'space' as 'irrelevant'. Implicitly they tap into the governance that shapes everyday life: one where the practical and ideological machinery of capitalism creates the impoverished lived conditions of the individual self. Their description here puts into words the fact that they feel terribly exhausted *all the time*, their confession revealing the pressures that they are put under. They don't have time to be lonely even if, implicitly, an existential loneliness sits behind these written thoughts.

By contrast, Gabriel does *have time* to be lonely and she makes time to creatively explore how she feels. She defines her notebooks or diaries as her loneliness room since it allows for 'proper reconnaissance or anagnorisis, so as to reach some sort of equilibrium between the inner and the outer worlds'. In describing what she writes into her loneliness room notebooks, Gabriel suggests:

> The world and the nation are [too complex] and full of risks, but also open to infinite possibilities. Each one is a miracle and a mystery, The limits of the soul are endless, as said Heraclito. So the notebooks reflect the path of an endless query. It is a matter of intelligence, conceived as intus legere and relegere which are the contrary to nec legere. So it is a search of meaning in the spiritual and cultural senses. It is a task of supreme care with oneself, the immeasurable others, the world and even with the deads and with them which will become after this so little pronoun named the I.

Gabriel defines her notebooks as the means through which she comes to understand not only her lived experiences but the mystery and miracle of the world itself. She writes to discover herself, to exercise a duty of care over her being-in-the-world. That this duality is employed to illustrate and evidence Gabriel's loneliness room is indicative of the way introspection and extrospection is spiritual, solitary, at the same time as it reaches out to connect with the social and 'cultural'.

When we write accounts of our life stories we often do so creatively. That is to say, we draw upon literary techniques, genres, and forms, using the aesthetics of language, story, plot, and narrative structure to create a version of events that is a mixture of realism and fiction, of verisimilitude and characterisation. As Kehily argues, 'Narrative and self-narration ... is more than the product of the individual writer or speaker; it is a highly constructed performance, drawing on a range of linguistic, literary and cultural repertoires, specially selected for a particular audience' (1995: 28).

Creative writing is itself a conduit for self-expression; for providing a form that allows one to connect feelings and emotions that are fragmented and fragmentary, or which sit so abstractly within the self they need allusion, metaphor, alliteration, and point of view to resurrect them from the depths of the barely visible unconscious self (Warzecha, 2015). Myfanwy's highly metaphorical, metaphysical response draws upon the lungs of language to explain what her loneliness room is:

> Within its extreme form it removes me from bodily existence and I am only my soul without body. It's black and it removes all matter and it breaks the soul. It, it, it. Without density and it crushes like a blackhole. Loneliness is a twin to nightmares and a brother to all the bullshit that my vine had to grow on, accepting less, less than certain. In the waking state I can best destroy its destruction by being with others or working busily on art projects. It is still there though when I am alone and disconnected from others. When I am alone day and night it pricks me when I think about it, loneliness is a prick,

> when I think I will not be accepted it pricks me. When I believe I am accepted it pricks me down. I began to be alone at age 4, the ground was unsteady, I began to not belong. Pressed to accept bullshit. 43 years since then and its hard to break and it has broken my mind many times which we recognise as bipolar, mania, psychosis, depression, anxiety, the rising of badness because that was something I knew, suggestions of schizophrenia. I lose my sense of direction. Sia 'push it down'. Loneliness rides on uncertainty. I'm ugly, overweight, old to be beginning. The best was not flourished. I flourish myself. My genes make me weird. Removing the ugliness, my family is society, learning from the TV, making films with fellows. Loneliness strangely gives me quietly me for art for love.

This is an infinitely powerful, mesmerising account of the way loneliness presses down on Myfanwy's shoulders. Loneliness is given a colour (black), a weightlessness, and an autobiographical trajectory, as we see its reach stretch across her life story. Loneliness is given a consciousness that lowers and reduces Myfanwy's self-image and self-esteem. Myfanwy reasons with it, blames herself ('my genes make me weird'), and yet draws attention to both the labelling and medicalisation that seeks to define her as Other ('suggestions of schizophrenia'). Nonetheless, as the narrative progresses, we also see that Myfanwy makes art, and works with other artists, to escape the clutches of her loneliness. In all her darkness, a rising note calls out beyond it: love.

Sonya also draws on the need for connection through art, explaining how her love of words, of story, generates a rich sense of belonging, keeping loneliness at bay as it does so:

> I think I love idea of finding words, language to convey a feeling in a book that somehow mitigates my sense of profound loneliness. The universal experience of needing connection, as per E. M. Forster's Only Connect in the covers of his book *Howard's End*. Stories and poems mean a lot to me for their power to evoke feelings and sensations.

Writing creatively about one's loneliness speaks directly to the schism that often operates in the way it is understood and as this book has explored. Language seeks to define the parameters of loneliness according to dominant cultural and social norms, while creative expression seeks to find a way to complexify and enrich and contest that which might over-determine or limit the way it is 'felt' and understood. These techniques of the self then, as alluded to above, are often in tension or contestation.

For the loneliness room project a number of poems and haikus were submitted, each one taking the fleshy expressions of the poetic form to capture what their loneliness room comprised. As O'Connor suggests, 'multiple, shifting and contested meanings are possible in the emotional utterances of poetry' (1996: 20). A poem often stands alone and is complete in itself: unmoored or untethered from other entries, chapters, narratives. The poem is a lonely art form, a solitary arrangement of verses and stanzas, that seeks connection through its delicious diction. The poem stands in an empty field, intending for its lines to seed the land. Its choice, then, as a representation or embodiment of the loneliness room was apt for a number of the participants.

In 'I Think the Loneliest I Have Ever Been', the participant captures the loneliness of a fresh start:

> It was
> nearly midnight,
> a Friday,
> barely a new year.
>
> Bedroom.
>
> I had
> just moved.
>
> I was
> hanging a mirror.
>
> I felt
> tentative with the hammer.
>
> I thought,
> what if this doesn't work?
>
> I thought,
> what if I miss?
>
> I thought,
> what if I hit too hard?
>
> I thought,
> who would fix the wall?
>
> I thought,
> what if the whole thing collapses?
>
> In fact I hadn't
> spoken in days.
>
> I blinked
> and drove the nail.

Here, in the shadow of the poem, is a broken relationship; the enigmatic ghost of the unnamed person who once would have helped repair or fix something that had newly broken. We are given a time and date: a new year has just rolled in, and the protagonist of the poem finds themselves alone in a bare flat at nearly midnight on a Friday – they are not out socialising nor cuddled up on the couch with their lover. In the poem, the mirror is used as a device to both personalise the space and to personify the lonely reflections of the teller. The rhythm of the two-line stanzas suggests floating thought patterns, but also the near exhaustion, the close to breaking point feeling, that envelops them. In the final stanza, the nail is finally driven into the wall, acting as a threshold moment – they are beginning to choose to leave the past behind.

In Ruth's beautiful poem, briefly discussed in the opening chapter to this book, we find the notion of separation etched into their deficient binaries – one where something essential to the 'coupling' is missing:

> *Everyday Loneliness*
>
> On Sunday, loneliness is a prayer room, in need of hope.
> On Monday, loneliness is a hallway, in need of light.
> On Tuesday, loneliness is a morning room, in need of conversation.
> On Wednesday, loneliness is a post room, in need of a message.
> On Thursday, loneliness is a vault, in need of treasure.
> On Friday, loneliness is a bedroom, in need of caressing.
> On Saturday, loneliness is an old barn, in need of support.

Ruth's poem takes us across the days of the week and various anthropomorphised spaces that are lonely because they lack a quality, purpose, or person to make them whole. Hope (prayer room), light (hallway), silence (morning room), emptiness (vault), and redundancy (post room), are the measurements by which loneliness enters the world. Ruth's penultimate line returns us to the poem, 'I Think the Loneliest I Have Ever Been', since they also imagine a bedroom where only one person dwells, but here they are looking, longing for the touch of a hand rather than the dead weight of a hammer. Ruth's poem finds the loneliness room to be both literal and metaphoric; it multiplies out in the poem, ending up as an old barn, aged and alone, needing the support of community to reconnect them with the social world.

In research settings, the use of poetry to help older people explore and creatively define or map their loneliness has been usefully employed since 'poetic representation provides a sense of what it means to be in the world' and introduces 'spirit, imagination and hope' into the way feeling is explored and expressed (Glesene, 1997: 214–215). Creative practices such as the writing of poetry help

> us push the boundaries of qualitative research, producing vivid and authentic representations of the lives and stories of participants. Poetry not only helps researchers to more deeply listen to the stories that participants so generously share …, but also to publicly share the intimate richness of lives that are being lived, composed and re-configured. It is a form of enquiry that helps the researcher to think with rather than about the participant's experience.
>
> (Miller et al., 2015: 416)

For this project, the haiku poem was also directly drawn upon through the online r/lonely group found on Reddit. Set the task/question, 'if you were to write a haiku poem about loneliness as a type of "room", what three lines (5/7/5 syllables) would you choose?', the following poems were submitted:

Ashley
A room with blank walls
Not a color to be seen
Alone forever

Ernesto
In this dimly lit room,
asleep and awake,
I spin in my grey.

Kent
nails clawing for air
my neck a cavern, enclosed.
i try to inhale.

James
Regrettably seeking solitude
While knowing its downfalls
Drifting into a room of my own void.

Anon
Walled in deception
Living chair/ished muted dreams
Floored by silent fear

Michael
Room without corners
Isolation in a throng
Painful paradox

Kevin
In my library of loneliness
I read the tomes
I alone have written

JT
Outside, all is mute
Here, I have my small comforts
but cannot share them

These haikus give creative embodiment and materiality to the conceit of the loneliness room. Each writer creates a space that is weighted down by loneliness, or else they capture the sensations and sentiments of what it feels like to be lonely. Colour and light are key for Ashley and Ernesto: the room is either blank or grey and its non-descript nature hints at the self-perceived invisibility of people who are lonely. A type of dizzying or confusing movement is central to the poems by Ernesto and James: they spin, fall, or drift, in a seemingly endless cycle of lonely repetition. Stillness and entrapment, however, are also a trope: Anon is 'floored by a silent fear'; Kent's neck becomes strangulated, pressed inwards; Michael inhabits a 'room without corners'; and Ashley and Anon describe the walls that keep them locked in the loneliness room. Silence and sound are also a repeated theme: Anon lives in a 'muted dream' and is knocked over by a 'silent fear'; JT describes a silenced world outside or beyond his loneliness room; Michael seems to silently walk among a noisy 'throng'; and Kevin retreats to the library, where silence invades every carrel desk. Each haiku captures a lone individual unable to take part in the social, unable to enact connection. Kent describes this condition as one that is suffocating, that takes place in his throat and lungs. He tries to breathe but breathing hurts.

In essence, these haiku poems describe a chronic form of loneliness. They speak to the way extreme loneliness has become the crisis condition of the contemporary age. The metaphors and allusions that are drawn upon are found more widely in the descriptions that are given about loneliness (Alberti, 2019), and are found across the stories found in this book. That the participants/poets are demographically placed in the 18–29 age range (64% of Reddit users are in this bracket) connects their responses to the way young adults, in particular, feel lonely. There is a world out there for them to join, to be a part of, but they are too anxious, too 'disconnected', to leave the rooms they find themselves in.

The haiku poems submitted for this project were, of course, done so through an online, social media meeting place. The poems were to be seen by anyone in the group – and more so, if the likes/votes propelled the thread upwards and could be commented on. In a very direct sense, then, these poems were both creative enterprises and attempts to explore the writer's loneliness and to connect to, and commune with, other Reddit users.

Nonetheless, as noted before, regular social media use is proven to be one of the reasons why young people feel increasingly lonely and disconnected. There is, in part, a perverse paradox in play. On the one hand, users of the Reddit r/lonely sub-community or subreddit, post and comment to express their feelings of loneliness and to find connection with other users. And yet, on the other hand, the r/lonely subreddit creates a space where isolation seems to double. Again, a double therapeutic consciousness is being enacted since the posts are often about confession and self-care, and about the need to have one's post recognised and supported. Loneliness becomes a type of virtual competition. Users upvote or downvote posts, with the former ensuring more people read it as it is elevated up the ranks and into people's feeds. These types of autobiographical or confessional discourses have a particular vexed relationship with the loneliness room, as I will now go on to explore.

I feel lonely

Autobiographical content drives much of social media content. Users create blogs, virtual diaries, video essays, and post confessional details on their pages and through the interest or community groups they join or identify with. This content can be signed/authored, with the user confessing or revealing personal details on sites where they are known to friends and family. Posts can also be made anonymously, with the user posting under a pseudonym or username to communities they may have no direct connection with beyond the virtual stage – although even in this context through repeat posting 'personalities' emerge (Sauter, 2014). When one reveals autobiographical detail, they can do so under 'private' settings so only those who they wish to read their posts can do so; or they can do so in the public arena, where what is revealed can be read and commented upon by anyone.

These online autobiographical musings and revelations change the nature of *writing things down* for two reasons. First, because 'engagement is intrinsically public, taking place within a circuit of larger connectedness' (Birkets, 1994: 122–123). Second, because through the process of sharing personal thoughts, lived biography is instantaneously 'interactive' – one posts to receive feedback, comments, and thus 'enhance that aspect of diary writing concerned not with solitary and private reflection, but with communication and community' (Sorapure, 2003: 10). In this public and interactive setting, autobiographical accounts are highly mediated: the reader is virtually present in the room and so the writer is conscious that it will be read and likely to be interacted with while they are online. A heightened level of creativity enters the composition by the very nature of the arena or stage on which it will be consumed – everything from spelling, syntax, grammar, to the aesthetics of written expression may be considered (Misoch, 2014). The writer becomes conscious of the reader, of how their post will be viewed. As such, on social media, personal autobiography becomes a performance, a type of spectacle of the self (Hall, 2016).

This spectacle of confession is particularly acute when it comes to crisis revelation or outpouring. The nomination of trauma, of pain and anguish, wets the writing with an emotional intensity, and levels of exaggeration, which are meant to withstand the needy lights of the virtual stage. There is in a sense a *triple consciousness* being enacted in such social media spaces: a need for therapeutic healing; a desire to be read, understood, and supported; and a longing to be centre stage (Berriman and Thomson, 2015).

What happens in these crowded confessional spaces is an incremental increase in the way trauma is written about and responded to: emotions are amplified and narrated so that they embody the psychology and physiology of pain. Words become instruments of revealing the self as being destroyed, negated, ripped apart. Similarly, the responses to posts take on heightened dimensions: cruelty can emerge, as may active suggestions on how to overcome the trauma being revealed – suggestions which may make matters worse. For example, in Zdanow and Wright's empirical research on Emo social networking groups they found 'a glorification, normalisation and acceptance of suicidal behaviours and determined that the potential for social networking sites to be used as a tool for the promotion and encouragement of such behaviours exists' (2012: 81). Madelyn Gould defines this correlation between the positive representation of suicide in online subcultural communities and suicide in the real world as 'suicide contagion' or 'the process by which one suicide becomes a compelling model for successive suicides' (2001: 200). Nonetheless, the sharing of personal biography, of confessing trauma, isn't solely one that promotes the behaviour that is being defined. Rather, they can be seen as 'counter-conducts' or 'anti-authoritarian struggles', which prevail as localised phenomena 'with subjects interacting with authorities in the present in order to object to forms of subjectivization' (Lilja, 2018: 421).

With regard to loneliness, particularly its chronic manifestations, one can see this struggle between glorification and resistance being played out in online sub-communities where people go to share their stories of feeling terribly alone. There has been a proliferation of such spaces on numerous platforms so that loneliness confessional discourse is writ large across social media, creating and sustaining it as an enveloping crisis (O'Day and Heimberg, 2021). The reddit sub-community, r/lonely, which I followed over a number of months and for an intensified 24 hours on 2 May 2020, demonstrates how loneliness is narrated, glorified, counselled, rejected, and transformed into a type of therapeutic spectacle where trauma and anxiety are performed and 'put on show' (Lovink, 2017). In this 'tense' space, the loneliness room emerges in all its diverse forms and formations.

r/lonely

r/lonely has 345,000 members or 'lonely hearts'. The community is 'a sub for all the lonely people. Everyone is welcome here, no matter your age, race, sex, sexuality, relationship status, all that we request is that you be accepting of people, and kind. Any problems at all, please let the moderators know'.

r/lonely has seven rules for posting and commenting: no discrimination, sexism, or racism; please be kind: 'this isn't so much as a rule, but just worth remembering. Most of us here are quite vulnerable, so please just if you can, spare a kind word, and if not, at the very least don't try and make someone feel worse'; no suicide encouragement, glorification, or notes; don't post personal information outside of PM's; No NSFW (Not Safe for Work) or posts looking for a relationship; don't spam, advertise or push your religion upon others; and use trigger warnings: 'please apply proper trigger warning post flairs on posts talking about suicide, abuse or drugs'. When it comes to posting on r/lonely, one may designate a filter for it to be filed or titled under. These filters are called Venting, when one needs to get something off their chest; Discussion, where comments are explicitly sought; TW: Wholesome, where the post is 'positive' and affirmative; and 'Looking for a long-term friendship', where the user seeks to make friends with fellow sub-ers.

One can see how r/lonely operates under a regime of governance that seeks and monitors for civility, safety, and which attempts to frame loneliness within acceptable or normative ideals. As noted above and in earlier chapters, it is a part of the wider therapeutic discourse that runs like a river across society and culture, providing a space to engage in affective revelation.

Surveillance, interior and exterior, of/from the self, and in relation to other users and moderators, polices the way loneliness is written about and responded to. Loneliness very often becomes a pathology, enunciated as a medical issue, a psycho-social individual abyss – a problem of the self and not ever recuperative, or produced in and by capitalist society and culture. Nonetheless, these public postings, wetted with feeling and emotion, trauma and doubt, represent 'the affect of change, of rupture with self', and have the potential to represent a 'break with one's past identity' (Foucault, 1990: 145). In speaking their loneliness room, r/lonely members often find new ways to be in the world.

r/lonely posts and comments have a number of recurring themes, in part shaped by the filters named above. These posts are also socially or contextually demarcated and often with temporal dimensions. Loneliness seems to be the user's fault, or is connected to broken or dysfunctional relationships. Past issues/events/relationships that have come to haunt their lonely imaginations fill the content of many of the posts. Past and present memories are seen to either bring loneliness on or prevent one from moving on – from making lasting or meaningful connections. Users post about their existing, of-the-moment temporal boredom; and about not being able to sleep, as if their loneliness keeps them awake in their rooms at night. Members also affirmatively post, checking in on other members of the sub-community, or to make new connections. A small number of the posts seem to break community guidelines by implying or suggesting suicide.

With regard to self-worth and self-loathing, r/lonely members often define themselves in a position of deficit:

I deserve to be alone

I came to realise late last year how shit I am as a person. I've improved but I don't think I will ever deserve another chance, I deserve the loneliness. I don't want sympathy in me saying this, I wonder how many of you guys on here feel the same? Somehow I have a partner but I do not deserve her. Never have, never will. Nor my family.

Hmmm? Maybe this is my fate

So I've been lonely now for a while (due to my anxiety and depression from events in my life) and tbh I think that because of how alone I've been etc I'm never gonna be able to hold conversation (even though I can speak to myself for hours) and now I'm beginning to think that maybe it's better to be alone if I've fallen this far as tbh I don't wanna bore people with what little I've done and that like my life story can be condensed into half a paragraph which is boring and shit and what, so after 5 seconds the convo is over? Nah, I'll be alone thanks! Sad truth but better to embrace it I guess.

In these two responses, the users say they deserve, or are deserving of, their chronic lonely state. The first user writes that they are a 'shit person' and questions how they are able to be in a romantic/sexual relationship. The drawing in of waste (here literally shit, and the wasteful nature of the relationship) returns the understanding of loneliness to the social margins and to the discourse that people are responsible for it (Ypsilanti et al., 2019). The second user also draws on the word shit, but their narrative is centrally about both the boredom they feel and how boring they imagine they are to read about. Anxiety and depression are referenced, and are given a causal relationship to their loneliness, but this is marginalised, as they recount how empty and meaningless their life appears to be. The metaphor of 'falling' is used as if they feel they are on a downward spiral, and yet the post ends with a resigned acceptance of their state. Of course, the posts are also a calling out to be understood and to be heard: they are punctuated with question marks and so engage in a rhetorical flourish, and directly invite comments in the hopeful search for validation.

Relationship failures are also drawn squarely into several of the responses, written as the cause for why, when, and how loneliness has emerged in their lives:

What do i have to get over doubt??

So in my life im only trust somebody once and never again, my life come from happy family, great friend, until it all come down, my parent pass away and i became silent for many years, until i met some good friend (what i think of that time) everything going well, normal thing friend do, hanging out, party ect ect. Until they all make me a laughstock by pouring floor cleaning water on me onfront of the whole school. From that i never trust anybody, always like to be alone, back of the bathroom, somewhere that nobody around, even that im home im still not like to talk to my sister and brother, when i feel like to be alone without being anoyed, im hide in a carton box (i know is weird) but is a good place nobody espect, i do not know how to start a conversation, i do not know how to asking out to a girl, i know nothing. Cause idk if they gonna say something bad to me, cause doubt is always onfront of my emotion. That what you can call my life is a life of a loser if that how your contry call idk. But im hope that some of you guys can give me some good advice and have a good day.

The people i thought cared about me dont care

Like everyone on this subreddit im fucking lonely and it makes it even harder to feel happy. People i thought i was close to dont talk to me anymore or even check in to see if im ok. I wonder what its like to never have been depressed or never hate yourself or never feel lonely to the point where you feel like your life is pointless ...

(F17) My Mom Hates Me, Is It My Fault?

Bare with me here; me and my mother have always had an okay relationship and she's comfortable enough to gossip about her dating life with me etc. There are just moments like today where I swear she regrets having kids ... So what's the issue?

I don't even fucking know. I literally (bit taboo topic here) ASKED FOR PADS. She swears that she got me some last time and gets mad because I don't even recall that ... and then she snaps and starts storming around looking for this box of pads she swears she gave me last time ... So now she's mad she can't find the box she claims she got from amazon and she's yelling and saying how she does everything and I just fuck it up. I'm not highly emotional on my period or anything, I'm genuinely a sensitive person so obviously, my eyes were watering but I just didn't say anything, just close my door and try to not make any sobbing noises that might make her get madder (she hates when I cry just because she's yelling, it makes her want to yell at me more) and then she says feed yourselves, I'm tired of doing shit for you. Okay, cool, a sandwich for dinner. I thought she'd calm down and I could hear her talking to the dogs and playing with them (we have two) and I thought it'd be safe to go out.

Nope, she gave me the death glare as soon as she saw me so I retreated back into my room and cried again ... she ignores my depression and anxiety and she doesn't even know I used to be suicidal. I literally slapped myself so hard it stung just because of how frustrated I was with myself an hour ago. I've made so much progress getting better by myself because she refused to think I needed a therapist and I had to work through my stuff alone and now here I am thinking about how happy it'd make her if I wasn't here since I ruin anything. Am I being selfish or something? Did I do something? I just can't deal with this anymore. ... Am I a bad daughter or something? Is it me? Please, someone, tell me what I'm supposed to do next ...

In these three incredibly moving responses we see relationship breakdowns as either framing lonely feelings, or as being caused by their lonely disposition. In the first response, the user plots a life event which becomes the trigger for his loneliness: the moment where his friends 'make me a laughstock by pouring floor cleaning water on me onfront of the whole school'. The user now no longer trusts people and finds it hard to make meaningful human connections. He hides away in a cardboard box and doubts that he will ever be able to have a girlfriend because 'he is a loser'.

In the second response, deep-seated feelings of self-loathing emerge because friends and family have absented themselves from the person's life. This alienation and disenfranchisement become circular, however, as the user defines their biography as one constantly beset by depression and self-hatred. Their response then is vortex-like: they are spinning in a web of lonely thoughts and feelings.

In the third response, the user recounts a recent event where they have rowed with their mother over the supply of sanitary pads. What we have in this response is plot points and narrative development, as the row leads to other revelations and new dramas. The user reveals that they suffer from anxiety and depression and have had suicidal thoughts. The post also becomes a cry for help: the run of question marks is again rhetorical but pleading: they seek comments where they will be understood and supported more than that which was offered by their mother. There is obviously a gender dimension to this post: the mother's voice is presented as an angry one and they are positioned as unsympathetic. Sympathy is looked for in this community of lonely people, where affordances and experiences are seen to match. Suicidal feelings are also shared in the following post:

I dont want to wait anymore

I am seeing not many people lately ... My friends after every vacation and almost every second weekend my friends told me about the cool and exiting stuff they did together. And i was never invited. I just was invited like once in my life to a little meetup in a garden of a friend of mine. Also in my childhood i was never asked to come and play with the others. I am missing the feeling of ever going in the local woods of my town and just having some childhood memories. But my friends never let it seem that they dislike me. I appears that hey just forget me everytime. I feel so forgotten and lost. My parents basically ignore me all the time and my friends forget me if i could call them Friends even. The only real friends i had was games. I wish i could go back in time and approach more people so i wouldn't become so forgettable. Am i this forgettable? It also didn't helped that i never had a girlfriend. Let alone any physical contact with a female in the whole last year ... I dont know a shit what to do if a girl shows interest to me or even detect if she does. Im going to graduate this summer and start a job as a mechanic in september. What happens then? Eventually they completely forget me ... Then i am left alone with no friends, boring and ignoring family and no love, ever. What reasons do i have to live then? I have been struguling with depression and suicidal thoughts wich i think will increase in the next few years. I have the fear that i wont have any will to live and just ... end it.

A set of relationship deficits centrally drives this response: they feel ignored or rejected by family and friends; they seek a romantic/sexual partner and yet do not feel emotionally equipped to form one. They feel 'forgettable' and 'boring' and yearn for the touch of a female lover that they do not believe they will be able to find. This response, then, connects loneliness to embodied separation, and to the desire for warm bodies that share spaces, rooms, and beds. Of course, this is again one of the criticisms of social media use: that it disconnects the body from direct physical contact and becomes a form of lonely dematerialisation (Yavich et al., 2019). This is a position that Sheryl Turkle superbly outlines:

> So, in order to feel more, and to feel more like ourselves, we connect. But in our rush to connect, we flee from solitude, our ability to be separate and gather ourselves. Lacking the capacity for solitude, we turn to other people but don't experience them as they are. It is as though we use them, need them as spare parts to support our increasingly fragile selves. We think constant connection will make us feel less lonely. The opposite is true. If we are unable to be alone, we are far more likely to be lonely. If we don't teach our children to be alone, they will know only how to be lonely.
>
> (Turkle, 2012)

The r/lonely responses so far analysed have a temporal dimension: that is to say, there is a time and temporality to how loneliness is defined and experienced. Some users see time stretching across the archaeology of their lives, an ever-present, while others find situations and events that give rise to their loneliness. Time is eventful and memorable, used to prove or evidence how loneliness emerged, or to show it as a 'room' that they have existed in since the day they were born. For this user,

Friday nights are the hardest...

Does anyone find a particular time the hardest when you're that lonely? Friday nights make me particularly sad. it's only a little after 6 and i just want to go to bed already so I don't have to sit here alone and think about how I don't have anyone.

Friday night is, culturally speaking, where the weekend begins and the 'social' takes over. However, for this user, and just as it was in the poem 'I Think the Loneliest I Have Ever Been', Friday nights confirm how alone and isolated they feel. Of course, the notion of the 'weekend' is constructed, serving to demarcate a gap between labour and leisure, and to allow consumption to take over. The romance for Friday night devours the lonely individual because its 'everyone is having fun' representations are found in marketing, advertising, and across the entertainment industries. This user considers going to bed to avoid the feeling that they are missing out. Sleep and insomnia are also a recurring theme in the posts under discussion:

> *it's 3am in my place and i can't sleep.*
>
> for the past 5 days i can't sleep for whatever reason. i may have developed insomnia. it's currently 3am in my place and my neighbors are being really loud and i can't sleep. i keep stressing out about something and i don't know what it is. my brain keeps reminding me of something embarrassing from 6 years ago. if anyone knows how to cure this, please let me know.

> *Anxious about sleep itself*
>
> I knew I 'needed' to get a good night's sleep because I'd be working a 24-hr shift the following day, and that pressure caused another zero-sleep night. Despite trialing mindfulness apps, guided meditation, exercise (2:00 AM jog anyone?), the more time that went on the more my heart pounded and the more pressure I put on myself to fall asleep. It's gotten to the point now that I get palpitations from merely laying in my bed (even in the daytime without the intention of sleeping) or from listening to guided meditation.
>
> A lot of times I've heard insomnia described as an ability to turn off one's mind, a problem with decompressing with the previous day, worrying about external things. For me, I get anxious thinking about the sleep itself, which in turn leads to no sleep, which feeds back to more anxiety. Does anyone else deal with the feedback loop, and if so, how do you deal with it?

In these two responses the night becomes their loneliness room: they struggle to sleep, their worries or anxieties becoming a noise that stops them from shutting their eyes and resting. The first response draws upon an embarrassing memory from years ago to narrate their sleeplessness, while the second describes how not sleeping becomes an anxiety-inducing repeating pattern. These descriptions of sleeplessness are somatic, felt in the body, the lungs, and the conscious/materialised mind. Sleeplessness becomes an entry to and from their loneliness room.

The final central thematic raised in these posts is one where users are directly reaching out for connections; to use r/lonely as a way to make new friends and develop new relationships:

27 [M4F] – Looking for someone, who prefers audio conversations – Arts, books, philosophy, music

Hey! I'm at such a point in my life where I have some time to talk, but a lot of people who reply, seem to have normal busy lives, so it's difficult to bond, especially given the time difference. So, my hope is to find a person in a somewhat similar situation (in other words, someone who doesn't have a well-measured, well-adjusted 9 to 5 lifestyle, but who is lost at their life's crosspath).

I'm looking for a FELLOW ADULT (sorry for caps), who's open-minded towards audio conversations (on an app). It could be entirely anonymous (no video), but I'm sadly not huge on texting, hence my preference for voice, which I find to be a more human-like medium and experience. I can understand obvious hesitance that some people could have; from my end I would do everything I could to preserve the sense of propriety and mutual respect.

General interests: literature, art history, philosophy, psychology, economics, languages, geography.

Don't have anyone to talk:(… I miss having someone …

19m who is just as lonely as you are atm Hobbies are photography editing and gaming and love watching tv shows if you watch the same shows as me I like you already. Fast replier as I have nothing to do nor I have anyone to talk Good listener and I give ok advices at least that's what I think. So text me if for any reason you're still reading this till here and if you are then thank you do comment or send me a chat if you wanna talk or be friends:)

PS4? Anybody?

Hey I'm very lonely, I need some friends, does anyone play GTA Online, Fortnite, Apex Legends, DC Online, or Fallout 76? Please share your usernames down below. I would really like it if you used your mic and spoke to me. My username is Kevin-point55 please add me.

Tell me anything

I'm not much of a talker and my world mostly plays out inside my head. I'm socially very anxious.

Right now my head is all dark inside. I'd like to talk, but then again I would not like to talk myself. I'd especially would like someone to talk to me. I just want to listen, to dissolve in someone else's talking …

So for whomever wishes to talk, please tell me anything in the comments. Any story. I'm broadly interested. I feel very empathic towards others and can easily drown in others' talking. So just know you're genuinely heard.

Is there depression on the other side?

Hey, My name is (?) I made a sad rain LoFi track for sad people who just wanna be alone. I have been lonely and sad all my life and tried to cope with depression in many ways. But I couldn't find a way to really make depression go away. I made this depression LoFi playlist to make you feel better. Life is not always fair. Depression is Real. Far more than what you think it is.

Spotify playlist: https://open.spotify.com/playlist/5CyR9VKY01BLw2FVYgzGZA?si=aYoNN7DbSSmemRm5mnJPRA

depression won't go away by doing anything. Take a look at my playlist will ya?

These four responses demonstrate how important communication and interaction is to these users. There is a desire for talk, conversation, messaging, as well as game playing. The last user has created a depression playlist that they hope will benefit other people who are feeling blue. Embedded in these responses is the desire for dialogical presence: they want to be both 'ear' and 'mouth', counsellor and counselled. The first user explains that they prefer to communicate via voice but without video. They hear and feel in the sound of speech the materialisation of the speaker – voice embodies them. That they dislike video, however, suggests a discomfort with seeing and being seen. In the third response, we see the user in despair, sitting in the depths of their loneliness, and wanting to 'dissolve' or 'drown' in the talk of others. In a sense, then, they want to be *liquid*, swimming in the thoughts and stories of others.

The r/lonely posts are textual/written: in an image-saturated society they refuse the call of the frenzy of the visible. This refusal to be seen (as body, flesh, face) may point to the way lonely people have low body image and lower self-care standards. It may also reject the tyranny of the objectified gaze found on platforms such as Instagram and TikTok where gendered beauty norms reign supreme (Lewallen and Behm-Morawitz, 2016).

I want to end this section with one final post and several of the comments it received since it draws attention to the tensions that operate in therapeutic confessional spaces about loneliness. The post was intended to be a positive one:

My positive message to you

Hey you who is reading this comment, I want you to know how important you are to this world, you are a beautiful person, don't let this world bring you down, know you can get through this hard time in your life, tell yourself things will get better, stay positive and happy and always know you can do it, always try and never give up.

> Just trying to make people feel better and happy who are going through a tough time in their life, just always tell yourself things will get better and know you can get through this difficult time in your life.
>
> I hope my message made a positive impact in your life. ☺
>
> Be who you are and live life to the fullest.
>
> You are on this world for a reason.
>
> I know some of y'all may not understand what I am trying to do but just to let y'all know that I am just trying to help people.

The post is written as a 'feel good' mantra, laying hope and positivity at the feet of those who are feeling lonely. Its discourse is part evangelical but also steeped in the utopian sentiments found in health marketing and promotions, and through the narratives of self-help gurus. Again, loneliness is something to get over, to overcome, with the message itself intended to be an activation point for that journey to recovery to begin. The post received 43 direct comments most of which were thankful, supportive:

> I was thinking about killing myself when i came across this. Thanks. I needed it.
>
> What sweet words! Thank you for taking the time to post them. I needed that today💜
>
> Thank youuu so much, can i copy this message to another subreddit?
>
> Your fucking amazing!! Never know how many people needed to hear this! I definitely did♥thanks

The positive responses either said that the post was directly helpful to their mental state or was welcomed as broadly affirmative. For the first user above, they directly cite how the post stopped them from 'killing' themselves. The positive responses collectively speak to the way r/lonely fosters community feeling and produces – in part through its posting rules – shared beliefs and attitudes. There were, however, more critical comments:

> *Player*
>
> Sorry, this isnt doing it for me. I need to hear this from someone I know for it to affect me. It just doesnt feel genuine coming from a stranger from the internet. But Im not here to hate, clearly you made people happy with this post so good on you:)
>
> *Sigma*
>
> Shut up, stay positive is the worst advice of all time. I'ts like fighting an uphill battle against a giant square block, you can push all you want but it will only wear you down.

> Stop with this fake wholesomeness. You don't know who am I. What if I'm a neo-nazi who drowns stray kittens every day, I wanted to kill myself because everyone hates me and your post saved my life? I'll just continue being a neo-nazi and I'll continue killing animals. Did you do a good thing then? I'm a beautiful person? Are you genuinely kidding me? You never saw me, you never saw my body and you never saw my face. I'm fucking ugly, I won't lie, and I'm used to see those lies. But imagine if an even uglier depressed person will see this? Their depression will get even worse because they see that people lie right into their face. This is just sad …

Player takes issue with the fact that it is a 'stranger' wishing them well. They see the post as generic or fake. The idea of the stranger, however, is a complex one since the r/lonely sub-community is one composed of intimate strangers who share personal stories. Sigma is more blunt or direct: he takes on the utopian sentiments of the post and the easy or sugary answers it seeks to provide. Self-hatred and self-loathing enter their response as they simultaneously turn inwards and project their disdain outwards. Implicitly, Sigma is engaging in a 'counter-conduct' activity, working against the rules of the sub-community, while drawing attention to the discourse the post is written within or through.

Sigma's post drew a backlash from other users, and particular from Faith who questioned his post by challenging how he understood the idea of love. In an exchange that lasts eight posts, Faith ends by saying:

> You know what I mean by that phrase.. quit giving shitty excuses.. your PC ain't human..
>
> And yo.. hate yourself all you want bro. No one gives a flying hoot.

The beginning of this exchange has Faith declaring that love happens both internally (love thy self) and through outward expression (love thy neighbour). However, each time, Sigma responds by either criticising or rejecting their definition of love, or how they will never be able to attain it. Love is, of course, an abstract concept, explored through both metaphor and expressed in ritual. In contemporary life, love is often considered to be liquid or ephemeral, turned into a commodity or fetish with a limited shelf-life (Bauman, 2013). Life without love, or with love that is sold on the altars of consumption, seems to create the conditions for loneliness to emerge. However, love remains one of the conduits for self-expression: it is very often the intimate register through which alienation and isolation are understood. This is something that I would like to explore in the final stopping off point in this chapter: the lonely intimacy of *The Red Hand Files*.

The lonely intimacy of *The Red Hand Files*

Nick Cave's *The Red Hand Files* are weekly email responses to questions that he has received from fans. The emails are laid out on what resembles cream-coloured watermarked paper, while the chosen Cambria font looks like it has been written on a typewriter by Cave's fingers and hands. The letters generally contain a central image, either a photograph or painting, that pictorially, if abstractly, anchors the questions and responses. There is a material, embodied intimacy to not only the way the letters appear, like they are accented analogue exchanges in a dematerialised digital world, but also in their imagined two-wayness, as if fan and Cave are privately writing to one another.

The questions and responses ignite the flames of closeness. Topics range from religion, death, love, loss, and longing to the taste distinctions that one might make over art, literature, music, and poetry. Cave responds personally, poetically, drawing on his own life experiences to answer biographical, metaphysical, and existential questions. He signs the letter 'with love', 'love', or 'much love, Nick', and a kiss, creating the sense that his response is not only authentic, written to and for 'you', but one drawn from the heart.

There is a long history of fan letters being written and of star and celebrity responses (Lewis, 2002). The entertainment industries energised such exchanges, most notably through fan magazines during the Hollywood studio system (Orgeron, 2003). In the contemporary celebrity marketplace, social media have become a series of connective zones where these star and fan exchanges increasingly occur (Hearn and Schoenhoff, 2016). These seemingly 'real-time' electronic responses orientate and authenticate connectivity, where it is felt that the star is directly addressing the fan who very often holds that message in their phone-hand, while ensuring fans remain commercially committed to the famous person in question. The star or celebrity's social media posts very often, then, seem to be both in the service of creating an intimate space for fans to gather in, and a form of commodity exaltation, since this communication is also the work of promotion where consumerist and individualist ideologies reign supreme (Orgeron, 2009).

While *The Red Hand Files* can be seen to also straddle both the communal and commercial nature of contemporary star and fan exchanges, their mode of communication is formally and experientially different to other mediated exchanges. Arriving as typed letters, they indicate a time that 'pre-dates' the digital world, recalling social practices that required a different type of emotive labour and set of materials – pen, paper, envelope, stamp (Barton and Hall, 2000). *The Red Hand Files* are not only formally nostalgic, however; they also carry an emotional intensity that certain forms of personal letter writing have historically done, including the love letter (Bazerman, 2000).

Further, *The Red Hand Files* are so unrelentingly raw that they carry a different level of shared intimacy when compared with other star and fan interactions. These email letters affectively 'leak'; they challenge normative morality; and they offer complex, messy, and often transcendent answers to the most difficult of 'life-based' questions.

As a cultish figure of transgression, a parastar (Sconce, 1995), this is in one sense to be expected: Cave is a subcultural figure whose worldview delves 'into the underbelly of human existence, being prepared to seek solace in heroin and the world that surrounded it, spending time in the areas of cities that combined the red-light districts, with bohemians, artists, all-night bars, transgressive behaviour, sexual encounters and transient lifestyles' (Webb, 2008: 119). However, these holy email letters speak to a number of more generalised and uncomfortable truths about the nature of contemporary experience, including the increased social dislocation and isolation that people experience in the modern world (Cacioppo and Cacioppo, 2018: 426); the need to confess, self-reveal, and in turn to be counselled and psychologically and spiritually healed (Taylor, 2010); and the power of experiential discourse to make sense of the alienation and cultural detritus that carries across all the tradewinds of modern life. Cave's star image fits this revelatory epistolary form, creating a space where shared biography and confession work to contest dominant ideology and to open his fans to new forms of re-enchanted feeling.

To date (27 December 2020), there have been 128 *The Red Hand Files* email letters, the first one published or delivered in September 2018. They generally arrive once per week, but the day can change, and more than one letter may be sent/received each week. This time elasticity creates both anticipation and excitement as one waits for the next letter to arrive. Cave has written that he reads all the questions that he receives and that he makes the decision about which questions are answered and published. This personal curation creates the sense that Cave is the editor and author and that through his selections and responses, a deeper understanding of who he is emerges. What we are supposedly witnessing, or reading, is Cave's real self and the revelation of his inner experiences and feelings cut free from star and public discourses. That is not to say, of course, that a level of performance isn't enacted through the letters, as it is with all communication produced by a famous figure (Meyers, 2009), but that Cave's responses open lines of flight, spools of insight, very rarely experienced or countenanced in star and fan exchanges.

One of the interconnected themes that emerges across the body of these letters is the relationship between loneliness and love. My method has been to read all the letters and to pull out the ones that speak to or of love and loneliness. However, this has not been a data-driven process, where I have used software or algorithm to number-crunch terms, words, adjectives. Rather, this is an aleatory response, and one, as you will see, that has been drawn from the heart.

As this book has contested, we live in the age of a confessional culture where stardom and celebrity are one of the key conduits for its revelatory transmission (Redmond, 2008). The cultural turn to public self-disclosure, the 'incitement to discourse' (Foucault, 1990), is 'individualized and a logic contrasted that pushes structural conditions and collective, interactive responsibilities out of the frame' (Macdonald, 2003: 85). On one level, the confessional can be understood as a coping strategy which centres dissatisfaction on the individual body rather than the body of the state. This is not always the case, however. On another level, as Sara Mills suggests, confessional discourse can act as a means of resisting oppression by 'locating oneself within a larger interest group or political group (such as feminists, or working-class women or lesbian women)' (1997: 82). Further, the environments where the confession takes place may actually create a Habermasian public sphere (Habermas, 1991), where minority opinions and modes of being actively engage with, and openly question, dominant mores.

The Red Hand Files straddles both perspectives. Fans readily and regularly share their burdens with Cave, and in his responses he shares his experiences, both to show empathy and to evidence his wise counsel. There is, on one level, something quite Catholic about these exchanges, with Cave taking on the role of the priest, *in persona Christi*, and absolving fans of their 'sins'. Reading *The Red Hand Files* 'brings a sense of Easter revival, of hope amid despair, inviting us to be still, be present in the moment, guided by a suited and booted vicar' (Cunningham, 2018). However, there is also an 'aesthetisation' of religious belief that 'awaken[s] experiences of inspiration and mystery' (Balstrup, 2020: 1). This is particularly the case for letters that address loneliness. For example, in response to the question (Issue #126, November 2020):

> Hey first I wanna say really like your music i have lost my beautiful wife in cancer and my dear brother in covid 19 my question to you is how keep you going on after lost your son its hard sometimes to keep going on with life.
> MATTI, STOCKHOLM, SWEDEN

Cave responds:

> One desperate morning, however, I did the most simple of things and perhaps this can help you with the loss of your wife, and your brother, more than my words. I sat by myself, in a quiet space, and called upon my son by name. I closed my eyes and imagined lifting him from my heart – this tormented place in which I was told he lived – and I positioned him outside of my body, next to

me, beside me. I said, 'You are my son and now you are beside me.' These few words had a powerful, vibrational effect, and this simple act of imagination was the first step in a process that would eventually lead me back to the world. By performing this act I was temporarily released from the rational world, a merciless place that gave me no peace, and given access to an *impossible realm* where I could form an increasingly resolute relationship with the spiritual idea of my lost child.

I began to feel Arthur's presence. I talked to him. He talked to me. I took him with me wherever I went ... It was a deeply powerful experience and testament to the restorative force of our imaginings – that child of God, that divine invention – rescuing me from my catastrophic heart and in doing so freeing himself from the convulsion of my grief ...

Love, Nick

In his response, Cave does two connecting things: he details how he moved beyond the grief he felt with the death of his son, as a way of showing how Matti may move beyond his own loss and longing. Cave's confession is couched as a religious parable, Father and Son walking beside one another, the latter resurrected through divine imagination housed under a sacred canopy. But it is also a mystical one, conjured up through an 'alternative spirituality' (Balstrup, 2020) that allows Cave – and his fans – to be the enchanted architect(s) of his/their own life story. This form of enchantment 'entails a state of wonder, and one of the distinctions of this state is the temporary suspension of chronological time and bodily movement. To be enchanted, then, is to participate in a momentarily immobilising encounter; it is to be transfixed, spellbound' (Bennett, 2001: 5).

However, we can also see that what touches the questions and answers in *The Red Hand Files* is a profound connection to a disenchanted world where Nick and fans are burdened by a crisis in loneliness. This is something that Lyn McCredden more generally identifies in Cave's lyrics, books, and poems, which she sees

> are in dynamic and conflicting conjunction, creating a sprawling, unsystematic and confrontational dialogue with divine forces which may or may not be 'there'. Institutional religion does not fare well in his lyrics, but nor is it ignored. What we find stamped across his songs, over and over, is the dark, lonely figure of a man caught up in desire for a divine source or balm.
>
> (McCredden, 2009: 167)

Issue #39 (May 2019) is (almost) entirely dedicated to the question of loneliness:

> What do you think is the best way to cope with loneliness?
> ELENA, REGGIO EMILIA, ITALY

How do you deal with loneliness?
LARS, ÖSTERBYBRUK, SWEDEN

Did you feel times of seemingly endless loneliness? What did you do against it?
FLORIAN, OPPONITZ, AUSTRIA

I'm writing right now to ask you for advice on how to deal with loneliness?
MEL, THESSALONIKI, GREECE

How long will I be alone?
LIII, KRAKOW, POLAND

Cave responds:

As we go through our lives we take on the expanding burden of our own distress – as we are abandoned, broken apart, betrayed, isolated, lost and hurt. This is essentially part of what it is to live. This despair will overwhelm us and turn inward into bitterness, resentment and hatred – worse, we will take it out upon the ones closest to us if we do not actively live our lives in the service of others and use what power we have to reduce each other's suffering. This, in my opinion, is essentially the key to living. This is the remedy to our own suffering; our own feelings of separateness and of disconnectedness. And it is the essential antidote for loneliness.

In the Philip Larkin poem 'The Mower', Larkin runs over a hedgehog while he is mowing the lawn. As he removes the body of the hedgehog from the blades of the mower, he muses on the nature of death and ends the poem with these words.

> *We should be careful*
> *Of each other, we should be kind*
> *While there is still time*

The urgency of these words came to me on that flight back from Marrakesh. The vision of the dying cat wrenched me from my own self-absorption and bitterness and isolation and loneliness and showed me that the world, in all its terrible wounded beauty, was in need of our urgent attention.

Much love, Nick

Cave's response again shows a form of double consciousness, that seamlessly moves from the individual to the collective, from the private to the social, and from the secular to the sacred. He sees himself existing in a cold and cruel world, one that leaves its violent and despairing impressions on the individual: on him. Cave's response reveals his own loneliness in the face of an uncaring world. Cave's suggested solution to this anomie is to live socially, in the service of others, to reduce each other's suffering. The Larkin poem that is quoted frames the discussion in terms of death, returning us to the theme of loss and the precarity of life. It is as if loneliness is death for Cave, shaped in a barbarity that renders one a violent self.

In this letter he also asks his fans to reach beyond the possessive individual to a shared and communal space where we all look after one another. In one sense, this is a decidedly socialist or humanist response: through social or societal action we together make the world a better place. In another sense, it is a particularly religious response whereby suffering is both inevitable and enabling in the world and leads to self-transformation. As the New Testament suggests: 'Not only so, but we also rejoice in our sufferings, because we know that suffering produces perseverance; perseverance, character; and character, hope. And hope does not disappoint us, because God has poured out his love into our hearts by the Holy Spirit, whom he has given us' (Romans 5:3–5 NIV). In Issue #23 (January 2019), Cave makes this connection to religious suffering explicit:

> Three and a half years ago I lost my wife and I was left to take care of my (then 2 year old) daughter. She's a happy little girl but I know she's happiest when her father is happy. I've been finding it hard to find happiness. It's not my loss – I made peace with that a while back. I just haven't found my life again …
> WILLIAM, BROOKLYN, USA

Nick answers:

> We are alone but we are also connected in a personhood of suffering. We have reached out to each other, with nothing to offer, but an acceptance of our mutual despair. We must understand that the depths of our anguish signal the heights we can, in time, attain. This is an act of extraordinary faith. It makes demands on the vast reserves of inner-strength that you may not even be aware of. But they are there. As your little daughter dances through her father's tears, she leads the way. The way lies there before us.
> With love, Nick.

Of course, within the hopeful discourses of *The Red Hand Files* the community that is being reached for is in a sense ready-made: the lonely questions set out in these issues are being answered within a fan community setting. These letters are an attempt to create a public space which will ease the sufferings of others, and that offers a wise counsel that increases the amount of love and kindness in the world. Cave is both icon and lonely prophet in *The Red Hand Files*.

That these questions and answers appear as typed letters is an attempt to remove them from the dematerialised digital world where there is a crisis of loneliness, and to take them back to a utopian time when there was more connection, more intimacy between people. This is again a romantic longing and is in some sense built on a paradox, since if suffering is inevitable and eternal, then the anguish free past it longs for never existed. These are romantic answers because loneliness is structural, economic, energised by the rancid politics of austerity: to suggest we can move beyond loneliness by being kind denies the inequalities built into late capitalist society.

And yet *The Red Hand Files* refuses to only argue from a deficit position: the loneliness of Cave is matched by the love he seeks to share. The affective qualities and intensities of these letters do move fans and they provide spaces of negotiation and belonging. As Joke Hermes writes in relation to the 'repertoire of melodrama' that emerges from reading women's magazines, the gossip that circulates between female friendship cells provides solace for readers experiencing similar issues:

> On an imaginary level it helps readers to live in a larger world than in real life – a world that is governed by emotional ties, that may be shaken by divorces and so on, but that is never seriously threatened. Sociological realities such as high divorce rates, broken families, children who leave home hardly ever to be seen again, are temporarily softened. The world of gossip is like the world of soap opera: whatever happens, they do not fall apart.
>
> (Hermes, 1995: 80)

In *The Red Hand Files* there is an attempt to soften the traumas of the world through the letters' own repertoire of melodrama. In Issue #64 (October 2019), when asked by Robin about the guilt they feel for having regrets, Cave responds with

> Perhaps it is useful to see our lives as a series of failed or abandoned dreams, but to also recognize that these dreams are the very architecture of our humanity; to lovingly accept our shortcomings and lay them to rest in the knowledge that growth and regret go hand in hand, as do failure and potentiality.

His answer here and elsewhere is an attempt to share and solve the person's dilemma. There is a therapeutic dimension to these instructions, but the mysticism and spirituality that entangles them complexifies their discourse. Cave's answers don't buy into therapy discourse but transcendental philosophy: an opening up beyond the (de)material world. In Issue #65 (October 2019), Barbara from Rome, Italy, asks

> I feel very bad about myself, I cannot see anything positive in my body, I hate to look at myself in the mirror and it makes me suffer a lot. I feel like everyone is better than me, even though I did very important things for being just 16 years old. How should I behave? What should I do for myself? Thank you for the possible answer.
>
> BARBARA, ROME, ITALY

Cave responds:

> That body that you 'can't see anything positive in' holds within it an unusually courageous, honest and intelligent heart. Your question is a testament to your specialness, and by asking it you have touched us all.
>
> Finally, you asked what you could do, how to behave. Please, take care of yourself. Seek out beautiful things, inspirations, connections and validating

friends. Perhaps you could keep a journal and write stuff down. The written word can put to rest many imagined demons. Identify things that concern you in the world and make incremental efforts to remedy them. At all costs, try to cultivate a sense of humour. See things through that courageous heart of yours. Be merciful to yourself. Be kind to yourself. Be kind.

With certain forms of fan and star exchanges it is recognised that the productive spaces offered for identity negotiation have empowering consequences, offering those on the cultural periphery a safe space to grow in. For example, Lady GaGa's Little Monsters write about how her open commitment to the LGTBQ communities inspires them. In *The Red Hand Files* we see a similar commitment to identity equality: the message to Barbara here is to recognise that the mirror she looks in is not full or clear and that she possesses a special kind of wonderfulness. The suggestion that she keep a journal completes the intimate circle: in the same way these letters conjure up paper and pen, Cave is asking her to write things down, to return to an epistolary age. Finally, of course, he asks her to be kind, to herself, and to the world. This is one of the dominant themes of *The Red Hand Files*: a call to be kind, to act out of love. As Cave writes in response to the question, 'What is love for you?' (Issue #103, July 2020):

> Love has something to do with the notion of being seen – the opposite of invisibility. The invisible, the unwitnessed, the unacknowledged, the isolated, the lonely – these are the unloved. Loving attention illuminates the unseen, escorting them from the frontiers of lovelessness into the observed world. To truly see someone – anyone – is an act that acknowledges and forgives our common and imperfect humanity. Love enacts a kind of vigilant perception – whether it is to a partner, a child, a co-worker, a neighbour, a fellow citizen, or any other person one may encounter in this life. Love says softly – *I see you. I recognise you. You are human, as am I.*

However, love itself can be considered to be cruel, particularly one set within capitalism which offers one the promise of forever but constantly weakens the chains of connection. Cruel optimism is 'when you're attached to objects or object worlds or forms of life that fundamentally get in the way of the attachment you brought to them, and of the optimism you brought to them' (Berlant, 2011: 2). The love that Cave prophesises seems to be of this cruel kind, or rather he sees cruelty as the very mechanism through which all love must flow. His love is lonely.

When asked why he wanted to talk to his fans and what he hoped to achieve by writing *The Red Hand Files* (Issue #19, January 2019), Cave responded,

> When I started the Files I had a small idea that people were in need of more thoughtful discourse. I felt a similar need. I felt that social media was by its nature undermining both nuance and connectivity. I thought that, for my fans at least, *The Red Hand Files* could go some way to remedy that.

He makes a similar point in Issue #97 (May 2020), where he writes,

> The questions that come in, so often naked and damaged and honest, offer me a form of salvation. I am the only one who accesses these questions, as I enter a sequestered world of mutual need. I read the questions each day, maybe fifty or so, sometimes more. It is like reading weird, brutal subterranean poetry, and like poetry they need to be read closely and with care. This exercise has become an essential part of my daily work.

One can see that in these responses a double consciousness again emerges: the letters are for fans cut adrift in an accelerated, cruel world; and they are for Cave, to find spiritual meaning and solace. For Cave, the world has been desacralised and he seeks to re-enchant it through his letters: he wants to let religion and mysticism back into the world. For fans, Cave is a star idol and prophet: his double consciousness increases the intimacies found in the letters. These letters of love, drawn from his scarred romantic heart.

A heart like mine

I gravitate to these letters with great excitement: I imagine that I am opening an envelope as I click open the email. Even though I read them through a phone or computer interface, I run my fingers down the letter's edges, touching the paper's watermarked impressions. The letter's double consciousness speaks to me: their messy sense of the world fits with my worldview, as do the flights of imagination they seek to name and set free. Cave's alternative spiritualism provides me with that level of mysticism that has always caressed my tissues and awoken my bones. When reading the letters, I feel like I am part of an extraordinary, *awe*some community, one on the edge of mainstream culture, washed in Cave's prophesising about the dual nature of love and suffering, and so, so romantically so.

And yet, I also feel guilty about these confessional pleasures: my head tells me that without structural changes to the world, then the coffins of chronic loneliness will keep on multiplying. *The Red Hand Files* fill me up but the unmoored wonder they leave me with is also truly terrifying.

Lonely words: a brief conclusion

We have seen in this chapter the way the written autobiography is a creative and confessional arena that enables people to share their stories of loneliness. The diary proved to be a way for people to write to themselves, opening corridors of self-reflection. However, here in the privacy of their own loneliness room, an imagined reader was waiting to be invited in. Diaries exist in the liminal space between private and public, secret and social, very like the nature of loneliness itself. The poetic form was used to transfer and transform the feelings of loneliness into metaphor, allusion, and alliteration, setting it free from regulatory discourse. The push and pull of what loneliness is or could be filled the stanzas and verses of the submitted poems: its chronic nature wounding the formalism of the haiku, while its existential properties sounded out in the beat of the hammer.

Online, in digital spaces, we found that whole communities of loneliness have emerged, filling virtual rooms with biographies of the lost, alienated, and isolated. Here the thoughts of a double consciousness were openly in play: people posted lonely thoughts for themselves and for those who will read them; as introspection and extrospection; and as techniques of healing for the self and for the community. This therapeutic discourse, however, was very often in the service of chronic loneliness, of loneliness as a pathology. While clearly for many of the responses this was *felt* to be the case, what also emerged was how people's posts were also shaped in and by the medicalisation of loneliness and the rampant discourses that suggest if one feels lonely then one is somehow in deficit.

What also emerged was the longing for communication, interaction; for touch, voice, text, words. That people used the dematerialised worlds of online communities to ask for this physical, somatic intimacy, not only points to the way communities have been driven online but that communities seem to have ceased to exist in the 'real world'. People seem to have given up on life, on hope, on love.

And yet not exactly, or fully: in the fan exchanges with Nick Cave we see these communities flourish; we see Cave prophesise not only on the ugly nature of the world but on the properties of love that can make it a less lonely place to live in. Cave recognises, as do his fans, that loneliness is natural, essential, if tempered by trauma and loss.

Cave is of course a rock star; he sits on the altar of cultural power. He provides a link back to *Joker*, to Amy Winehouse, to those numerous creative responses that connect loneliness to invisibility and not having any 'worth' if one cannot be seen. We see fame culture across these threads as having a dramatic effect on the quilts of loneliness. It's as if our lonely words are wetted in the red ink of renown.

7

A pandemic of creative loneliness

Prelude: lonely in lockdown

Day 1

I stand at the apartment window and take a photograph of the mesmerising morning light shadows that appear to dance on the exterior walls. The communal garden below is empty, and the chill wind of winter runs its fingers over grass and hedge. I sip black coffee from a chipped mug and eat burnt toast, letting the butter melt on my tongue. Music plays in the background.

Day 10

The sky is black and the rain falls as if it has nowhere to go. Splashes of water hit the patio tiles creating a percussion of sound and swell. I lie on my leather couch and flick through the channels and streaming options, resting on curated menu items: that suggestion, this possibility. I choose to watch an old black and white film noir: its nihilism, entrapment, and loneliness matching my mood. Popcorn falls in a chiaroscuro pattern onto the floor.

Day 27

I take a slow walk by the river which is within my 5km 'exercise' bubble. I have made a circular route that takes me through tunnels and across bridges, criss-crossing silenced container warehouses, messy marshes, and wavering grassland. The walkway is full of people doing the same: slow walking, keeping their distance, dropping their gaze as you approach. In many respects this could be any normal day except there are too many people slowly walking and the face masks that we all now wear throw us into the drama of an apocalyptic present. I imagine each walker is a zombie, the masks concealing their rabid orifices and that I am the last man alive on earth.

Day 46

It is early evening, the sun has retreated and the blue sky is coloured with a crimson red that streaks itself across the apartment windows. I am in the kitchen slowly peeling, chopping, cutting up vegetables for dinner. I finely chop carrot, gut yellow capsicum, dice field mushroom, and deflower a purple headed broccoli. I love the way their colours and textures seem to innately feel healthy; they smile back at me. I have a play list for cooking: songs that provide both a rhythm to the knife work, and a lyrical and musical energy that fills my place with life. I haven't spoken to a single person all day and so I sing, sing loudly, letting my voice duet with Bowie, Cave, and Beyoncé. I throw the vegetables in the pan and look out the window and at the stars beginning to open themselves up to the night sky.

Day 64

I have begun to exercise in my apartment. My routine involves skipping, squats, and jumps, and running its length for 20 to 30 minutes. I put on a headband, an old Bruce Lee riding a skateboard t-shirt, and baggy shorts that nearly cover my knees. When I run I create scenarios, write fantasies with my imagination, ones where I am hero and heroic, or where I succeed at things that matter to me. I have travelled across galaxies, saved the universe multiple times, and still been home for tea. I decide to video my run, my star jumps, to share with my children who I haven't been able to see in person in over 64 days. I run up to the camera, jump over it. I point my finger at the lens, pout, letting the music that plays behind me amplify the swagger. My children think I could become a TikTok sensation. I miss my children. I miss their human touch. I am lonely in lockdown.

A pandemic of creative loneliness

The loneliness room project had been gathering its data for approximately 12 months when the COVID-19 pandemic was declared. As national and international borders were closed and the first lockdowns manifested across the world, in March 2020, a series of affordances were gifted its design. It would allow new situational and contextual factors to be explored, and it would serve as a 'test case' for what forms of creativity might spontaneously emerge from the ground up, from the lives of ordinary people placed under restrictions. The COVID-19 pandemic would allow the project to not only see how loneliness was represented under these unprecedented circumstances, but it would provide a canvas to look across many of the art forms addressed in this book so far, to see how they would manifest when presented with the isolation brought on by lockdowns. What follows then is an exploration of loneliness and the creative forms that blossomed under its iron cage. I term this phenomenon a pandemic of creative loneliness.

Lonely in lockdown

One of the dominant media narratives of the first wave of the coronavirus had been the way that people in lockdown, or quarantine, newly experienced isolation as a withering form of loneliness. In response, numerous health bodies, across a range of nation states affected by the virus, released promotional material on how to remain socially connected while alone.

In particular, the social media were awash with 'how to keep connected' video posts and updates, each offering advice on how to avoid temporal boredom while being confined in limited spaces. In this pandemic of loneliness, time and space were – and for many, remain – newly delineated: time became 'longer' while space seemed to grow 'smaller'. In the official discourses of the pandemic, one was asked to build new routines, social ties, and networks out of being newly boxed in. Exercise daily. Prepare meals slowly. Virtually share books and movies. Telephone talk to loved ones on a daily basis. Practice meditation. Routinise your new 'clocks'.

These discourses were again in part shaped by a neoliberal logic that attempted to position the individual as responsible for their health and wellbeing through the lifestyle choices they make, rather than through inequalities and inequities in the capitalist, health-market system. This 'normative' definition of loneliness suggested that it rests with(in) the individual, who needs to be counselled or supported back into the social. As such, these discourses were not 'new' at all but continued the threads of how loneliness was designated and as detailed across this book.

For example, during the March 2020 lockdowns, various health authorities in Australia developed campaigns on 'staying connected while being physically apart: wellbeing in the time of social distancing'. The Queensland Health Authority developed a series of interactive advice and support pages with this explanation (now archived):

> We also know that feeling socially isolated can impact your mental wellbeing. It can make people feel sad, anxious, lonely and depressed. We want to make sure that during this time, you have ways to stay connected to your family, friends and community, even if you can't see them in person.

This is something that the r/lonely Reddit users (see Chapter 6) were also motivated by; they sought to understand it through the vectors of connections and well-being. The lockdown became a mirror that either revealed to them how isolated they really were, or allowed them to newly assess their relationship to partners, family, and friends:

Lonelier than other people in lockdown

Since lockdown I've been texting loads of people trying to stay sane but it's apparent most other people have phone calls, drunk Zoom group calls with family and friendship groups going on most evenings. The only person who calls me is my ex-girlfriend, and that's when she's bored and it's a reminder that part of the fact she left is because I had no real friends, and her extroversion and ability to make friends is what I wish I could be but just can't seem to do.

My evenings are sitting playing PS4 alone wondering what's wrong with me, why I don't ever form close friendships or have a group to fit into. I'm starting to believe that I've missed the boat and wonder if family and the friends you make in early life are really the only dependable close bonds. And it's not like I don't try, I probably text about 10 different 'friends' a day but it doesn't seem to help.

I'm dreading lockdown lifting as well as I don't really have anyone [whose] house I'll be rushing round to hang out. For all intents and purposes I have the appearance of someone with a packed social life but lockdown has just showed me how few really close friends I have. Tinder convos have also been leading nowhere and feel like a waste of time as the enthusiasm just slowly fades out …

Anyone can empathise?

I have lost all feeling

Isolation for this long has driven me mad with self-hatred. I don't blame anyone for not caring about me. This needs to end …

Suffering from mild depression

I have no eagerness to do anything anymore and it may be because of quarantine but my family are angry all the time and it feels like none of them want me here anymore. I literally just had to stop my sister from walking out of the house and we both sat there crying for a full 10 minutes, it just feels like my family are full of anger and they don't want me to be here anymore and to be honest neither do I.

I get very lonely when i go out.

why everytime i go out, i feel lonely and anxious and whenever i'm alone i feel way better, it just feels like when i'm at school, i always have this anxiety and loneliness and scared that people hate me since i dont have any friend and i always end up replaced by people, during quarantine i never a felt a tiny bit of loneliness i was enjoying my time alone, and not scared that i'll be replaced by anyone, but when all of this ends and when i start to go out again, i'll start feeling worthless and unwanted by people.

The first three responses detail how isolated they felt in lockdown, with few if any contacts or networks existing that they can be part of. The first response moves between demonstrating a heart-felt desire to want to communicate with friends, while recognising that any friendship ties they have are superficial. They begin to question themselves, their awkwardness in social settings, and consequently fear lockdown ending.

The second response describes how numb they have become under lockdown, developing a degree of self-loathing as their enforced isolation is taken as if it is they who are responsible for it. The third response also details that they feel as if it is they who are the source of family conflict in the claustrophobic conditions of lockdown. They want to escape the situation, but one can see how trapped they felt.

The final response has the user not wanting lockdown to end because they will again be thrust into social situations which make them feel lonely, anxious, unwanted. They have enjoyed their lonely room experiences. Collectively, these responses point to perhaps the way chronically lonely people experienced isolation as both normal and extreme – taking away any, and all, opportunity to be socially connected.

Of course, not everyone experienced the same time and space in the pandemic lockdowns. For example, the living conditions of the poor, the homeless, and those in migration camps were often marked by privation and a further stretching of temporal boredom – since these people may have lived in overcrowded dwellings with limited access to entertainment and exercise (Warrior et al., 2020). When, in July 2020, the residents of the '9 Towers' in Melbourne, Australia, were put into a 'hard lockdown' without notice, and prohibited from leaving their flats for any reason, it was because of the tacit recognition of overcrowding and high population density in these public commissioned housing blocks. Of course, social class and capital were also being *obliquely* drawn attention to: these towers had been neglected, were run down, and the lockdown exacerbated these materially impoverished conditions. While a crisis in chronic loneliness existed before the pandemic, as this book gives truth to, the various lockdowns not only exacerbated it, but drew swathes of new people into its disabling, chronic arms (Luchetti et al., 2020).

Alongside these 'official' self-help loneliness narratives there also emerged the production of creative responses, where ordinary people used the media to share their own stories of overcoming pandemic loneliness. On the one hand, the sharing of these creative responses was an attempt to reconnect with significant others, and to establish new communities of togetherness. They took all manner of forms and genres: song parody, imitation and mimicry, poetry readings, live music recordings, photo essays, dance-offs, drawings and paintings, fanzines, street art, yarn bombing, short 'genre' films, and video diaries.

On the other hand, these self-made media productions were also a form of DIY citizenship, in which 'individuals and communities participate in shaping, changing, and reconstructing selves, worlds, and environments in creative ways that challenge the status quo and normative understandings of "how things must be"' (Ratto and Boler, 2014: 5). Further, these creative works were often activist in nature and explicitly drew on class, gender, and ethnic perspectives to politicise their responses. This creative making was a critical activity, one 'that provides both the possibility to intervene substantively in systems of authority and power and that offers an important site for reflecting on how such power is constituted by infrastructures, institutions, communities, and practices' (Ratto and Boler, 2014: 1). Through the pandemic's lonely, creative imagination, then, one got to *directly* see the power of inequalities circulating at the heart of late, liquid capitalism (Doogan, 2009).

A *pandemic of creative loneliness* did two central things. First, it demonstrated the rich agency that ordinary people had in shaping and sharing their experience of lonely isolation, reaching out from their lonely rooms to touch and connect with other lonely people. Second, through the generation and circulation of these creative works, they revealed or put under a spotlight the inequalities inherent in modern systems of governance. That is to say, the creative artwork produced as a response to the loneliness of the pandemic had an activist and resistance quality. This chapter is divided into two main sections: the first looks at a range of creative works made by ordinary people to reconnect them to the social world. The second section looks at the creative works that were explicitly politicised and activist in nature, turning the lonely imagination into a political project.

A final note: the case study material that follows has been chosen from the first four months of the pandemic, March to June 2020, during the so-called first wave. This is to make the analysis 'bordered' and temporally 'meaningful'. The case studies are chosen from around the world, as anchoring exemplars, to show the variety of creative responses, and to connect the lonely imagination to what it sees as pressing activist and political issues as they emerged in various international contexts during this period.

Staying creatively connected

Research points towards the role that emotionally actioned, everyday creativity can play in offering points of contact and a means of expression that releases the imagination from its lonely state. Everyday creativity is characterised by

> openness, flexibility, autonomy, playfulness, humor, willingness to take risks, and perseverance. These characteristics are also consistently emphasized in

models of 'normal' personality growth, so that the possibility of promoting mental health arises by fostering creativity in day to day life.

(Cropley, 1990: 167)

One early example of using creative art to deal with the 'missing' human connections that people faced due to the coronavirus lockdowns was organised by the UK-based community artist Naz Syed, who ran the Lost Connections project. This had the aim of 'telling the stories of the community ... – of hope, isolation, worries, memories, things that we hold close to us. What are we holding onto? What will we take forward from all of this?' (Powell, 2020). In one submission, a respondent supplied a photo poem composed of an image of a red-headed girl with two blue painted handprints –one on their shoulder and one on their face – with the following opening stanza:

> Skin stone cold where hands used to hold me
> I'm sick and tired of being this lonely
> A thousand miles from home
> Small, sometimes lost, I'm on my own

The Lost Connections project used art to both represent the loneliness that people were experiencing, and to create new spaces of connections where these works would be 'gifted' and shared. However, these works were intended to be viewed online, in a forum of digital belonging, itself a form of untethered connectivity (Buckingham, 2007), as Chapter 6 has also explored.

I will now explore two forms of pandemic creativity where locality played a central part: the role that site-specific music had in keeping loneliness at bay; and the way that street art and yarn bombing 'redrew' the deserted streets, turning 'spatial capital' (Marcus, 2010) into forms of creative empowerment.

Song and dance

One of the dominant modes of creative expression that emerged in the first wave was through song and dance. Fiona Flores Watson, a Spanish journalist, translator, and guide, recalls a moment that lifted her spirits during the State of Emergency in Spain:

> My favourite was a man singing a saeta (a heartfelt flamenco-religious lament addressed to statues of the Virgin Mary in Holy Week processions) to a woman who was walking her dog in the street below. 'Peeerrrooooo!' he wailed. What's more, the Spanish never miss a chance to show their collective approval or protestation. Every night at 8pm people all around Spain take to their balconies to applaud the efforts of the Spanish health service, stretched

more thinly each day. Last night, kids sang 'Hola Don Pepito, Hola Don Jose' in a call and response for (Spanish) Father's Day.

(Watson, 2020)

These song events were found across numerous nation states and extended to song videos and performances. In Italy, for example, a new form of social interaction emerged: the flashmob sonoro or sound flashmob, where 'every evening around 6pm classical musicians, folk singers, and even DJs have been giving impromptu concerts on their balconies to raise the spirits of their neighbours' (Lorenzon, 2020). In Milan, this extended to neighbours in adjacent blocks of flats bringing out traditional southern Italian tambourines for a singalong. In relation to these events, Tim McKenry writes that

> the isolation we are experiencing hits some people very hard – that disruption to routine, that denial of sunlight in some instances, that separation from friends and families. [It] is a real form of grief. Music is able to help people process that grief and try and find some joy and connection in the context of a pretty miserable situation.
>
> (quoted in Kelsey-Sugg, 2020)

Unsettled Scores, an amateur New York choir ensemble, decided to continue rehearsing via Zoom, holding

> musical movie nights, watching and singing along with *The Rocky Horror Picture Show*, *Moana* and *Moulin Rouge!*. They also put together a tribute video for Adam Schlesinger, the *Fountains of Wayne* singer-songwriter, who had died because of complications due to contracting coronavirus. Ms. Candori, one of the choirists, explained that 'it gave me something to focus on that didn't involve all the desperation'.
>
> (Garcia, 2020)

Such creative events and activities are more generally seen to have material health benefits. For example, the *COVID-19 Social Study* tracked arts participation and mental health in a cohort of 72,000 UK adults aged 18 and older on a weekly basis, from March 2020: 'The data suggests that people who have spent 30 minutes or more each day during the pandemic on arts activities like reading for pleasure, listening to music, or engaging in a creative hobby have lower reported rates of depression and anxiety and greater life satisfaction' (Fancourt, 2021).

The UK-based project Live Music Now at Home developed a series of interactive music workshops where musicians facilitated participatory music-making with people living and working in aged care and disabled settings. This work provided a new community thread for residents to participate together, using music as a way to emotionalise well-being and connectivity. The project delivered 'outside' concerts, where artists would play in the courtyard or garden, bringing live music into the 'locked down' care settings. At the Leeds Recovery Club, musician Simon Robinson provided a live outdoor performance which people could see and hear in the central courtyard: 'a massive thank you to Simon@srobinson1990 for coming to the RecoveryHub@EastLeeds in the rain to play some music and sing for our customers. It really lifted their spirits and they enjoyed singing along! Thank you again!' (Live Music Now, 2020).

Kimmo Lehtonen suggests that for older people 'music forms a certain kind of meaningful space' (Musikraum), one in which memories are activated and 'emotional life' is rekindled (2001). The sociality of music, and the way it reaches into 'connected' memories, keeps loneliness at bay. During the pandemic, when aged care centres were in their own state of emergency, without visits allowed, or human 'touch' being countenanced, music became the connecting tissue for older people. Here the lonely imagination takes flight through song.

These forms of creative connectivity were not limited to interiors, homes, virtual highways, memories, however, but exploded out into the cities, which had been emptied and made quiet by various lockdown orders, as the chapter will now go on to explore.

Repainting the city

One of the most powerful visualisations of the impact that the coronavirus had on social connectivity was through ground-level and drone/aerial footage of cities rendered silent and still. This 'spatial dread' (Thompson, 2012: 85), where movement, activity, noise, were no longer present in the image but, nonetheless, continued to haunt its representation, created a profound sense of uncanny isolation. Cities themselves appeared distinctly 'lonely' and evoked or projected the very sensation of human disconnection. For example, the lockdown video, *Wuhan: The City Under Coronavirus* (7 February 2020), followed the city's bridges, skylines, roadways, into inner-city streets that had been emptied of people. In a city of 11 million people, this sense of emptiness carried through the sensation that the world had ground to a halt. ABC's *7.30 Show* (2020) produced a similar video of Melbourne during lockdown, this time with George Stirling from the Australian Boys Choir performing 'Meet Me in the Middle of the Air' over the images of empty parks, stadiums, fairgrounds, laneways, and rivers.

The spatial and temporal qualities of cities during lockdown seemed to create two simultaneous, albeit seemingly contradictory impressions: first, one of claustrophobia; and second, one of expansiveness. The cities lay silent because people were at home, restricted to their houses and neighbourhoods, and only allowed out for exercise or to fetch groceries and medicines. Their world had visibly shrunk. Montages of usually busy, kinetic urban environments absented people but existentially ghosted them into private settings – seemingly everyone was now living alone and lonely behind 'net curtains'.

And yet the emptied, clean, and clear vistas of the city created the feeling of openness, of new sightlines, where one could move more freely. There was an economic aspect to this spatial democracy: the city, usually the heart of commerce and consumption, was now one where one could imaginatively dwell without needing capital to do so. The paradoxical caveat here, of course, was that the lockdown both created this new condition for free dwelling and forbade or limited it.

This is exactly the dialectical space that the street artist enters: they see the city as a participatory canvas, but one where the rules and regulatory norms of the city – turned over to capital – closes off, closes down creative expression. Street artists are often

> dwellers dissatisfied with the ugliness of our cities [who] may endorse an ideology of resistance to the alienation of public space. Overall, they claim entitlement to and sharing of city walls and thus question the boundaries of appropriation in public contexts. They observe that city walls, although privately owned, are nonetheless visible to everyone and thus made consumable to a larger set of stakeholders.
>
> (Visconti et al., 2010: 518)

The street art created during the first wave of coronavirus offered narratives that attempted to alleviate or explore the lockdowns through different lenses and materials. There were street canvases painted which aimed to bring communities together, such as the 'stay home, save lives' pastes that sprung up across many cities in the world. There were street murals that foregrounded the heroic role of frontline health workers, such as the mural of 'Sophia' the nurse smashing the virus with a club, painted on a derelict wall in Vila Nova de Gaia, a suburb of Porto in Portugal. And there were installs that lampooned and criticised those political leaders who were deemed to be failing the people, such as John D'oh's stencil art of Donald Trump holding a bottle of 'Trump's Covid disinfectant' spray which kills '99.9% of Americans'. What interests me in this chapter, however, is the street art designed to explicitly reconnect people, and which recognised the alienation, the loneliness that the coronavirus lockdowns had on sociality.

In Mark Titchner's *Please Believe these Days will Pass* poster and billboard series – installed in ten UK cities during the first coronavirus lockdown – he used strong black typeface and vibrant background colours to message the recognition that the present was both traumatic and temporary. Commenting on the colourful background to these installs, Titchner suggests that

> it seemed more appropriate, thinking about being stuck inside. When you think about the dream scenario for escape, it is being on a beach looking at the sunset, a Turner-esque moment, so that kind of backdrop seemed more appropriate really. A lot of the works will be going up in very grey, concrete locations, so I wanted the colours to be strong, positive.
>
> (quoted in Simpson, 2020)

The utopian dimension to these public artworks hints at the loneliness that is occurring because of people being trapped *indoors*. However, Titchner also recognises that the spaces that street art is often found in/on – 'hospitals, stations and libraries' – are ones 'where we share the experience, but we don't engage with each other. It's about being present but not there. It's a very disembodied version of shared space. It's a means to an end' (Simpson, 2020).

Titchner is here alluding to the idea of the 'non-place' or nondescript spaces of transience where human beings remain anonymous, disconnected, *lonely-in-space* (Augé, 1995), as this book has already addressed. In a similar fashion, Ann Cvetkovich suggests that this is in fact a facet of late capitalism: one that has shaped ordinary public life so that it is experienced as a depressive state in which 'the felt sensations of the lived environment renders one as emotionally down' (2012: 11). However, Marc Augé also powerfully suggests that the non-space has other qualities and intensities which make its definition and experiential qualities more complex:

> You know where this definition begins to break down, though? When you spend way too much time in non-place. All of a sudden, in a process that somewhat resembles a figure/ground reversal, these putatively anonymous and interstitial zones take on texture and resolution of their own ... [Then, one] can no longer see non-places ... as entirely flat and featureless: I've learned that everything has texture if you see it often enough.
>
> (Sturm, 1995)

Street art gives this 'texture' to liminal spaces, in part because it calls for people to stop, stare, and take the moment in. Flashes of aerosol paint, wrinkled stickies, and giant murals give 'flesh' to identikit corporate buildings. Street art often encourages interaction, co-creation, where these primary canvases are added to, 'mixed up'. In a very real sense, street art takes the non-space and renders it inviting, pleasurable, and collectively meaningful. As Visconti et al. argue:

> The ideology of street democracy demands active and collective participation in the design and use of cityscapes. It refuses both the excesses of the appropriation of public space by single individuals and the lack of conscious consumption. This is the idea of street democracy, since it relates to the set

of rights and duties that citizens have in democratic political settings. These artists acknowledge the right of collectively consuming public space as a collective good, while calling for participation, responsibility, and planning from its entitled owners.

(Visconti et al., 2010: 517)

One of the most powerful sets of street art murals that emerged during coronavirus was of two people/lovers kissing with face masks on. In Milan, Italian urban artist Salvatore Benintende, known as Tvboy, reinterpreted the 1859 painting *The Kiss* by Francesco Hayez. In his reimagining the lovers have been provided with face masks and hand sanitisers. A mural by artist Ponywave appeared on a wall in Venice Beach in Venice, California, depicting, in close-up, two lovers kissing while wearing flower-strewn, brightly coloured face masks. In Melbourne, Australia, street artist Peter Seaton painted a mural, titled 'Trapped in the 3rd Dimension', depicting a man and a woman wearing gas masks locked in a passionate embrace. Seaton, better known as CTO, said he painted the work 'to remind people of the importance of relationships and intimacy' during the pandemic and that 'one of the most human things that we have is our connection with one another and the coronavirus has sort of tested that' (Jeffery, 2020).

These murals speak to the way the lockdowns had uncoupled lovers and partners who may have not been living together. Street art that placed them in lover-like settings – near the beach, under the subway at 'night', and outside cafes and bars – inserted romantic coupling into their narratives, recognising the loneliness that separation causes while filling this 'gap' with impressions of touch, tactility, and love.

Retexturing the city

Yarn bombing was used or drawn upon for similar effect/affect during the first wave of coronavirus. The practice often centres on its insertion into public space through a remoulding and re-texturing of hard, cold, urban spaces, or by entangling the yarn works around natural forms, such as trees. Yarn bombing exists in a 'dialogic relationship' formed by the collaborative nature of yarn bombing projects, and is linked to feminine and feminist traditions:

> The clear demarcation between the handmade, often associated with the feminine desire to create useful objects and/or decorate domestic space ... and yarn bombing is marked in the fact that yarn bombing has no interest in producing functional, wearable pieces: most of the yarn squares are ultimately discarded or recycled into other yarn projects. Finally, yarn bombing is often about social involvement, social awareness, and social interactions between like-minded people, mainly women.

(Myzelev, 2015: 60)

One powerful example of raising social awareness that emerged during the first wave of coronavirus was the Healthy Families Yarn project initiated by the Mount Isa Domestic Violence Action Group in collaboration with Mount Isa City Council and the Mount Isa Tourism Association, in Northern Queensland, Australia. The project encouraged locals to get involved in yarn bombing their yards and homes during lockdown to 'promote healthy yarns surrounding domestic and family violence'. The project encouraged 'families to have the yarns: to talk among themselves around what keeps their family healthy, strong, and safe. We'd love for families to come up with the answers that work for them – there is no right or wrong' (Campbell, 2020).

What sits beneath this initiative is the belief that both separation (from other family members you may not live with) and disconnection from normal routines (such as going to work or school) fuels forms of domestic violence in the home – which was a major problem before the pandemic but here is exacerbated by lockdown conditions. Both emotional loneliness and social loneliness are seen to be catalysts for various forms of violence – physical, psychological, symbolic – and the reason why one might feel lonely (Kunst and van Bon-Martens, 2011). The act of yarn bombing the home is here a strategy to creatively 'connect' house members and to provide an opportunity to yarn or story tell together for both cathartic and bio-political reasons. Here the creative, participatory work of yarn bombing is an attempt to colour and texturise loneliness, so it doesn't tail off into violent becomings.

Yarn bombing took on different forms during the first wave of coronavirus, some of them highly individualistic. For example, in Desert Hot Springs, California, Stephanie Buriel knitted a series of community messages that she put up on fences: 'we are all in this together'; 'we will rise above this'; and 'kiss this virus goodbye' (News Channel 10, 2020). The knitting involved a rainbow design, with either masked faces or a large kiss as part of the patterning. These yarns were placed on chain-link fences, softening their appearance. Buriel commented, 'We're all experiencing the same things at home, or we've been laid off, or we have the kids at home all day. I mean, whatever it is, we're all going through the same thing, and so I thought it was an important message to send to the community' (News Channel 10, 2020). Similarly, Nina Elliott developed a series of knitted and crocheted textile art alongside a two-kilometre strip of the Twillingate Roadway in Newfoundland, Canada. These works were intended to help people who were feeling anxious and isolated: 'It's definitely stressful. And you come home and check in to the news and it's all about coronavirus and it's really difficult to get away from. It's nice to be able to provide an offer of some mental reprieve' (Hawthorn, 2020).

The lonely imagination is here seen as a balm to the isolating trauma of the pandemic: art that soothes as it simultaneously 'space-moulds' existing public settings. However, creative responses during the pandemic were also highly politicised – an attempt to use creative works to draw attention to the inequities that lockdowns produced, or which were there hiding in plain sight.

The lonely capital of the pandemic

Coronavirus has been defined by various scholars as the 'pandemic of inequality' because of its disproportionate effect on already disadvantaged and marginalised communities (Nassif-Pires et al., 2021). Joan Benach observes: 'The pandemic constitutes an enormous threat to the poorest and most vulnerable social groups and neighborhoods in many countries, living with fragile and even dire social determinants of health: poor housing; poverty; precariousness; lack of basic services, water, and food; environmental pollutants, etc.' (2021: 51).

Such inequalities were, of course, directly experienced by refugees who found themselves cut off from community and with limited access to material, economic resources. This pandemic of inequality, however, can be recuperated and re-sourced through everyday creative practice. Artist and human rights activist, Salma Zulfiqa, developed ARTconnects to 'promote social cohesion, tolerance and wellbeing and to bring together refugees, asylum-seekers and other vulnerable people' (quoted in Saltmarsh, 2020).

During the first wave of coronavirus they organised Zoom workshops where refugee women and girls from countries as diverse as Bangladesh, Ethiopia, Greece, Iraq, Niger, the United States, and Yemen shared their experiences during lockdown, as well as their paintings, poetry, mixed-media photographs, and music. One participant, Tasneem, said the sessions helped her to understand that she was not alone: 'It was really fantastic to feel like you could share your problems with another person who you have never met before … For me, it was like therapy' (Saltmarsh, 2020).

The idea that sharing lockdown isolation stories and developing creative responses to both represent and express these experiences again speaks to the way everyday creative practice assists with positive mental health. However, here it was also activist in nature, since the sharing of these art pieces demonstrated commonality in lonely inequalities and inequities for refugee women and girls, creating a resistant and oppositional space for their voices to be heard and shared. *The Migration Blanket*, the documentary that was made to collect the paintings created by the girls and women during the Zoom sessions, represented 'both isolation and solidarity during the pandemic' (Saltmarsh, 2020). Its comforting nature, imagined as a warming blanket, connected these participants to all the spaces and places where refugees were found, including leaking boats on the Mediterranean Sea. The contraction in space produced by lockdowns is again here opened – the blanket wraps itself around the whole world – but with an added political dimension since people are on the run from inequality and persecution, from the cold hands of capitalised loneliness, everywhere.

There were also 'small' and localised stories of resistance to pandemic loneliness, shaped around self-identity and (not) belonging. Queer artist KT Taylor developed the *Not Alone, Never was Penpal Zine 4 Rural Queers* as part of the initiative Artists Respond: Combatting Social Isolation, a project of Springboard for the Arts. Inspired by gay newsletters that were circulated in the (pre-digital) 1970s and 1980s, KT put out a call for letters to be sent in, on how queer people were experiencing lockdown in rural Minnesota. The zine illustrates seven of these letters including this one from Kayden:

> Imagine living in a world that isn't this shitty, this lonely, this terrifying. Personally, I can't picture one off the top of my head. Maybe you can't either. And that could paralyze us both, shut us down because there isn't any hope. But I don't think that's what actually will happen. I believe that with some imagination, we might be able to picture an ideal world. Just our own, not the whole world by any means. But a little slice of ideal world for us. Mine includes a few plants and some good cheese. Yours might look entirely different. But if we chose to make imagine those worlds, we can make them happen.
> (Taylor, 2021: 3)

KT wanted to give gay people 'the experience of having something arrive in their mailbox. Something they could read through, feel the pages ... almost this talisman that's a physical piece connecting them across separation' (Ross, 2021). Arriving as printed zines, they indicate a time that pre-dates the digital world, recalling social practices (Barton and Hall, 2000) that required a different type of emotive labour and set of materials (pen, paper, colours, staples). KT's zines are not only formally nostalgic, however, since they carry an emotional intensity that certain forms of fan literature have historically done. They return us implicitly to the fan letters that emerge from *The Red Hand Files* (see Chapter 6 for a discussion of this).

Further, the *Not Alone, Never Was* zines are so unrelentingly raw that they carry a level of shared intimacy that collapses distance and difference. These zines affectively 'leak' (Sobchack, 2000); they challenge normative narratives of loneliness; and they offer complex, messy, often transcendent answers to the most difficult of 'life-based' questions raised and shared in the age of coronavirus. Space and time are recalibrated here: the zines are delivered to the home and brought inside it. Slow time is being imagined that people in lockdown will now have more time to read and dwell. The fanzine is a gift, delivered without cost, attempting to empty the rural queer reader of their loneliness.

A pandemic of creative loneliness: a brief conclusion

Hong Kong-based artist Louise Soloway-Chan's *Contactless* series of 22 ink paintings on rice paper captures 'the bustling scenes of everyday life amid an epidemic. Louise's figurative works suggest that the disconnection and isolation measures may have the unintended consequence of inducing loneliness, fear, and panic in the community' (Boundless Artists Collective, 2020).

In *Too Cool for School II* we see a young girl (daughter) sitting on a woman's (mother's) knee in a setting that resembles a bus stop or a carriage on a train. Mother and daughter are wearing different types of facemasks: the former, a cloth covering, and the latter, a full-face shield. The drawing is full of both ease and tension: the daughter, wearing a bright spotted skirt, lazily sits between her mother's knees, who holds her closely, while they both tensely stare at someone not presented in the image. The face shield dwarfs the child's visage: she peers out as if through a giant window. The mother's hair falls down over her face, and it is her stare that carries or captures a/their sense of shared fear. The face coverings recast the drawing as a coronavirus one and present into the image the invisible virus and the concern that other people (commuters, parents) might carry it. The face coverings also take away some of the intimacy between mother and daughter: there are added, medical layers between them. Loneliness runs its fingers over the drawing as isolation and fear of others' touch produce a 'tightness' between mother and daughter and a separation from/within space. They are together but alone.

All the drawings in the *Contactless* series capture the new conditions of entering public space: people wear masks; attempt to socially distance; look into their cell phones as a way of avoiding eye contact; and service workers endlessly clean surfaces. What these drawings draw attention to is the new formations of time and space in the coronavirus city that is not locked down: people exist in iso bubbles as they quickly move on, not dwelling, not resting. Of course, the echoes and traces of the pre-coronavirus city remain: commuters and city workers didn't dwell before the time of the virus but then it was the flows of 'capital' that moved them on. Capital is lonely, even when it attempts to affectively register on human interaction, on the human psyche, since it orientates one to be a productive worker, while fetishising this labour. These new temporal and spatial relations, then, share traces of the past but they are not of the same affective registers.

Capital seems used up, exhausted in the pandemic spaces conjured up by the lonely imagination.

It is creative works that have drawn and reformed temporal and spatial relationships and shown how art can reveal inequality and inequity while reconnecting us as human beings. On the one hand, everyday creativity brought people together, to share their experiences of loneliness, and through these gatherings, to keep it at bay. Time was slowed, space remoulded, a different way of living was found that was both desperately 'cold' and constrained and yet, paradoxically, freer than before. On the other hand, these acts of creativity that sprang from individuals, communities, or art initiatives revealed what was already at the heart of liquid capitalism: an emptiness, an unfairness, a velocity that withered one. That is to say, this pandemic of creative loneliness was able to do multiple things: create and establish new forms of DIY citizenship and shine a light on the inequitable way the virus affected different groups and communities. This was the power of the lonely imagination set free.

But to what end? Were these examples and instances of creativity demotic rather than democratic – without power to effect real change? Will both the strings and bows of liquid capitalism return, and with it 'normalised' forms of loneliness, when the pandemic ends? Or have new ways of being in the world been forever rooted: has everyday creativity recalibrated lifeworlds?

Capitalism has an uncanny ability to appear to be on the point of exhaustion and expiration only to survive and reorient itself. It takes on forms of creative resistance and very often monetarises them, such as is the case with street art. Against this, the power of the imagination, lonely or not, is able to creatively remake the world: a perpetual 'act' of resistance. This set of forces and relations, as I have explored throughout this chapter, seems to offer both hope and restraint. Perhaps, then, they are a form of cruel optimism, to paraphrase Lauren Berlant (2011), forever destined to fail. Or, conversely, in their potentiality have the ability to transform who we can be. All the art forms and creative practices taken up in this pandemic of loneliness have shown this potential, and it is through this agency where my hope ultimately lies.

Conclusion: if nobody speaks of loneliness rooms

In the roaring traffic's boom
In the silence of my lonely room
I think of you night and day

Cole Porter, Night and Day

In Jon McGregor's novel, *If Nobody Speaks of Remarkable Things* (2002), we follow a day in the life of the inhabitants of one street in a British city, experiencing 'the vast multiplicity of stories which were happening there'. We get to see how these 'stories interact with each other in an environment where people are constantly moving in and out and rarely know each other's names'. These stories are of the mundane, the everyday, and yet as they are revealed the reader sees them connect in ways that render them truly extraordinary. McGregor finds in the minutiae of everyday life the complexity and artistry of the human condition. He also finds, implicitly at least, the way that loneliness permeates the houses that the novel visits.

Which song for you best captures what it feels like to be lonely?

'Wicked Game', Chris Isaak

Briefly explain why this song captures the feeling of loneliness. Please feel free to comment on its arrangement, lyrics, composition.

the chord the song is recorded in rings through my heart strings, the plucked guitar riff is so iconic, bold, yet very sad, it reminds me of being in a desert at night with no petrol!

Can you recall where you first heard it and how it made you feel? Please describe.

I stopped in my tracks, very confused, was this country music or something else? Immediately I sensed an emptiness inside me that the guitar seemed to pinpoint. Every time I hear it, I am thrown back to a highly contemplative space, alone, looking out.

In many respects the 'narrative' of *The Loneliness Room* takes a similar route to McGregor's novel. The stories of loneliness are culled and curated from the ordinary and the everyday and they connect and intersect in a richly woven tapestry which reveals remarkable things about the lonely imagination. By spending time in the rooms of the lonely we have been able to see and hear its variations, intensities, and possibilities. That these stories of loneliness have emerged from the remarkable selection of artwork submitted demonstrates how the ground between ethnography and creative practice can be fruitfully brought closer together.

In this submission by a painter, they offer two versions of their loneliness room: 'Figure and window' (Figure 8.1) and 'Spirit garden' (Figure 8.2). For me, they capture the disorientating spatial qualities of loneliness, with 'Figure and window' disproportionately sized and cold and immobile, and 'Spirit garden' full of greenery which seems to magically 'dance'. And yet, the white Spirit is absent against the fecundity of the Garden, and Figure abstracts itself into a mirrored bloody nothingness. Modernity and Eden may both be this painter's loneliness room.

The Loneliness Room also clearly questions the pathology narrative that has come to determine the way loneliness is presented and discussed in the

Figure 8.1 Figure and window

Figure 8.2 Spirit garden

political, cultural, and medical arenas. While chronic loneliness *is* the crisis of the age, it is not the fault of individuals but of neoliberal capitalism and the unequal rooms that it homes people in. What this book has shown is how and why the discourse of chronic loneliness disables, labels, and marginalises anxiously lonely people. What *The Loneliness Room* has also demonstrated is the rich agency that chronically lonely people have when asked to use their lonely imaginations. The book's findings go some way to destigmatising the way loneliness is presently understood in dominant discourse, offering its readers (and participants) new representations and insightful ways with which to see its manifestations in art and audiovisual culture.

For Johnny, the film which best captures what it feels like to be lonely is *Taxi Driver* (Scorsese, 1976):

> *Taxi Driver* has always had a profound impact on me and I think that's particularly because of its focus on loneliness. Travis is always on the outside of society, his friends, his dates and his passengers. His detachment and isolation are so compelling and terrifying. I think it's such a bold examination of mental collapse brought on by isolation.
>
> There's a great scene where Travis tries to reach out to Peter Boyle's character and explain his thoughts and feelings, but Boyle misses the point. Travis' last attempt at stopping his own descent is missed and his sense of detachment complete. I think as an only child I've always had an awareness of being alone and that fundamentally life is us stuck within our own head, only we can reconcile that. *Taxi Driver* speaks to that literal and metaphorical loneliness that life is.

What *The Loneliness Room* has also explored is the way loneliness is connected to a number of identity markers, including gender, class, race, and age. Not only is loneliness not a singular condition, but the way it affects people is shaped by how they are positioned in the social and cultural world, in the neoliberal marketplace. The book has shown how lonely marriages and the limitations put on the subjectivity of women create a particular type of loneliness room.

Similarly, we have seen how time and space affect the way loneliness is defined and experienced. *The Loneliness Room* has explored numerous environments and ecologies, from the isolating city streets to the rural idyl, and from middle-class suburbia to the wilds of the wilderness. The bedroom at home, the transient hotel, and the mobile car became three rooms to house loneliness in.

The time of loneliness also matters: we see it changed by night, by day, and by the breaking of dawn. We have seen how loneliness affects the time of young children, teenagers, middle-aged married couples and single men, and those who are aged. We have seen loneliness rooms appear in all of life's stories, from the cradle to the grave.

What is your lonely room song?

'After the Lights Go Out' – The Walker Brothers

Briefly explain why this song captures the feeling of loneliness. Please feel free to comment on its arrangement, lyrics, composition.

the whole song is just devastatingly lonely from the opening line of 'my silent little room goes dim' and the protagonist even pondering if a pigeon he sees 'love has also flown away' its just slow and mournful sound and slow meandering beat too, plus just how hard loneliness hits at night

Can you recall where you first heard it and how it made you feel? Please describe.

late at home on a late night and it just really stuck with me how perfectly it encapsulated late-night loneliness

The Loneliness Room has not employed a straight division between the art submitted by its participants and the art forms that were analysed. Very often they are addressed together or exist in threaded relationships. The book largely refuses a hierarchy between professional art and the art of its participants. Instead, *The Loneliness Room* uses their shared representations and impressions to forge connections and articulations – allowing it to demonstrate how everyday art sits in rooms with extraordinary photographs, films, documentaries, songs, and poems. Further, the book's iterative research design has shown how art and culture not only impact upon the way its participants came to express what they understood loneliness to be but were the stimulus for their own creative practice. Again, this participant-led deployment of art and culture to get to the heart of loneliness opens up ethnography to the sheer power of creativity and its ability to reveal something new.

Where is your loneliness room?

Walking alone has the element of being able to reflect. To be both present and absent at the same time. To have a corporeal connection with the world while the world shows you the possibilities (and impossibilities) it generates.

Why do you go there?

It is important to have space away from others. I talk to myself when I walk, I am not sure if this is genuinely because it is a better class of conversation, or because I am verging on madness. Perhaps the fact that I do talk to myself stops me from going mad.

The book has shown how its request to 'talk' about loneliness sits within confessional and therapeutic discourses, and yet this chatter very often challenges and resists orthodoxy and convention. Participants move seamlessly across, and readily undermine, terms and concepts such as solitude and aloneness, equating them with loneliness. The book's intentionally open, and deliberately porous, definition of loneliness enabled its participants to respond to the conceit of the loneliness room as they understood and felt it. Shibboleths fell away. Startling truths about loneliness emerged.

The Loneliness Room has shown how objects, possessions, smells, and sensations have shaped the way loneliness is embodied and expressed. As such, it evidences not just the cognitive or psychological nature of loneliness but its phenomenological, sense-based attributes. Water becomes a particular quality that loneliness is washed in – at the car wash, in the sea or swimming pool, in a flood of tears, in the cleansing shower:

Where is your loneliness room?

The shower.

Why do you go there?

Societal expectations surrounding hygiene, mostly. But sometimes I just have a shower to feel warm and in control. The water reminds me to relax but the smallness of the cubicle reminds me that it's just me in there.

Using as many words as you like, describe your loneliness room. Please feel free to be poetic or to write your answer as a 'story'.

It's crowded, tiled, claustrophobic and it steams up way too quickly. But because it's a shower, it's warm and familiar. It's a small part of my day where I can just focus on washing my hair and not about the anxiety I face at work, or the panic attacks i'll surely have around lunchtime. I wish showers could last forever and I didn't have water bills to pay.

Nonetheless, the senses of loneliness have also been connected to waste, refuse, and shit, revealing a self-loathing, a self-hatred of the participant who lives in that particular room. Again, this sense of disgust at being a loner is orientated by outside discourses and representations; by the biopolitics of neoliberalism which only wants what it sees as productive, working, consuming citizens, turning the wheels of capitalism.

One of the rivulets of *The Loneliness Room* has been the theme of invisibility and visibility, of mask-wearing and renown. Fame culture has sat like a changeable sky over many of the submissions. Participants very often exercised a double consciousness: a desire to belong to the centre of social life; a fear of doing so.

The Loneliness Room has threaded in elements of fiction: the book not only presents the lonely stories that were submitted but engages in storytelling itself. Its embedded poetry, its sensory sentences, align the various elements of the book together, refusing to hold a line between traditional scholarship and creative practice. Further, it draws on moments of autoethnography; it draws on my loneliness room. It does this to cross boundary lines, and to recognise this author's creative investment in the lonely imagination.

At the start of the project, I engaged in my own form of creative practice. I developed a sticker/sticky campaign, going to the places and spaces where I felt loneliness would dwell. I visited the beach (Figure 8.3), the park, and

Figure 8.3 The loneliness room

Figure 8.4 Around-and-around

the city. I looked in the fridge. I watched a washing machine at the laundromat go round and round (Figure 8.4). I walked along the railway tracks at night; sat in a library during the weekday; and looked back at the contents of my bedroom as I settled into bed, alone (Figure 8.5). I rested in my car, parked up at a roadside café. I looked out of the train window on the morning commute, counting rain drops as I did so. At each destination, I left my lonely room sticker, imagining, hoping, intending it to resonate with those who came across it. Of course, many of the spaces and places I visited became the stories and artworks of this book – the loneliness of my imagination was the loneliness of theirs.

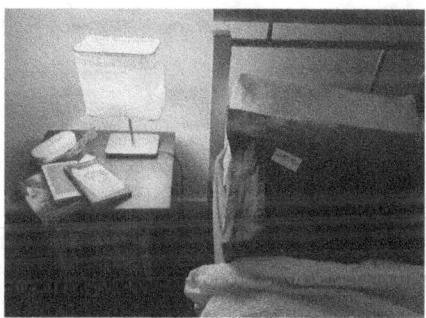

Figure 8.5 Bedroom blues

If nobody speaks of loneliness rooms, then we are left with pathology and literalness. We impoverish the way that loneliness is variously and complexly lived, and we deny its poetic and creative expressions and the way that these reveal so much more about the lonely imagination. If nobody speaks of loneliness rooms, we come to limit our methodology and methods, narrowing our insights, lessening our analytical power. When we speak of loneliness rooms we invite imagination into the academic arena, freeing us to invest in its power for revelation. When we speak of loneliness rooms, our words and images run counter to dominant discourse, resisting and challenging neoliberal capitalism as it does so.

And I taste sea salt on tongue.

Appendices

Appendix 1

The loneliness room

For the purpose of this project the loneliness room is defined as a real or imagined space or place where we feel lonely or go to find loneliness.

Each of us will have our very own version of the loneliness room: it could be the hills we walk on; a morning swim at the beach or local swimming pool; listening to a certain song in our bedroom; writing in our diary; or the park we go to sit in at lunchtime.

Loneliness may be a feeling of solitude or isolation, or a space of contemplation or renewal. One may go to a loneliness room in melancholy or as a recuperative place to feel whole again.

Please use the link below to read the plain language statement and to access the consent and withdrawal form.

Please now answer the following questions:

Q1. Where is your loneliness room?
Q2. Why do you go there?
Q3. Using as many words as you like, describe your loneliness room. Please feel free to be poetic or to write your answer as a 'story'.
Q4. If you could choose one artist who for you best captures loneliness, who would it be and why?

If loneliness is at times for you overwhelming, please see this supportive site: https://au.reachout.com/challenges-and-coping/isolation-and-loneliness. If you are happy having your answers identified for research purposes, please fill out the below:

Name:

Location (Country, City):

Email address (not to be published):

Appendix 2

Lonely films

This questionnaire is part of the loneliness room project which looks at the way various art forms represent loneliness.

For further details about the project see here: https://www.facebook.com/profile.php?id=100063647824826

For this questionnaire, we are looking at the way film captures this state and are asking participants to choose one film that for them powerfully or affectively encapsulates what it feels like to be lonely.

Please use the link below to read the plain language statement and to access the consent and withdrawal form.

Please now answer the following questions:

Q1. Which film for you best captures what it feels like to be lonely?
Q2. Describe or explain the reasons for your choice?
Q3. Choose one scene or sequence that particularly resonated with you in terms of its portrayal of loneliness and describe its impact upon you.

If you are happy having your answers identified for research purposes, please fill out the below:

Name:

Location (Country, City):

Email address (not to be published):

If loneliness is at times for you overwhelming, please see this supportive site: https://au.reachout.com/challenges-and-coping/isolation-and-loneliness

Appendix 3

Lonely photographs

This questionnaire is part of the loneliness room project which looks at the way various art forms represent loneliness.

For further details about the project see here: https://www.facebook.com/profile.php?id=100063647824826

For this questionnaire, we are looking at the way photography captures this state and are asking participants to choose one photographer that for them powerfully or affectively encapsulates what it feels like to be lonely.

Please use the link below to read the plain language statement and to access the consent and withdrawal form.

Please now answer the following questions:

Q1. Which photographer for you best captures loneliness?
Q2. Describe or explain the reasons for your choice.
Q3. Choose one photograph by this artist in terms of the way they capture loneliness. Describe the photo and its impact upon you.

If you are happy having your answers identified for research purposes, please fill out the below:

Name:

Location (Country, City):

Email address (not to be published):

If loneliness is at times for you overwhelming, please see this supportive site: https://au.reachout.com/challenges-and-coping/isolation-and-loneliness

Appendix 4

Lonely songs

This questionnaire is part of the loneliness room project which looks at the way various art forms represent loneliness.

For further details about the project see here: https://www.facebook.com/profile.php?id=100063647824826

For this questionnaire, we are looking at the way music captures this state and are asking participants to choose one song that for them powerfully or affectively encapsulates what it feels like to feel lonely.

Please use the link below to read the plain language statement and to access the consent and withdrawal form.

Please now answer the following questions:

Q1. Which song for you best captures what it feels like to be lonely? Provide its title, and the band, musician or composer who wrote and/or performs it.
Q2. Briefly explain why this song captures the feeling of loneliness. Please feel free to comment on its arrangement, lyrics, composition.
Q3. Can you recall where you first heard it and how it made you feel? Please describe.

If you are happy having your answers identified for research purposes, please fill out the below:

Name:

Location (Country, City):

Email address (not to be published):

If loneliness is at times for you overwhelming, please see this supportive site: https://au.reachout.com/challenges-and-coping/isolation-and-loneliness

References

Alberti, Fay Bound. 2019. *A Biography of Loneliness: The History of an Emotion*. Oxford: Oxford University Press.
Allen, Kim, Tyler, Imogen, and De Benedictus, Sara. 2014. 'Thinking with "White Dee": The Gender Politics of "Austerity Porn"'. *Sociological Research Online*, 19:3. www.socresonline.org.uk/19/3/2.html (accessed 20 October 2020).
Alpert, Patricia T. 2011. 'The Health Benefits of Dance.' *Home Health Care Management & Practice*, 23:2, 155–157.
Anderson, Benedict. 2006. *Imagined Communities: Reflections on the Origin and Spread of Nationalism*. New York: Verso.
Andrews, Hannah. 2017. 'From Unwilling Celebrity to Authored Icon: Reading Amy (Kapadia, 2015)'. *Celebrity Studies*, 8:2, 351–354.
Arnold, Emma. 2021. 'Photography, Composition, and the Ephemeral City'. *Area*, 53:4, 659–670.
Asimov, Isaac. 1986. *Pebble in the Sky*. London: Grafton.
Augé, Marc. 1995. *Non-Places: Introduction to an Anthropology of Supermodernity*. Trans. by John Howe. London and New York: Verso.
Ayala, Nicolas. 2021. 'The Killing of a Sacred Deer's Greek Tragedy Inspiration Explained'. *Screenrant*. 29 January. https://screenrant.com/killing-sacred-deer-movie-greek-tragedy-story-inspiration-explained/ (accessed 23 February 2023).
Baelo-Allué, Sonia. 2019. 'Transhumanism, Transmedia and the Serial Podcast: Redefining Storytelling in Times of Enhancement'. *International Journal of English Studies*, 19:1, 113–131.
Balstrup, Sarah K. 2020. 'Religion, Creative Practice and Aestheticisation in Nick Cave's The Red Hand Files'. *Religions*, 11:6, 304.
Barrett, Frederick S., Grimm, Kevin J., Robins, Richard W., Wildschut, Tim, Sedikides, Constantine, and Janata, Petra. 2010. 'Music-Evoked Nostalgia: Affect, Memory, and Personality'. *Emotion*, 10:3, 390–403.
Barthes, Roland. 1975. *The Pleasure of the Text*. Trans. by R. Miller. New York: Hill and Wang.
Barthes, Roland. 1977. 'The Death of the Author'. In Stephen Heath (ed. and trans.) *Image-Music-Text*. New York: Noonday, 142–148.
Barthes, Roland. 1981. *Camera Lucida: Reflections on Photography*. New York: Hill and Wang.
Barton, David, and Hall, Nigel (eds). 2000. *Letter Writing as a Social Practice*. Vol. 9. Amsterdam: John Benjamin.
Baruah, Trisha Dowered. 2012. 'Effectiveness of Social Media as a Tool of Communication and its Potential for Technology Enabled Connections: A Micro-Level Study'. *International Journal of Scientific and Research Publications*, 2:5, 1–10.

Bauman, Zygmunt. 1988. 'Strangers: The Social Construction of Universality and Particularity'. *Telos*, 78, 7–42.

Bauman Zygmunt. 2000. *Liquid Modernity*. Oxford: Blackwell.

Bauman, Zygmunt. 2013. *Liquid Love: On the Frailty of Human Bonds*. London: Polity.

Bazerman, Charles. 2000. 'Letters and the Social Grounding of Differentiated Genres'. In Barton, D., and Hall, N. (eds), *Letter Writing as a Social Practice*. Amsterdam: John Benjamin, 15–30.

Berman, Marshall. 1983. *All That is Solid Melts into Air: The Experience of Modernity*. London: Verso.

Benach, Joan. 2021. 'We Must Take Advantage of This Pandemic to Make a Radical Social Change: The Coronavirus as a Global Health, Inequality, and Eco-Social Problem'. *International Journal of Health Services*, 51:1, 50–54.

Bennett, Jane. 2001. *The Enchantment of Modern Life: Attachments, Crossings, and Ethics*. Princeton, NJ: Princeton University Press.

Berg, Freja Sørine Adler. 2021. 'Independent Podcasts on the Apple Podcast Platform in the Streaming Era'. *MedieKultur: Journal of Media and Communication Research*, 37:70, 110–130.

Bergefurt, Lisanne, Kemperman, Astrid, van den Berg, Pauline, Borgers, Aloys, van der Waerden, Peter, Oosterhuis, Gert, and Hommel, Marco. 2019. 'Loneliness and Life Satisfaction Explained by Public-Space Use and Mobility Patterns'. *International Journal of Environmental Research and Public Health*, 16:21, 1–20.

Berlant, Lauren. 2011. *Cruel Optimism*. Durham, NC: Duke University Press.

Berman, Marshall. 1983. *All that is Solid Melts into Air: The Experience of Modernity*. New York: Verso.

Berriman, Liam, and Thomson, Rachel. 2015. 'Spectacles of Intimacy? Mapping the Moral Landscape of Teenage Social Media'. *Journal of Youth Studies*, 18:5, 583–597.

Björk, Jonas, Albin, Maria, Grahn, Patrik, Jacobsson, Hanna, Ardö, Jonas, Wadbro, Per-Olof, Östergren, John, and Skärbäck, Erik. 2008. 'Recreational Values of the Natural Environment in Relation to Neighbourhood Satisfaction, Physical Activity, Obesity and Wellbeing'. *Journal of Epidemiology & Community Health*, 62:4, e2.

Birkerts, Sven. 1994. *The Gutenberg Elegies*. Boston: Faber.

Bloom, Lynn Z. 1996. '"I Write for Myself and Strangers": Private Diaries as Public Documents'. In Suzanne Bunkers and Thia Huff (eds), *Inscribing the Daily: Critical Essays on Women's Diaries*. Amherst: University of Massachusetts, 23–37.

Boundless Artists Collective. 2020. *Contactless*. www.boundlessart.com/liveshowroom (accessed 6 March 2023).

Brandt, Ros, Duffy, Michelle, and MacKinnon, Dolly (eds). 2009. *Hearing Places: Sound, Place, Time and Culture*. Cambridge: Cambridge Scholars.

Bratman, Gregory N., Anderson, Christopher B., Berman, Marc G., Cochran, Bobby, De Vries, Sjerp, Flanders, Jon, Folke, Carl, et al. 2019. 'Nature and Mental Health: An Ecosystem Service Perspective'. *Science Advances*, 5:7. www.science.org/doi/full/10.1126/sciadv.aax0903 (accessed 20 February 2020).

Brown, Jeffrey. 2021. 'A City without a Hero: Joker and Rethinking Hegemony'. *New Review of Film and Television Studies*, 19:1, 7–18.

Brown, Steven Caldwell, and Knox, Don. 2017. 'Why go to Pop Concerts? The Motivations Behind Live Music Attendance'. *Musicae Scientiae*, 21:3, 233–249.

Bruno, Giuliana. 1987. 'Ramble City: Postmodernism and *Blade Runner*'. *October*, 41, 61–74.

Buckingham, David. 2007. *Youth, Identity, and Digital Media*. Cambridge, MA: MIT Press.

Bull, Michael. 2001. 'Soundscapes of the Car: A Critical Ethnography of Automobile Habitation'. In Daniel Miller (ed.), *Car Cultures*. Oxford: Berg, 185–202.

Bullock, Janis R. 1998. *Loneliness in Young Children*. ERIC Clearinghouse on Elementary and Early Childhood Education, University of Illinois. www.vtaide.com/png/ERIC/Loneliness.htm (accessed 5 March 2023).

Cacioppo, John T., and Cacioppo, Stephanie. 2018. 'The Growing Problem of Loneliness'. *The Lancet*, 391:10119, 426.

Campbell, Samantha. 2020. 'Yarn Bombing Continues Across City and into People's Yards'. *North West Star*. 17 April. www.northweststar.com.au/story/6724566/yarn-bombing-continues-across-mount-isa-city-and-into-peoples-yards/ (accessed 5 March 2023).

Cassidy, Jude, and Asher, Steven R. 1992. 'Loneliness and Peer Relations in Young Children'. *Child Development*, 63:2, 350–365.

Cave, Nick. 2023. *The Red Hand Files*. www.theredhandfiles.com/ (accessed 30 April 2023).

Charles, Ashleigh, and Felton, Anne. 2020. 'Exploring Young People's Experiences and Perceptions of Mental Health and Well-being Using Photography'. *Child and Adolescent Mental Health*, 25:1, 13–20.

Chittenden, Tara. 2013. 'In My Rear-view Mirror: Female Teens' Prospective Remembering of Future Romantic Relationships through the Lyrics in Taylor Swift Songs'. *Journal of Children and Media*, 7:2, 186–200.

Coldwell, Michael C. 2022. *The Disappearing City (2014–2019)*. www.michaelcoldwell.co.uk/disappearingcity.html (accessed 11 January 2022).

Connell, John, and Gibson, Chris. 2003. *Sound Tracks: Popular Music Identity and Place*. London: Routledge.

Copeland, Stacey. 2018. 'A Feminist Materialisation of Amplified Voice: Queering Identity and Affect in *The Heart*'. In D. Llinares, N. Fox, and R. Berry (eds), *Podcasting: New Aural Cultures and Digital Media*. Basingstoke: Palgrave Macmillan, 209–226.

Cropley, Arthur, J. 1990. 'Creativity and Mental Health in Everyday Life'. *Creativity Research Journal*, 13:3, 167–178.

Cunningham, Russell. 2018. 'Nick Cave is Showing Us a New, Gentler Way to Use the Internet'. *The Guardian, International Edition*. 27 November. www.theguardian.com/commentisfree/2018/nov/27/nick-cave-red-hand-files (accessed 5 March 2023).

Curtis, Meagan E., and Bharucha, Jamshed J. 2010. 'The Minor Third Communicates Sadness in Speech, Mirroring its use in Music'. *Emotion*, 10:3, 335–348.

Cvetkovich, Ann. 2012. *Depression: A Public Feeling*. Durham, NC: Duke University Press.

D'Aloia, Adriano. 2009. 'Cinematic Enwaterment: Drowning Bodies in the Contemporary Film Experience'. Emergent Encounters in Film Theory: Intersections between Psychoanalysis and Philosophy. Kings College, London, 21 March 2009.

Dawson, Jane. 2003. 'Reflectivity, Creativity, and the Space for Silence'. *Reflective Practice*, 4:1, 33–39.

Davidson, Susan, and Rossall, Phil. 2015. 'Age UK Loneliness Evidence Review'. www.ageuk.org.uk/globalassets/age-uk/documents/reports-and-publications/reports-and-briefings/health--wellbeing/rb_june15_loneliness_in_later_life_evidence_review.pdf (accessed 5 April 2021).

de Certeau, Michel. 1985. '*Practices of Space*'. In M. Blonksy (ed.), *On Signs*. Baltimore, MD: Johns Hopkins University Press, 122–145.

de Jong Gierveld, Jenny. 1998. 'A Review of Loneliness: Concept and Definitions, Determinants and Consequences'. *Reviews in Clinical Gerontology*, 8:1, 73–80.

Deleuze, Gilles. 1983. *Cinema 1: The Movement-Image*. London: Athlone.

Deleuze, Gilles. 2003. *Francis Bacon: The Logic of Sensation*. Minneapolis: University of Minnesota Press.

Dennis, Richard. 2008. *Cities in Modernity: Representations and Productions of Metropolitan Space, 1840–1930*. Cambridge: Cambridge University Press.

Di Piero, W. S. 2010. 'On Edvard Munch'. *The Yale Review*, 98:1, 58–64.

Diekema, David A. 1992. 'Aloneness and Social Form'. *Symbolic Interaction*, 15:4, 481–500.

Doane, Mary Ann. 2004. 'Pathos and Pathology: The Cinema of Todd Haynes'. *Camera Obscura*, 19:3, 1–21.

Doogan, Kevin. 2009. *New Capitalism?* New York: Polity.

Dyer, Richard. 1981. 'Entertainment and Utopia'. In R. Altman (ed.), *Genre: The Musical*. London: Routledge, 175–189.

Eakin, Paul. 1985. *Fictions in Autobiography: Studies in the Art of Self-invention*. Princeton, NJ: Princeton University Press.

Edwards, Elizabeth. 2009. 'Thinking Photography Beyond the Visual?'. In J. J. Long, A. Noble, and E. Welch (eds), *Photography: Theoretical Snapshots*. London: Routledge, 31–48.

Elan, Maika. 2015. *Inside Hanoi*. http://maikaelan.com/photos/inside-hanoi.html (accessed 19 October 2019).

Elan, Maika. 2017. 'It Felt Safe Here'. *Witness*. 21 December. https://witness.world pressphoto.org/it-felt-safe-here-adcb41725fc2 (accessed 19 October 2019).

Emin, Tracey. 2008. 'Her Soft Lips Touched Mine and Every Thing became Hard'. www.mutualart.com/Artwork/Her-soft-lips-touched-mine-and-every-thi/5B877 E98F1832FA9 (accessed 10 June 2020).

Fancourt, Daisy. 2021. 'We Asked 70,000 People how Coronavirus Affected Them – What they Told us Revealed a Lot about Inequality in the UK'. *The Conversation*. 17 February. https://theconversation.com/we-asked-70-000-people-how-coronavirus-affected-them-what-they-told-us-revealed-a-lot-about-inequality-in-the-uk-143718 (accessed 6 April 2021).

Felperin, Leslie. 2005. '*The 3 Rooms of Melancholia*'. *Sight and Sound*, September. http://old.bfi.org.uk/sightandsound/feature/439 (accessed 15 February 2020).

Ferriss, Suzanne. 2008. 'Fashioning Femininity in the Makeover Flick'. In Suzanne Ferriss and Mallory Young (eds), *Chick Flicks: Contemporary Women at the Movies*. London: Routledge, 41–57.

Fisher, Mark. 2012. 'What is Hauntology?'. *Film Quarterly*, 66:1, 16–24.

Foucault, Michel. 1990. *The History of Sexuality, vol. 1: An Introduction* (trans. R. Hurley). New York: Vintage.

Foucault, Michel. 1994. *Ethics: Subjectivity and Truth* (trans. R. Hurley). New York: New Press.

French, Lisa. 2021. 'The "Female Gaze".' In *The Female Gaze in Documentary Film*. London: Palgrave Macmillan, 53–70.

Friedberg, Mark. 2019. *Vision and Fury*. *Joker*. Blue-Ray Extras. Warner Brothers. www.blu-ray.com/movies/Joker-Blu-ray/254136/ (accessed 5 March 2023).

Frith, Simon. 1996. 'Music and Identity'. In S. Hall and P. Du Gay (eds), *Questions of Cultural Identity*. Thousand Oaks, CA: Sage, 108–128.

Furedi, Frank. 2003. 'Get Off That Couch'. *The Guardian Online*. 6 October. www.theguardian.com/books/2003/oct/09/health.mentalhealth (accessed 20 November 2019).

Garcia, Sandra E. 2020. 'How to Stay Creative while Stuck at Home'. *New York Times*. 4 April. www.nytimes.com/2020/04/23/arts/coronavirus-creatives-artists-musicians-photographers.html (accessed 6 April 2020). (Subscription required.)

Garrison, John, and Krejcarek, Philip. 2017. 'Gregory Crewdson's Twilight: Domesticity, Liminality, Sensuality.' *Photography and Culture*, 10:3, 233–246.

Gill, Jo. 2013. *The Poetics of the American Suburbs*. New York: Palgrave MacMillan.

Giroux, Henry A. 2002. 'Teen Girls' Resistance and the Disappearing Social in *Ghost World*'. *The Review of Education, Pedagogy & Cultural Studies*, 24:4, 283–304.

Glesene, Corrine. 1997. 'That Rare Feeling: Re-presenting Research through Poetic Transcription'. *Qualitative Inquiry*, 3:2, 202–221.

Goffman, Erving. 1959. *The Presentation of Self in Everyday Life*. New York: Doubleday.

Goodden, Nico. 2020. *Capturing the Beauty of Urban Solitude*. www.nicholasgooddenphotography.co.uk/london-blog/solitude-urban-street-photo (accessed 10 November 2021).

Gould, Madelyn S. 2001. 'Suicide and the Media'. *Annals of the New York Academy of Sciences*, 932:1, 200–224.

Gotesky, Rubin. 1965. 'Aloneness, Loneliness, Isolation, Solitude'. In J. Edie (ed.), *An Invitation to Phenomenology*. Chicago, IL: Quadrangle, 221–239.

Grainge, Paul. 2000. 'Nostalgia and Style in Retro America: Moods, Modes and Media Recycling'. *Journal of American and Comparative Cultures*, 23:1, 27–34.

Grannan, Katy. 2014. *The 99 Series*. https://fraenkelgallery.com/exhibitions/katy-grannan-the-99 (accessed 10 November 2021).

Grierson, John. 1946. *Grierson on Documentary*. London: Collins.

Grosz, Elizabeth. 1998. 'Bodies – Cities'. In H. Nast and S. Pile (eds), *Places Through the Body*. London: Routledge, 42–51.

Habermas, Jurgen. 1991. *The Structural Transformation of the Public Sphere: An Inquiry into a Category of Bourgeois Society*. Cambridge, MA: MIT Press.

Hall, Kimberly. 2016. 'Selfies and Self-writing: Cue Card Confessions as Social Media Technologies of the Self'. *Television & New Media*, 17:3, 228–242.

Hannell, Briony. 2019. 'Celebrity, Aspiration and Contemporary Youth: Education and Inequality in an Era of Austerity'. *Celebrity Studies*, 10:2, 309–311.

Hawker, Rosemary. 2013. 'Repopulating the Street: Contemporary Photography and Urban Experience'. *History of Photography*, 37:3, 341–352.

Hawthorn, Andrew. 2020. 'Lifting Spirits with Yarn-bombing: How Coronavirus Inspired a Twillingate Facelift'. *CBC*. 17 May. www.cbc.ca/news/canada/newfoundland-labrador/twillingate-yarn-art-elliott-1.5563026 (accessed 3 June 2020).

Hearn, Alison, and Schoenhoff, Stephanie. 2016. 'From Celebrity to Influencer: Tracing the Diffusion of Celebrity Value Across the Data Stream'. In P. David Marshall and S. Redmond (eds), *A Companion to Celebrity*. Chichester: John Wiley & Sons, 194–212.

Hermes, Joke. 1995. *Reading Women's Magazines. An Analysis of Everyday Media Use*. Cambridge: Polity.

Hesmondhalgh, David. 2008. Towards a Critical Understanding of Music, Emotion and Self-Identity. *Consumption, Markets and Culture*, 11:4, 329–343.

Hoffner, Cynthia, and Cohen, Elizabeth. 2018. 'Mental Health-related Outcomes of Robin Williams' Death: The Role of Parasocial Relations and Media Exposure in Stigma, Help-seeking, and Outreach'. *Health Communication*, 33:12, 1573–1582.

Holbrook, Morris B., and Schindler, Robert M. 2003. 'Nostalgic Bonding: Exploring the Role of Nostalgia in the Consumption Experience'. *Journal of Consumer Behaviour: An International Research Review*, 3:2, 107–127.

Holmes, Su. 2006. 'When Will I Be Famous? Reappraising the Debate About Fame in Reality TV'. In David S. Escoffery (ed.), *How Real Is Reality TV: Essays on Representation and Truth*. Jefferson, NC: McFarland, 7–25.

Hsieh, Ning, and Hawkley, Louise. 2018. 'Loneliness in the Older Adult Marriage: Associations with Dyadic Aversion, Indifference, and Ambivalence'. *Journal of Social and Personal Relationships*, 35:10, 1319–1339.

Hubbard, Phil. 2003. 'A Good Night Out? Multiplex Cinemas as Sites of Embodied Leisure'. *Leisure Studies*, 22, 255–272.

Hunt, Mia. 2014. 'Urban Photography/Cultural Geography: Spaces, Objects, Events'. *Geography Compass*, 8:3, 151–168.

Huron, David. 2011. 'Why is Sad Music Pleasurable? A Possible Role for Prolactin'. *Musicae Scientiae*, 15:2, 146–158.

Icarus Films. nd. 'The 3 Rooms of Melancholia'. https://icarusfilms.com/if-3r (accessed 26 February 2023).

Imada, Adria L. 2018. 'Lonely Together: Subaltern Family Albums and Kinship During Medical Incarceration'. *Photography and Culture*, 11:3, 297–321.

James, Peter, Banay, Rachel F., Hart, Jaime E., and Laden, Francine. 2015. 'A Review of the Health Benefits of Greenness'. *Current Epidemiology Reports*, 2:2, 131–142.

Jamison, Leslie, and Litovsky, Dina. 2021. 'Dark City: Manhattan Last Spring'. *VQR: A National Journal of Literature and Discussion*. Spring. www.vqronline.org/photography/2021/03/dark-city (accessed 19 September 2021).

Jeffery, Marco Holden. 2020. 'Street Art Unites in Time of Isolation'. *Southbank News*. 9 June. www.southbanklocalnews.com.au/editions/article/street-art-unites-in-time-of-isolation_9713/ (accessed 5 March 2021).

Jerrems, Carol. 1975. *Vale Street*. www.artgallery.nsw.gov.au/collection/works/46.1979/ (accessed 16 September 2023).

Jordan, Glenn. 1995. 'Flight from Modernity: Time, the Other and the Discourse of Primitivism'. *Time & Society*, 4:3, 281–303.

Juhasz, Alexandra, and Lebow, Alisa (eds). 2015. *A Companion to Contemporary Documentary Film*. New York: Wiley-Blackwell.

Juslin, Patrick, N., and Laukka, Petri. 2004. 'Expression, Perception, and Induction of Musical Emotions: A Review and a Questionnaire Study of Everyday Listening'. *Journal of New Music Research*, 33:3, 217–238.

Kehily, Mary Jane. 1995. 'Self-narration, Autobiography and Identity Construction'. *Gender and Education*, 7:1, 23–32.

Kelsey-Sugg, Anna. 2020. 'We're Turning to Music Amid the Coronavirus Crisis – and that's a Little Bit of History Repeating'. *ABC News*. 29 April. www.abc.net.au/news/2020-04-29/coronavirus-history-music-helps-in-times-of-crisis/12175952 (accessed 5 May 2021).

Kerins, Mark. 2021. 'Hearing Reality in *Joker*'. *New Review of Film and Television Studies*, 19:1, 89–100.

Kleinman, Arthur, Das, Veena, and Lock, Margaret, M. (eds). 1997. *Social Suffering*. Berkeley: University of California Press.

Klinenberg, Eric. 2013. *Going Solo: The Extraordinary Rise and Surprising Appeal of Living Alone*. New York: Penguin.
Knibbs, Kate. 2022. 'The Rise of Sad Voice Sci-Fi'. *Wired*. 13 April. www.wired.com/story/rise-of-sad-voice-sci-fi/ (accessed 15 April 2022).
Kolker, Robert. 2011. *A Cinema of Loneliness*. Oxford: Oxford University Press.
Koutsourakis, Angelos. 2012. 'Cinema of the Body: The Politics of Performativity in Lars Von Trier's *Dogville* and Yorgos Lanthimos' *Dogtooth*'. *Cinema: Journal of Philosophy and the Moving Image*, 3, 84–108.
Kunst, Maarten J. J., and van Bon-Martens, Marja J. H. 2011. 'Examining the Link Between Domestic Violence Victimization and Loneliness in a Dutch Community Sample: A Comparison Between Victims and Nonvictims by Type D Personality'. *Journal of Family Violence*, 26:5, 403–410.
LaBelle, Brandon. 2010. *Acoustic Territories: Sound Culture and Everyday Life*. New York: Continuum.
Laing, Olivia. 2016. *The Lonely City: Adventures in the Art of Being Alone*. Edinburgh: Canongate.
Laurie, Timothy, and Stark, Hannah. 2021 'The End of Intimate Politics in Yorgos Lanthimos' *The Lobster*'. *New Review of Film and Television Studies*, 19:2, 200–216.
Leach, Jim, and Grant, Barry, K. 1998. *Documenting the Documentary: Close Readings of Documentary Film and Video*. Detroit, MI: Wayne State University Press.
Lehtonen, Kimmo. 2001. 'Some Ideas About Music Therapy for the Elderly'. *Voices: A World Forum for Music Therapy*. https://voices.no/index.php/voices/article/view/1600/1359 (accessed 3 September 2020).
Levinson, Jerrold. 1997. *Music in the Moment*. Ithaca, NY: Cornell University Press.
Lewallen, Jennifer, and Behm-Morawitz, Elizabeth. 2016. 'Pinterest or Thinterest?: Social Comparison and Body Image on Social Media'. *Social Media + Society*, 2:1, 1–9.
Lewis, Lisa A. 2002. *The Adoring Audience: Fan Culture and Popular Media*. London: Routledge.
Lieberman, Alicea, Schroeder, Juliana, and Amir, On. 2022. 'A Voice Inside My Head: The Psychological and Behavioral Consequences of Auditory Technologies'. *Organizational Behavior and Human Decision Processes*, 170, 104–133.
Lilja, Mona. 2018. 'The Politics of Time and Temporality in Foucault's Theorisation of Resistance: Ruptures, Time-lags and Decelerations'. *Journal of Political Power*, 11:3, 419–432.
Lim, Michelle. 2018. 'Australian Loneliness Report: A Survey Exploring the Loneliness Levels of Australians and the Impact on their Health and Wellbeing'. http://hdl.handle.net/1959.3/446718 (accessed 12 September 2023).
Lim, Song Hwee. 2014. *Tsai Ming-liang and a Cinema of Slowness*. Hawaii: University of Hawaii Press.
Liu, Chen. 2021. 'Rethinking the Timescape of Home: Domestic Practices in Time and Space'. *Progress in Human Geography*, 45:2, 343–361.
Live Music Now. 2020. 'LMN North East Musicians are 'Singing in the Rain' at Leeds Recovery Hub'. 30 April. www.livemusicnow.org.uk/lmn-news/title/LMN-North-East-musicians-are-Singing-in-the-rain-at-Leeds-Recovery-Hub/item/69805 (accessed 3 June 2020).

Lorenzon, Matthew. 2020. 'Musicians in Italy Perform on Balconies during Quarantine'. *ABC Classic*. 18 March. www.abc.net.au/classic/read-and-watch/news/musicians-in-italy-perform-on-balconies-during-lockdown/12066476 (accessed 5 June 2020).

Lovink, Geert. 2017. *Social Media Abyss: Critical Internet Cultures and the Force of Negation*. Cambridge: Polity Press.

Luchetti, Martina, Lee, Ji Hyun, Aschwanden, Damaris, Sesker, Amanda, Strickhouser, Jason E., Terracciano, Antonio, and Sutin, Angelina R. 2020. 'The Trajectory of Loneliness in Response to COVID-19'. *American Psychologist*, 75:7, 897–908.

Luckett, Moya. 2010. 'Toxic: The Implosion of Britney Spears's Star Image'. *The Velvet Light Trap*, 65, 39–41.

Macdonald, Myr. 2003. *Exploring Media Discourse*. London: Arnold.

Marcus, Lars. 2010. 'Spatial Capital'. *The Journal of Space Syntax*, 1:1, 30–40.

Markman, Kriss. 2012. 'Doing Radio, Making Friends, and Having Fun: Exploring the Motivations of Independent Audio Podcasters'. *New Media & Society*, 14:4, 547–565.

McCredden, Lyn. 2009. 'Fleshed Sacred: The Carnal Theologies of Nick Cave'. In Karen Welberry and Tanya Dalziel (eds), *Cultural Seeds: Essays on the Work of Nick Cave*. Farnham: Ashgate, 167–185.

McGraw, John G. 1992. 'God and the Problem of Loneliness'. *Religious Studies*, 28:3, 319–346.

McGregor, Jon. 2002. *If Nobody Speaks of Remarkable Things*. London: Bloomsbury.

Mendick, Heather, Allen, Kim, and Harvey, Laura. 2015. '"We Can Get Everything We Want if We Try Hard": Young People, Celebrity, Hard Work'. *British Journal of Educational Studies*, 63:2, 161–178.

Metz, Christian. 1982. *The Imaginary Signifier: Psychoanalysis and the Cinema*. Bloomington: Indiana University Press.

Meyers, Erin. 2009. '"Can you Handle my Truth?": Authenticity and the Celebrity Star Image'. *Journal of Popular Culture*, 42:5, 890–907.

Michels-Ratliff, Emelia, and Ennis, Michael. 2016. 'This is your Song: Using Participants' Music Selections to Evoke Nostalgia and Autobiographical Memories Efficiently'. *Psychomusicology: Music, Mind, and Brain*, 26:4, 379–384.

Mijuskovic, Ben Lazare. 2012 *Loneliness in Philosophy, Psychology, and Literature*. 3rd edn. Bloomington, IN: iUniverse.

Miller, Evonne, Donoghue, Geraldine, and Holland-Batt, Sarah. 2015. '"You Could Scream the Place Down": Five Poems on the Experience of Aged Care'. *Qualitative Inquiry*, 21:5, 410–417.

Miller, Susan. 2013. *Disgust: The Gatekeeper Emotion*. London: Routledge.

Mills, Sara. 1997. *Discourse*. London: Routledge.

Misoch, Sabina. 2014. 'Card Stories on YouTube: A New Frame for Online Self-Disclosure'. *Media and Communication*, 2:1, 2–12.

Monbiot, George. 2014 'The Age of Loneliness is Killing us.' *The Guardian*. 15 October. www.theguardian.com/commentisfree/2014/oct/14/age-of-loneliness-killing-us (accessed 9 March 2020).

Montgomery, Robert. 2013. Light Poem Series. www.robertmontgomery.org/recycledsunlightpoems (accessed 10 June 2020).

Mousavi, Seyyedeh Fatemeh, and Dehshiri, Gholamreza. 2021. 'The Predictors of Loneliness in Adolescents: The Role of Gender, Parenting Rearing Behaviors, Friendship Quality, and Shyness'. *Journal of Woman and Family Studies*, 9:4, 1–20.

Moustakas, Clark. 1961. *Loneliness*. New York: Prentiss Hall.

Myzelev, Alla. 2015. 'Creating Digital Materiality: Third-Wave Feminism, Public Art, and Yarn Bombing'. *Material Culture*, 47 (Spring), 58–78.

Nassif-Pires, Luiza, de Lima Xavier, Laura, Masterson, Thomas, Nikiforos, Michalis, and Rios-Avila, Fernando. 2021. 'Pandemic of Inequality: Crisis at the Intersection.' Working Paper. https://archive-ouverte.unige.ch/unige:147177 (accessed 29 July2021).

News Channel 10. 2020. 'Yarn Bomber' Shares Message of Hope during COVID-19 Crisis'. 6 May. www.newschannel10.com/2020/05/06/yarn-bomber-shares-message-hope-during-covid-crisis/ (accessed 22 March 2021).

Nichols, Bill. 2017. *Introduction to Documentary*. Bloomington: Indiana University Press.

Nixon, Rob. 2011. *Slow Violence and the Environmentalism of the Poor*. Boston, MA: Harvard University Press.

Nuttal, Mark. 1997. 'Packaging the Wild: Tourism Development in Alaska'. In Simone Abram, Jacqueline Waldren, and Donald MacLeod (eds), *Tourists and Tourism: Identifying with People and Places*. Oxford: Berg, 223–238.

O'Connor, Kay. 1996. 'Glossary of Validities'. *Journal of Contemporary Ethnography*, 25:1, 16–21.

O'Day, Emily B., and Heimberg, Richard G. 2021. 'Social Media Use, Social Anxiety, and Loneliness: A Systematic Review'. *Computers in Human Behavior Reports*, 3. www.sciencedirect.com/science/article/pii/S245195882100018X (accessed 10 January 2022).

Oliver, Mary Beth. 2008. 'Tender Affective States as Predictors of Entertainment Preference'. *Journal of Communication*, 58, 40–61.

Orgeron, Marsha. 2003. '"Making It" in Hollywood: Clara Bow, Fandom, and Consumer Culture'. *Cinema Journal*, 42:4, 76–97.

Orgeron, Marsha. 2009. '"You Are Invited to Participate": Interactive Fandom in the Age of the Movie Magazine'. *Journal of Film and Video*, 61:3, 3–23.

O'Toole, Isabelle. 2019. 'Sleeping by the Mississippi'. *The Independent Photographer*. https://independent-photo.com/news/alec-soth-sleeping-by-the-mississippi/ (accessed 12 May 2020).

Palmgreen, Philip, Cook, Patsy L., Harvill, Jerry G., and Helm, David M. 1988. 'The Motivational Framework of Moviegoing; Uses and Avoidances of Theatrical Films'. In B. A. Austin (ed.), *Current Research in Film: Audiences, Economics, and Law*. Norwood, NJ: Ablex, 1–23.

Papinczak, Zoe E., Dingle, Genevieve A., Stoyanov, Stoyan R., Hides, Leanne, and Zelenko, Oksana. 2015. 'Young People's Uses of Music for Well-being'. *Journal of Youth Studies*, 18:9, 1119–1134. www.southwalesargus.co.uk/news/18888939.lost-connections-share-coronavirus-inspired-art/ (accessed 5 December 2020).

Phillips, Todd. 2019. *Joker: Vision and Fury*. Blue-Ray Extras. Warner Brothers. www.blu-ray.com/movies/Joker-Blu-ray/254136/ (accessed 5 March 2023).

Pickering, Michael, and Keightley, Emily. 2006. 'The Modalities of Nostalgia'. *Current Sociology*, 54:6, 919–941.

Pilgrim, Leanne, Norris, Ian J., and Hackathorn, Jana. 2017. 'Music is Awesome: Influences of Emotion, Personality, and Preference on Experienced Awe'. *Journal of Consumer Behaviour*, 16:5, 442–451.

Pink, Sarah. 2004. *Home Truths: Gender, Domestic Objects and Everyday Life*. Berg: Oxford.

Pinkerton, Nick. 2012. 'Alps: The Full Range'. *Village Voice*. www.villagevoice.com/2012/07/11/alps-the-full-range/ (accessed 22 March 2020).

Pistrick, Eckehard, and Isnart, Cyril. 2013. 'Landscapes, Soundscapes, Mindscapes: Introduction'. *Etnográfica. Revista do Centro em Rede de Investigação em Antropologia*, 17:3, 503–513.

Plath, Sylvia. 1965. *Ariel*. London: Faber and Faber.

Plath, Sylvia. 1972. *The Bell Jar*. London: Faber and Faber.

Powell, Leah. 2020. 'Lost Connections: How to Share Coronavirus Inspired Art'. *South Wales Argus*. 22 November. www.southwalesargus.co.uk/news/18888939.lost-connections-share-coronavirus-inspired-art/ (accessed 23 August 2023).

Polaschek, Bronwyn. 2018. 'The Dissonant Personas of a Female Celebrity: *Amy* and the Public Self of Amy Winehouse'. *Celebrity Studies*, 9:1, 17–33.

Qualter, Pamela. 2018. *The BBC Loneliness Experiment*. www.seed.manchester.ac.uk/education/research/impact/bbc-loneliness-experiment/ (accessed 12 January 2020).

Quinto, Lena, Thompson, William Forde, and Keating, Felicity Louise. 2013. 'Emotional Communication in Speech and Music: The Role of Melodic and Rhythmic Contrasts'. *Frontiers in Psychology*, 4. www.frontiersin.org/articles/10.3389/fpsyg.2013.00184/full (accessed 5 March 2023).

Ratto, Matt, and Boler, Megan. 2014. *DIY Citizenship: Critical Making and Social Media*. Cambridge, MA: MIT Press.

Redmond, Sean. 2008. 'Pieces of Me: Celebrity Confessional Carnality'. *Social Semiotics*, 18:2, 149–161.

Redmond, Sean. 2013. *Celebrity and the Media*. London: Palgrave.

Reiffenrath, Tanja. 2015. 'Re-writing Cure: Autobiography as Therapy and Discursive Practice'. In Kerstin W. Shands, Giulia Grillo Mikrut, Dipti R. Pattanaik, and Karen Ferreira-Meyers (eds), *Writing the Self: Essays on Autobiography and Autofiction*, English Studies 5. Huddinge, Sweden: Södertörns högskola, 359–368.

Ribbat, Christoph. 2013. *Flickering Light: A History of Neon*. London: Reaktion Books.

r/lonely. 2023. Reddit. www.reddit.com/r/lonely/ (accessed 30 April 2023).

Roe, Annabelle Honess, and Pramaggiore, Maria (eds). 2019. *Vocal Projections: Voices in Documentary*. New York: Bloomsbury Academic.

Rokach, Ami. 2012. 'Loneliness Updated: An Introduction'. *Journal of Psychology*, 146:1–2, 1–6.

Ross, Jenna. 2021. 'Minnesotans Discover that Art can Offer a Cure for Loneliness in the Pandemic'. *StarTribune*. 15 January. www.startribune.com/minnesotans-discover-that-art-can-offer-a-cure-for-loneliness-in-the-pandemic/600011126/?refresh=true (accessed 10 March 2021).

Rotenberg, Ken J., and MacKie, Jennifer. 1999. 'Stigmatization of Social and Intimacy Loneliness'. *Psychological Reports*, 84:1, 147–148.

Salinger, J. D. 1969 (1951). *The Catcher in the Rye*. London: Penguin.

Saltmarsh, Matthew. 2020. 'UK Art Therapy Group Moves Online to Support Refugees in Lockdown'. UNHCR.UK. www.unhcr.org/uk/news/stories/2020/4/5e98652f4/uk-art-therapy-group-moves-online-to-support-refugees-in-lockdown.html (accessed 5 April 2021).

Sauter, Theresa. 2014. '"What's on your Mind?" Writing on Facebook as a Tool for Self-Formation'. *New Media & Society*, 16:5, 823–839.

Schäfer, Katharina, Suvi, Saarikallio, and Tuomas, Eerola. 2020. 'Music May Reduce Loneliness and Act as Social Surrogate for a Friend: Evidence from an Experimental Listening Study'. *Music & Science*, 3, 1–16.

Schwartz, Joan, and Ryan, James. 2003. *Picturing Place: Photography and the Geographical Imagination*. London: Routledge.

Sconce, Jeffrey. 1995. '"Trashing" the Academy: Taste, Excess, and an Emerging Politics of Cinematic Style'. *Screen*, 36:4, 371–393.

Sedikides, Constantine, Wildschut, Tim, Arndt, Jamie, and Routledge, Clay. 2008. 'Nostalgia: Past, Present, and Future'. *Current Directions in Psychological Science*, 17, 304–307.

Seller, Merlin. 2021. 'Repeated Failure: Time, Dressage and Thingness in *Joker*'. *New Review of Film and Television Studies*, 19:1, 41–53.

Shaw, R. J., Cullen, B., Graham, N., Mackay, D., Ward, J., Pearsall, R., and Smith, D. J. 2018. 'Loneliness, Living Arrangements and Emotional support as Predictors of Suicidality: A 7-year follow-up of the UK Biobank Bohort'. *Journal of Epidemiology and Community Health*, A30–A31.

Shields, Meg. 2018. 'Four Essential Films About Solitude'. *Nonfics*. https://nonfics.com/essential-films-about-solitude-cfa538dacecf/ (accessed 5 March 2023).

Simmel, Georg. 1950. 'The Stranger'. In K. H. Wolff (trans. and ed.), *The Sociology of George Simmel*. New York: Free Press.

Simpson, Veronica. 2020. 'Mark Titchner – Interview: "Language is How we Relate to the World, There's No Separation"'. *Studio International*. 6 May. www.studiointernational.com/index.php/mark-titchner-interview-please-believe-these-days-will-pass-language-is-how-we-relate-to-the-world (accessed 19 September 2020).

Smith, Douglas, Leonis, Trinity, and Anandavalli, S. 2021. 'Belonging and Loneliness in Cyberspace: Impacts of Social Media on Adolescents' Well-being'. *Australian Journal of Psychology*, 73:1, 12–23.

Smith, Jennifer L., Thomas, Virginia, and Azmitia, Margarita. 2022. 'Happy Alone? Motivational Profiles of Solitude and Well-Being Among Senior Living Residents'. *International Journal of Aging and Human Development*, 1–23.

Sobchack, Vivian. 2000. 'What my Fingers Knew: The Cinesthetic Subject, or Vision in the Flesh'. *Senses of Cinema*, 5:4. www.sensesofcinema.com/2000/conference-special-effects-special-affects/fingers/ (accessed 10 January 2020).

Soloway-Chan, Louise. 2020. *Contactless*. Boundless Art Exhibition. www.boundlessart.com/liveshowroom (accessed 4 February 2021).

Sorapure, Madeleine. 2003. 'Screening Moments, Scrolling Lives: Diary Writing on the Web'. *Biography*, 26:1, 1–23.

Sperb, Jason. 2004. 'Ghost without a Machine: Enid's Anxiety of Depth (Lessness) in Terry Zwigoff's *Ghost World*'. *Quarterly Review of Film and Video*, 21:3, 209–217.

Stack, Steven. 1998. 'Marriage, Family and Loneliness: A Cross-national Study'. *Sociological Perspectives*, 41:2, 415–432.

Stanley, Liz. 1993. 'On Auto/biography in Sociology'. *Sociology*, 27:1, 41–52.

Star Trek: The Next Generation. 1991. 'Data's Day'. Season 4, Episode 11.

Stever, Gayle, S. 2009. 'Parasocial and Social Interaction with Celebrities: Classification of Media Fans'. *Journal of Media Psychology*, 14:3, 1–39.

Sturm, Sean. 1995. 'Marc Augé Interviewed: "Places and Non-Places – A Conversation with Marc Augé"'. *Broken Vessel*. https://seansturm.wordpress.com/2009/07/09/marc-auge-interviewed-places-and-non-places%E2%80%94a-conversation-with-marc-auge/ (accessed 10 September 2019).

Svendsen, Lars. 2017. *A Philosophy of Loneliness*. London: Reaktion.

Taylor, Chloë. 2010. *The Culture of Confession from Augustine to Foucault: A Genealogy of the 'Confessing Animal'*. London: Routledge.

Taylor, KT. 2021. *Not Alone, Never was Penpal Zine 4 Rural Queers*. Self-published. https://documentcloud.adobe.com/link/track?uri=urn:aaid:scds:US:2a33d6f7-9be3-4923-877a-7320b77bc135 (accessed 4 November 2021).

Taylor, Matthew. 2012. 'Not with a Bang but a Whimper: Muen Shakai and Its Implications'. *Anthropoetics* 28:1 (Fall). http://anthropoetics.ucla.edu/ap1801/1801taylor/ (accessed 12 September 2023).

Tefertiller, Alec C., Maxwell, Lindsey Conlin, and Morris, David L. 2020. 'Social Media goes to the Movies: Fear of Missing Out, Social Capital, and Social Motivations of Cinema Attendance'. *Mass Communication and Society*, 23:3, 378–399.

Thompson, Kirsten Moana. 2012. *Apocalyptic Dread: American Film at the Turn of the Millennium*. New York: SUNY Press.

Tishkov, Leonid. 2022. *Private Moon Series*. www.leonidtishkov.com/Private-Moon (accessed 22 March 2022).

Turkle, Sheryl. 2011. *Alone Together: Why We Expect More from Technology and Less from Each Other*. Philadelphia: Basic Books.

Turkle, Sheryl. 2012. 'The Flight from Conversation'. *New York Times*. 21 April. http://popcultureandamericanchildhood.com/wp-content/uploads/2012/04/The-Flight-From-Conversation-NYTimes.pdf (accessed 26 February 2023).

Van Dijck, José. 2006. 'Record and Hold: Popular Music Between Personal and Collective Memory'. *Critical Studies in Media Communication*, 23:5, 357–374.

Visconti, Lucas M., Sherry, John, Borghini, Stefania, and Anderson, Laurel. 2010. 'Street Art, Sweet Art? Reclaiming the "Public" in Public Place'. *Journal of Consumer Research*, 37 (October), 511–529.

Walber, Daniel. 2016. 'The Furniture: *The Lobster's* Phony Flowers'. *The Film Experience*. http://thefilmexperience.net/blog/2016/8/15/the-furniture-the-lobsters-phony-flowers.html (accessed 6 April 2020).

Wang, Caroline, and Burris, Mary Ann. 1997. 'Photovoice: Concept, Methodology, and use for Participatory Needs Assessment'. *Health Education & Behavior*, 24:3, 369–387.

Warrior, Lakshmi, Kim, Christine Y., Burdick, Daniel J., Ackerman, Daniel J., Bartolini, Luca, Cagniart, Kendra R., and Dangayach, Neha S. 2020. 'Leading with Inclusion during the COVID-19 Pandemic: Stronger Together'. *Neurology*, 95:12, 537–542.

www.theguardian.com/world/2020/mar/21/life-in-lockdown-spain-curtailed-by-coronavirus-but-still-rocking (accessed 4 April 2020).

Warzecha Daniel. 2015. 'From Autobiography to Storytelling: The Works of C. S. Lewis'. In Kerstin W. Shands, Giulia Grillo Mikrut, Dipti R. Pattanaik, and Karen Ferreira-Meyers (eds), *Writing the Self: Essays on Autobiography and Autofiction*, English Studies 5. Huddinge, Sweden: Södertörns högskola, 103–112.

Watson, Fiona Flores. 2020. 'Our Lives in Virus-stricken Spain: Locked Down but still Rocking'. *The Guardian*. 22 March.

Webb, Peter. 2008. '"Infected by the Seed of Post-industrial Punk Bohemia": Nick Cave and the Milieu of the 1980s Underground'. *Popular Music History*, 3:2, 103–122.

Webster, Frank. 2005. 'The End of the Public Library?'. *Science as Culture*, 14:3, 283–287.

Weiss, Robert. 1974. *Loneliness: The Experience of Emotional and Social Isolation*. Boston, MA: MIT Press.

Wells, Liz. 2021. *Land Matters: Landscape Photography, Culture and Identity*. London: Routledge.

White Cube. 2005. 'Gregory Crewdson, *Beneath the Roses*'. https://whitecube.com/exhibitions/exhibition/gregory_crewdson_hoxton_square_2005 (accessed 19 October 2019).

Williams, Raymond. 1975. *The Country and the City*. Oxford: Oxford University Press.
Wilson, Margaret E., Megel, Mary E., Enenbach, Laura, and Carlson, Kimberly L. 2010. 'The Voices of Children: Stories about Hospitalization'. *Journal of Paediatric Health Care*, 24:2, 95–102.
Woods, Heather Cleland, and Scott, Holly. 2016. '#Sleepyteens: Social Media use in Adolescence is Associated with Poor Sleep Quality, Anxiety, Depression and Low Self-esteem'. *Journal of Adolescence*, 51, 41–49.
Yanchyk, Brandy. 2019. *Breaking Loneliness*. Brandy Y Productions. https://brandyyanchyk.com/breakingloneliness (accessed 10 March 2021).
Yavich, Roman, Davidovitch, Nitza, and Frenkel, Zeev. 2019. 'Social Media and Loneliness – Forever Connected?' *Higher Education Studies*, 9:2, 10–21.
Ypsilanti, Antonia, Lazuras, Lambros, Powell, Phillip, and Overton, Paul. 2019. 'Self-Disgust as a Potential Mechanism Explaining the Association between Loneliness and Depression'. *Journal of Affective Disorders*, 243, 108–115.
Zdanow, Carla, and Wright, Bianca. 2012. 'The Representation of Self Injury and Suicide on Emo Social Networking Groups'. *African Sociological Review/Revue Africaine de Sociologie*, 16:2, 81–101.
Zentner, Marcel, Grandjean, Didier, and Scherer, Klauss, R. 2008. 'Emotions Evoked by the Sound of Music: Characterization, Classification, and Measurement'. *Emotion*, 8:4, 494–521.

Filmography

A Day in the Country. 1946. Directed by Jean Renoir: French, Panthéon Productions.
Aloneliness – A Short Documentary. 2019. Director by Ross Field: UK, Videoblog Productions.
Alps. 2011. Directed by Yorgos Lanthimos: Greece, Haos Films.
Amy. 2015. Directed by Asif Kapadia: UK, A24 Films.
Blade Runner. 1982. Directed by Ridley Scott: USA, the Ladd Company, Shaw Brothers.
Breaking Loneliness. 2019. Directed by Brandy Yanchyk: Canada, CBC.
Brokeback Mountain. 2005. Directed by Ang Lee: USA, River Road Entertainment.
Carol. 2015. Directed by Todd Haynes: USA/UK, Number 9 Films.
Charulata/The Lonely Wife. 1964. Directed by Satyajit Ray: India, R. D. Bansal & Co.
Children of Men. 2006: Directed by Alfonso Cuarón: UK, Strike Entertainment.
City Lights. 1931. Directed by Charlie Chaplin: USA, United Artists.
Dogtooth. 2009. Directed by Yorgos Lanthimos: Greece, Boo Productions.
Gilda. 1946. Directed by Charles Vidor: USA, Columbia Pictures.
Ghost World. 2001. Directed by Terry Zwigoff: USA, Advanced Median.
Gravity. 2013. Directed by Alfonso Cuarón: USA, Warner Brothers.
Happy Together. 1997. Directed by Wong Kar-wai: Hong Kong, Jet Tone Production.
Her. 2013. Directed by Spike Jonze: USA, Warner Bros Pictures.
In the Mood for Love. 2000. Directed by Wong Kar-wai: Hong Kong, Jet Tone Production.
Interstellar. 2014. Directed by Christopher Nolan: USA, Paramount Pictures.
Joker. 2019. Directed by Todd Phillips: USA, Warner Brothers.
Late Spring. 1949. Directed by Yasujirō Ozu: Japan, Shochiku Studios.
Leaving Las Vegas. 2015. Directed by Mike Figgis: USA, United Artists.
Loneliness: The Silent Health Crisis. 2019. SBS, Australia.

Lost in Translation. 2003. Directed by Sofia Coppola: USA, American Zoetrope.
Red Road. 2006. Directed by Andrea Arnold: UK, British Film Council.
Rizi/Days. 2020. Directed by Tsai Ming-Liang: Taiwan, Homegreen Films.
Shall We Dance. 1937. Directed by Mark Sandrich: USA, RKO Radio Pictures.
Solaris. 1972. Directed by Andrei Tarkovsky: Soviet Union, Mosfilm.
Taxi Driver. 1976. Directed by Martin Scorsese: USA, Columbia Pictures.
The Lobster. 2015. Directed by Yorgos Lanthimos: UK, Element Pictures.
The Killing of a Sacred Deer. 2017. Directed by Yorgos Lanthimos: USA, New Sparta Films.
The King of Comedy. 1982. Directed by Martin Scorsese: USA, Embassy International Pictures
The Favourite. 2018. Directed by Yorgos Lanthimos: UK, Fox Searchlight Pictures.
The Road. 2009. Directed by John Hillcoat: USA, Dimension Films.
The 3 Rooms of Melancholia. 2004. Directed by Pirjo Honkasalo: Finland, Millennium Film Oy.
Two Years at Sea. 2011. Directed by Ben Rivers: UK, Soda Pictures.
Under the Skin. 2013. Directed by Jonathon Glazer: UK, A24 Films.

Index

A Day in the Country 15
ABBA 65
abjection 82, 144
absence 35–36, 38, 74, 87, 94, 107, 129, 150
acoustic territories 125
Adams, Ansel 60
'After the Lights Go Out' 208
Age UK 4
alienation 6, 17, 26, 30, 48, 56, 76, 78, 133, 142, 148, 169, 175, 177, 196
alone 3, 5, 9–12, 15, 17, 20, 27, 36, 43, 46, 51, 56, 63, 66, 71, 75, 79–81, 83, 86–89, 91–92, 102, 104–107, 109–111, 117–119, 124, 126–129, 131–133, 135–136, 140, 142, 147, 149–150, 158–159, 162, 167–168, 170, 173, 190, 200, 202, 211
Alone Together 31, 148–151
Aloneliness – A Short Documentary 116
aloneness *see* alone
Alps 27, 85
Amy 29–30, 116–118, 121, 147, 185, 217
anonymity 110, 116
architecture 48, 91, 143, 182
ART connects 200
'Asleep' 140
auditory life 125
austerity 91–92, 99, 109, 181
authenticity 7–8, 16, 76–77, 99, 161, 176
autobiographical 131, 138, 151, 159, 164

autobiography 105, 156–157, 164, 184
autoethnography 24, 210–211

Bacon, Francis 13
Badu, Erykah 136
beach
 sea 2, 22, 38, 63–65, 67, 125, 197, 210
bedroom 19, 39–42, 45, 53–56, 66, 80, 88, 102–104, 144, 156, 160–161, 208, 211, 213
Beneath the Roses series 45
'Bitter Glass' 137
Blade Runner 28, 89
boredom 72–74, 78, 100, 139, 166–167, 189, 191
breakdown 105, 142
Breaking Loneliness 16
Brokeback Mountain 15

capitalism 1, 10, 17, 20, 33, 53, 56, 73, 114, 115, 116, 121, 147, 151, 152, 157, 166, 181, 183, 189, 192, 197, 203, 207, 210, 212
Carol 44, 74–75, 81
cars 39, 43–45, 48, 50, 81, 110, 123–124, 131–134, 151
carwash 132
 see also water
catharsis 131
Cave, Nick 32, 124, 176–180, 182, 184–185
celebrity 29, 117, 136, 176–178

Charulata/The Lonely Wife 74, 78, 84
children ix, 29, 44, 83–84, 87, 118–121, 125, 137, 157, 170, 182, 188, 208
Children of Men 28, 87
chronic loneliness 2, 6, 8, 9, 10, 11, 16, 18, 31, 45, 48, 55, 66, 71, 83, 91, 93, 94, 98, 99, 114, 115, 116, 121, 126, 142, 151, 163, 165, 167, 184, 185, 191, 207
  see also existential loneliness
cinema 5, 14–15, 24, 27, 28, 69–72, 74, 79, 86, 98
City Lights 14
Coldwell, Michael C 50
'Come on up to the House' 133
confession 20–21, 32, 118, 149, 151, 156–157, 163–165, 177–179, 184, 209
Contactless series 202, 217
contagion 1, 132, 165
  see also virus
counselling 4, 149, 165, 173, 177, 189
  see therapy
creative loneliness ix, 32, 187–189, 192, 202–203
creative practice *see* ethnography
creative writing 158–159
Crewdson, Gregory 45, 55, 221
crowd 14, 51–52, 54, 126–127, 136, 144

dance 8, 14, 18, 26, 37, 65, 97, 107–109, 135, 142, 145–146, 187, 191, 193, 206
darkroom 35–36, 49
death 4, 19, 29, 32, 84, 89–90, 92–93, 104, 119, 133–134, 140, 168, 176, 179–180
depression 4–5, 8, 29, 31, 127–128, 136–137, 143, 147, 159, 167–170, 173, 175, 189–190, 194
diaries 155–157, 164, 185, 191
disgust 210
documentary 16, 24, 28–29, 85, 99, 112–118, 120–121, 149, 200
documentary film 16, 29, 112
Dogtooth 27, 83–85
domestic time 100

'Down to Zero' 136
'Dusty in Here' 140–141
dwellers 12, 27–28, 48

Elan, Maika 26, 29, 48, 52–55, 81
embodied experience 3, 112
Emin, Tracey *see* neon art
emotional loneliness 5, 199
  see also social loneliness
enchantment 50, 138, 177, 179, 184
epidemic 114
escapism 9–11, 14, 21, 31, 46, 55, 57–58, 63, 65, 71, 74, 77, 79, 97, 102, 110, 118, 126, 129, 144, 147, 159, 191, 197
ethnicity 26, 56, 192
ethnography 208
eudaimonic 71
existential loneliness 2, 8, 9, 11, 12, 13, 15, 16, 17, 18, 31, 37, 42, 45, 47, 48, 57, 66, 67, 71, 79, 86, 90, 93, 98, 105, 111, 121, 125, 130, 134, 138, 145, 151, 157, 176, 185
  see also chronic loneliness
exposure 12–13, 35

faith 111, 121, 181
'Falling Up' 137
family albums 37–38
'Field Below' 129
fine art photography 49
friendship 4, 73, 89, 115, 119–120, 166, 182, 190–191

garden 2, 22, 62, 65, 78, 84, 97–98, 125, 151, 155, 169, 187, 195, 207
gazing 48, 54, 74
gender 15, 26–28, 44–45, 74, 76–77, 81, 93, 142, 169, 192, 207
Ghost World 27, 76–77, 221, 227, 229
ghosts 11, 35–36, 49, 86, 93, 123
Gilda 15
Grannan, Katy 13
Gravity 28, 86
Gray, David 135

haiku 24, 155, 159, 162–163, 185
Happy Together (film) 17

'Happy Together' (song) 44
hauntology 86
Healthy Families Yarn 199
Her 27, 89–90
hikikomori 26, 52–55, 66, 105
Hopper, Edward 12
hotels 27, 49, 79, 82

If Nobody Speaks of Remarkable Things 205
Iggy Pop 43, 133
In the Mood for Love 72
individualism 4–5, 91, 116
Inside Hanoi series 26, 55–56, 62, 66, 81
Interstellar 87–88, 229
invisibility 10, 13, 101, 116–117, 163, 183, 185, 210
isolation 2–4, 6, 9, 11, 14–15, 17, 27–28, 32–33, 36–37, 41, 43, 45, 51, 77–79, 81, 83–86, 89, 92, 99–101, 104–105, 115, 120–121, 124, 127, 137, 139, 142, 147, 151, 157, 163, 175, 177, 180, 189–195, 200, 202, 207, 213, 217

Jerrems, Carol 91
Joker 30–31, 142–143, 145–148, 151, 185, 218
joy 14, 26, 35, 37–38, 55, 59, 63–64, 87–88, 92, 129, 132, 136, 138, 141, 146, 151, 194
Joy Division 59

Kahlo, Frida 105
King of Comedy 147
kodokushi 4
   see also muen shakai

Lady GaGa 183
Lanthimos, Yorgos 27, 82, 84, 93, 223, 229–230
Late Spring 15
Leaving Las Vegas 76
liminal 11, 42, 63, 88, 110, 185, 197
liquid capitalism 1
liquid modernity 5, 91
Litovsky, Dina 50

Live Music Now at Home 194
lockdown 32, 139, 187–191, 195–196, 198–202
lone wolf 151
Loneliness: The Silent Health Crisis 114 114
'Lonely' 138
lonely imagination ix, 2, 8, 16, 18, 21, 24–25, 36–37, 49, 59, 71, 93–94, 98, 102, 109, 121, 132, 151, 192, 195, 200, 203, 206, 210, 212
loners 26, 40, 61–62
losers 168–169
Lost Connections 193
Lost in Translation 27, 80
love 5, 10–11, 14, 17–18, 32, 37, 44, 46–47, 58, 60, 63, 65, 72, 79, 83–84, 90–91, 105, 118, 123–124, 134–138, 141, 151, 155, 159, 170, 172, 175–177, 180–185, 188, 198–199, 208
'Lua' 136

maps 49, 73
marriage 44, 46, 84, 118
masculinity 27, 90, 142
masks 105–106, 121, 123, 147, 187, 198, 202
McCubbin, Frederick 61
'Meet Me in the Middle of the Air' 195
melancholy 11, 13, 16, 26, 35, 47, 50, 58, 62–63, 86, 89, 99, 123, 128, 132, 134, 143, 147, 213
memory 13, 18, 21, 30, 50, 65–66, 76, 88, 110, 124–125, 132, 134–135, 137–140, 156, 171
men 4, 17, 24, 26, 30, 38, 45, 53, 66, 75, 90–92, 94, 100–102, 104, 114, 117–118, 208
'Metal Heart' 152
modernity 48–49, 91, 102, 157, 206, 218
Montgomery, Robert 11
moon 2, 39, 46–47
mothers 45
muen shakai 4
   see also kodokushi

music 2–3, 15, 17–18, 22, 24, 30–32, 59, 65–66, 73, 100–101, 103, 108, 115, 120, 128–140, 142–144, 146, 155, 172, 176, 178, 188, 191, 193–195, 200, 205, 216

nature 8, 11–13, 16, 18, 23, 33, 35–37, 42, 45, 50, 57–60, 62, 64, 66, 71–73, 76, 81, 84, 86–87, 93, 99, 102, 108–109, 115, 117–118, 124, 126–128, 132, 142, 144–145, 148, 150–151, 163–164, 167, 176–177, 180, 183–185, 192, 198, 200, 209
neoliberalism *see* liquid capitalism
neon art 11–12
'None but the Lonely Heart' 140–141
nostalgia 124, 128, 131, 134, 137–140, 151
Not Alone, Never was Penpal Zine 4 Rural Queers 201

On the Wallaby Track 61–62
online 3, 151, 162–165, 185, 193

painting 3, 7, 12–13, 21, 24, 47, 61, 81, 101–103, 176, 198
pandemic ix, 10, 31–33, 50, 187–189, 191–195, 198–203, 217–218
pathology 77–78, 99, 114, 117, 121, 145, 166, 185, 206, 212
'Pictures of You' 18
Plath, Sylvia 19
Please Believe these Days will Pass series 196
podcasts 11, 30, 148–150
poems 11, 19, 24, 110, 159–163, 179, 185, 208
precarity 99, 180

r/lonely 24, 32, 105–106, 116, 162–163, 165–167, 170, 172–175, 189, 217
realism 16, 27–28, 82, 85, 99, 112–113, 121, 131, 139, 158
Red Road 27, 78–79, 81
reminiscentia 26

river 26, 46, 62, 63, 67, 139, 156, 187
  see also water
Rizi 72–73
'Rock 'n' Roll (Part 2) 146
rural 8, 13, 25, 26, 57, 58, 59, 60, 61, 62, 65, 66, 101, 115, 125, 201, 208
  see also wilderness

sad speech 128
sadness 1, 11, 14, 26, 47, 55, 63, 71, 92, 98, 123, 125, 128–129, 139–141
science fiction 16–17, 27–28, 85, 87–90, 93, 120, 127–128
Scott of the Antarctic 127
sea 2, 38, 47, 58, 63, 64, 65, 67, 110–111, 212
  see also beach water
self-loathing 167, 169, 175, 191, 209
Shall We Dance 144, 230
shame 53, 73, 99, 106, 114–115
shed 2, 100, 104, 107, 110, 126, 141, 151
shit 146, 167–168, 170, 209
shower 53–54, 76, 77, 126–127, 209
  see also water
silence 17, 27, 35, 40, 69–70, 72, 85, 87, 98, 109, 120, 126, 142, 144–145, 151, 161, 163, 205
Sleeping by the Mississippi 26, 62, 225
slow cinema 73, 93
slow time 36, 201
slow violence 76, 115
social class 26–28, 45, 53, 56, 74, 82–84, 92–93, 117, 151, 191–192, 208
social isolation 4–5, 16, 28, 100, 139
social loneliness 5, 31, 199
  see also emotional loneliness
social media 4, 31–32, 105–106, 116, 155–156, 162–165, 170, 176, 183, 185, 189
sociality 20, 65, 70–71, 104, 110, 116, 146, 195–196
solace 78, 83, 111, 149, 157, 177, 182, 184
Solaris 28, 85–86

solitude 2, 9–10, 14, 40, 47, 50–51, 58, 61, 63–64, 67, 82, 85, 92, 109, 118, 126, 170, 209, 213
songs 11, 18, 29–30, 121, 123, 127, 132, 134–136, 138, 140–141, 150–151, 179, 188, 208
sound 2, 14, 17–18, 24, 30–31, 40, 43, 48, 65, 69, 72, 77–78, 85, 93, 98, 112, 117, 120–121, 125–127, 129, 134, 136, 143–145, 148, 151, 163, 173, 187, 194, 208
Soth, Alec 26, 48, 62–63
'Spanish Blue' 139
spectacle 36, 54, 79, 145, 164–165
Star Trek: The Next Generation 89
stranger 27, 123, 174–175
street art 197–198
street photography 49, 52
sublime 8–9, 35, 48, 60, 64, 66, 86–87, 124, 130, 144
suburban 44–46, 125
surveillance 28, 45, 49–50, 75, 78, 81
swimming pool 63, 65–66, 67, 209
  see also water

Taxi Driver 27, 207
Tchaikovsky, Pyotr Ilyich 140
tears 30, 47, 129, 132, 134, 136, 141, 148, 168, 181, 209
  see also water
technology 90, 103
The 3 Rooms of Melancholia 29, 119–120, 217
The Catcher in the Rye 19
the city 48
The Dirty Three 43, 133
The Favourite 85
The Killing of a Sacred Deer 27, 84
The Kiss 198
The Lobster 27, 82–84
The Loneliness Experiment 4
The Migration Blanket 200
'The Old Soft Shoe' 146
'The Passenger' 43, 133
The Red Hand Files 32, 176, 178–179, 181–184, 219

The Road 87
The Scream 102
therapeutic 1, 20, 21, 148, 151, 156, 157, 163, 165, 166, 173, 182, 185, 209
  see also counselling
therapy 21, 43, 99, 115, 182, 200
  see also counseliing
Tishkov, Leonid 47
Titchner, Mark 196–197
'Trapped in the 3rd Dimension' 198
trauma 8, 11, 37, 53–54, 78, 105, 114, 119–120, 137, 164–166, 182, 185, 200

Under the Skin 17, 27, 90–92
Unsettled Scores 194
urban *see* the city

Vale Street 44, 222
virus 1, 189, 196, 199, 202, 203
  see also contagion
voice 2, 16, 25, 29–30, 38–39, 78, 89, 92–93, 97, 112–113, 116, 121, 123–124, 126–129, 135–136, 140–141, 148–152, 169, 172–173, 185, 188

waste 15, 53, 63, 73, 83, 89, 146, 148, 167, 190, 209
water 45, 58, 62, 97–98, 129, 142, 187, 209
Welfare in Australia Report 17
'Wicked Game' 205
wilderness 9, 22, 60–61, 63, 66, 87, 118, 127, 151, 208
  see also rural
women 4, 38, 44–45, 74–76, 90–92, 94, 114, 137, 178, 182, 198, 200, 208
Wuhan: The City Under Coronavirus 195

yarn bombing 191, 193, 198–199
youth 26, 28, 54, 77, 84, 93, 120, 134, 139, 151

EU authorised representative for GPSR:
Easy Access System Europe, Mustamäe tee 50,
10621 Tallinn, Estonia
gpsr.requests@easproject.com

www.ingramcontent.com/pod-product-compliance
Lightning Source LLC
Chambersburg PA
CBHW051610230426
43668CB00013B/2058